D1253706

AN ADAMS BUSINESS ADVISOR

All-In-One
Business
Planning
Guide

Other titles in
THE ADAMS BUSINESS ADVISORS

Bob Adams books are appropriate for professional development seminars, training programs, premiums, and specialized reprint activities. They can be ordered through retail outlets everywhere, or by calling the Special Sales Department at 800-872-5627 (in Massachusetts 617-767-8100).

AN ADAMS BUSINESS ADVISOR

All-In-One Business Planning Guide

HOW TO CREATE COHESIVE PLANS
FOR MARKETING, SALES, OPERATIONS,
FINANCE, AND CASH FLOW

CHRISTOPHER R. MALBURG, CPA, MBA

BOB ADAMS, INC.
Holbrook, Massachusetts

Acknowledgments

Every author calls on people whose opinions and professionalism he respects. These treasured sages provide insight and know-how from their real-world experiences. For this book I was helped by Marilyn Cohen, Fran Adams, and Pat Bannister. Many thanks to you all.

Published by Bob Adams, Inc. 260 Center Street, Holbrook, MA 02343

ISBN: 1-55850-348-X (hardcover)
ISBN: 1-55850-347-1 (paperback)

Printed in the United States of America.

J I H G F E D C B A (hardcover)
J I H G F E D C B A (paperback)

Library of Congress Cataloging-in-Publication Data
Malburg, Christopher R.
   All-in-one business planning guide : how to create cohesive plans for marketing, sales, operations, finance and cash flow / Christopher R. Malburg.
      p.   cm. — (An Adams business advisor)
   Includes bibliographical references and index.
   ISBN 1-55850-348-X : $29.95 — ISBN 1-55850-347-1 (pbk.) : $10.95
   1. Small business—Management. I. Title. II. Series.
HD62.7.M336   1994
658.02'2—dc20   94-8709
                                                                                CIP

COVER DESIGN: Marshall Henrichs

This book is available at quantity discounts for bulk purchases.
For information, call 1-800-872-5627.

Other books by Chris Malburg:
Accounting for the New Business (Bob Adams, Inc.)
The Cash Management Handbook (Prentice-Hall)
The Property Tax Consultant's Guide (Prentice-Hall)
The Professional Investor's Tax Guide (Prentice-Hall)
Business Plans to Manage Day to Day Operations (John Wiley & Sons)
How to Fire Your Boss (Berkley Publishing Group, Division of G.P. Putnam's Sons)
The Controller's and Treasurer's Desk Reference (McGraw-Hill)
How to Write a Knock-em-Dead Book Proposal (Writer's Resource Group)

To Bert Cohen

Some people treat life as a test. There are those who tiptoe through it,
careful never to miss one question. (You aren't one of them.)
Others barge right through, taking risks and having a great time.
They're happy if they have a few more right answers than wrong ones.
These are the people who really succeed.
Congratulations, you pass!

Table of Contents

Introduction

The All-In-One Business Planning Guide shows how to create a single business plan that ties all the company's functions together. This book demonstrates how to chart a course for your company *and then follow it*. The book addresses the unique planning needs of small-business managers. We'll dispense with all the fancy verbiage and drop-dead presentations so often found at larger companies. What we need, and what this book provides, is a no-nonsense blueprint for creating a single business plan that works.

The All-In-One Business Planning Guide takes the mystery out of a useful management tool that's been mired in the haze of crystal-ball gazing for too long. The book thoroughly describes the most effective ways of small-business planning. We begin with the basics, such as how to structure your plan so that it becomes a tool to manage profits. The book gives examples and cases in which use of specific techniques moved a company a little closer to its objectives.

Very little of the material and concepts in this book is of a technical nature. If concepts or analytical tools may be foreign to most small-business managers, the book identifies them, puts them into simple terms, and walks you through easy-to-use applications. Chances are that you may be using some of them right now or in the near future.

Regardless of your position or responsibilities, charting your firm's course, *then following it* is a necessity. This book delivers the mechanics of how to do it. We won't waste time on things of little or no direct use to managers of small companies. For example, eight chapters are devoted to showing and explaining how the different departments in your company contribute their special knowledge to the planning effort. Included among these are creating plans for

- Marketing • Sales • Operations • Major purchases
- People • Salaries and wages • Finances • Cash flow

Purpose of the Book

The All-In-One Business Planning Guide covers the subject beginning with the determination of the company's current position. It takes you through the entire exercise of creating a workable business plan. But it doesn't stop there. Equally important are the *implementation* of the plan and *monitoring* interim results. You'll find the techniques involving benchmarks and motivating employees among the most useful in making and executing midcourse changes.

Wherever practicable, the book uses real-life examples, charts, and graphs to simplify and illustrate the presentation. It purposely separates business planning into its component parts. Each step is explained, and the relationship is established between the effects different departments have on the plan and its implementation.

Even people who already have some knowledge of business planning will benefit from the streamlined and simplified explanations. This accelerates the planning task of busy decision makers.

Scope

The topics covered were carefully selected to be

- Relevant to the issues faced every day by managers of small businesses
- Easily applicable
- Quickly implemented in your own business

You don't have to be a financial or forecasting whiz to use this book. In fact, I assume you aren't. We'll begin with the basics. Then we'll advance to the details you need in order to design and implement an effective business planning routine in your company.

This isn't a textbook for MBAs. I promise that the subjects included here are of immediate use to you in understanding how a small business creates and implements its business plan. We won't waste time on subjects that probably aren't relevant right now to a company the size of yours. Instead, we'll focus on how to install an effective planning mechanism to assist you in taking your business from where it is today to where it should be tomorrow.

Who Can Benefit from the Book?

The All-In-One Business Planning Guide was written for a variety of individuals specifically involved in small business enterprises. You don't have to be the boss to benefit from this book. You don't even have to be the person charged with creating the plan. The more you know about planning a small business, the better you'll be able to contribute to your area—whether it's the whole company or a department. This book was written for

- General managers who are responsible for directing the entire company
- People who help in planning the business' goals
- Those who are responsible for implementing the plan in each department
- Anyone else who is interested in helping plot the company's course

The All-In-One Business Planning Guide helps bridge the gap between the executive and technical sides of the company. Often a fissure develops between senior management and those who make top-level decisions happen. The book explains in plain English how each area relates to the others in the business plan.

How the Book Differs from Others

The style emphasizes a user-friendly approach. The objective is to develop and implement a business plan, then monitor its progress and identify areas that need attention. You won't find long, irrelevant discussions of the theory behind each issue—that's for textbooks. Instead, we'll describe how each technique works and the best ways to use it, and then move on.

Each chapter employs major and minor headings for the topics. This helps you locate the exact discussion you want without wasting time thumbing through the parts you don't need right now. All examples and illustrations appear within the text where they'll be of most benefit, not elsewhere in the book where space permits.

Features of the Book

Along with the use of streamlined headings and concise discussions, often followed by examples that demonstrate the techniques, you'll see aids like worksheets. Some help you identify your company's current position, others assist in defining your company's goals, and still others show you how to report monthly progress toward benchmark targets. These make needed midcourse corrections pop right out. All worksheets are intended for copying from the book and use in designing and implementing your business plan.

Examples offer practical illustrations that quickly clarify a technique by showing how someone in a similar situation solved the problem.

How to Use the Book

There are three features of the book designed to help you locate the exact topic or issue in which you're interested:

- Master table of contents at the front of the book • Index
- Heading structure within each chapter

To locate a subject, look first in either the master table of contents or the Index. Then locate the exact discussion using the headings within the text.

The book also was intended for reading from cover to cover. Each topic builds on the prior discussions. The chapters begin with the basics and progress to state-of-the-art practices in the field of small-business planning.

Chapter Summaries

Chapter 1: Why Plan Your Business?

The first chapter identifies the reasons for a written business plan. It immediately lays to rest many small-businesspeople's natural fear that this is the same busywork they left a corporate job to avoid.

Chapter 2: Structuring Your Business Plan

Chapter 2 provides an overview of the entire planning process presented in the chapters that follow. Included are introductions to such topics as

- Assessment of your present position

- How to identify your company's goals
- How to create subplans in each department

Chapter 3: Where Is the Company Today?

Chapter 3 begins the first step of the planning process. It shows readers how to assess their company's current position. The process involves honest appraisals of financial resources, product lines, market share, market potential, customers, production equipment, technology, competition, employee skills, and more. This section serves as the starting point from which the business plan goes forward.

Chapter 4: Setting Company Goals

Chapter 4 shows how to draw up effective, achievable, and specific companywide goals. Too many small-business owners believe they're at the mercy of larger competitors. In some cases that's true. But more often we see small businesses compete effectively because they've created a unique niche for themselves. Producing such a niche doesn't usually happen by accident. It's forged by establishing specific goals for the company, then hitting the target.

Chapter 5: Setting Department Goals

Chapter 5 demonstrates how to establish specific goals for each department—goals that work together to get the company where it must go. We'll concentrate on focusing employees' attention on the single thing each of them does that helps the firm achieve its main goal. The intent is to demonstrate how to identify those goals in each department that flow upward, moving the company that much closer to its overall objectives.

Chapter 6: Identifying the Capability Gap

Effective goals must be realistic. Even so, often there's a gap in the firm's present capability to achieve a specific goal. Sometimes it's customer-induced. Other times there are barriers to a market the firm must penetrate. Often the gap results from the firm's borrowing capacity or a lack of knowledge by its employees.

Whatever the cause, Chapter 6 shows how to identify capability gaps and the steps the business plan must take to bridge them.

Chapter 7: Writing the Business Plan

We're not talking about a fancy document written by a team of MBAs. Nor even something that's very lengthy. Chapter 7 describes the business plan as a working document. It's intended to be as short and concise as possible, but with enough detail to communicate exactly where the company intends to go. It demonstrates the sections to cover and the financial and performance information it should contain.

The emphasis is on clarity, specifics, and creating a document for reference throughout the implementation and the inevitable midcourse corrections.

Chapter 8: Creating the Sales Plan

Sales plans are the driving force behind most small companies' business plans. It is here that the gross revenue is forecasted. Chapter 8 demonstrates how to translate the marketing plan into a monthly sales revenue timetable. This is used not only by the production schedulers but also by purchasers of raw material or subassemblies and by the controller who schedules collection of accounts receivable for cash flow purposes. Though no book can tell you how much revenue to forecast, this one demonstrates a systematic method of arriving at those numbers. Equally as important, the format and techniques offered provide for future reference to monitor progress toward your goals.

Chapter 9: Creating the Marketing Plan

Sales and marketing drive most small businesses. Chapter 9 shows how to create a marketing plan for the firm's products that integrates with the company's overall goals.

Chapter 10: Creating the Operations Plan

The operations plan is key to most companies, particularly manufacturing or assembly businesses. It includes new uses of technology, production schedules, inventory costs and purchases, and labor costs. The operations plan influences the purchasing schedule and the cash disbursement timetable. It creates the acquisitions schedule for the purchase of expensive machinery and equipment used throughout the company.

Chapter 11: Creating the Plan for Major Purchases

What may be a major purchase for a small business probably isn't for larger companies. Nevertheless, the capability gap identified earlier defines the need for purchases of such durable goods. Since they represent significant increases in manufacturing capability, often lower production costs, and usually a substantial cash outlay, they must be included in the plan.

Chapter 11 shows how to schedule these purchases so that all the departments involved know how and when they'll be affected.

Chapter 12: Forecasting Labor Expenses

Chapter 12 offers specific instructions on how to schedule employee raises and bonuses for use in the financial plan. Additionally, contingencies such as the need for overtime, temporaries, or consultants can be forecasted and incorporated into the plan. Chapter 12 shows you how to create a logical schedule of all salary and wage costs for other areas of the company to use in planning their expenses.

Chapter 13: Creating the Financial Plan

This section describes the components of the financial plan. It takes information from all over the company and reduces it to projected numbers for every month throughout the year. The emphasis is on creating a plan that can be compared against actual results. The financial plan assists in determining what midcourse corrections should be made along the way to achieve the company's goals.

Included in this chapter are specific issues such as the accounts receivable collection plan, how to track compliance with loan requirements, and managing the outflow of cash.

Chapter 14: Creating the Cash Flow Plan

The cash flow plan is one of the most important spinoffs of the financial plan. For small businesses strapped for cash, this part of the planning effort answers two all-important questions:

- How much do we need? • When do we need it?

Creating a cash flow plan isn't difficult once the financial plan is in place. Chapter 14 shows you how.

Chapter 15: Establishing Benchmarks

Careful monitoring of the business plan throughout its implementation requires establishing specific interim targets along the way. We call these benchmarks—measurements by which we can judge how the plan is progressing. Chapter 15 shows how to establish meaningful benchmarks in each critical area of the plan.

Chapter 16: Automating the Plan

Simple spreadsheet programs are extremely useful, especially for the quantitative components of the business plan. Chapter 16 demonstrates how to use a PC for such components as production scheduling, sales projections, and the financial plan. Additionally, this section unveils simple programming tips such as avoiding so-called hard programming of assumptions—that streamline the entire process.

Chapter 16 also teaches you the use of what-if scenarios, sensitivity analysis, and simulation analysis. Additionally, graphical representations of the business plan components are provided to better illustrate ways to communicate the overall objectives.

Chapter 17: Monitoring Progress Toward Plan Goals

Chapter 17 shows how to monitor the business plan to keep it on track. That's done by creating an easy method of monitoring progress—one that quickly identifies departures from the plan and suggests possible solutions. You'll find quick ways to simulate various solutions to problems you encounter as the plan is executed. If you used the automated spreadsheets discussed earlier, the discussion takes on added value.

Chapter 18: Updating the Plan

Business plans are living documents. They can't possibly foretell everything that will happen during the course of the planning year. Chapter 18 demonstrates when to update the plan. In many cases, much of the plan is still on track. But some departments may have faced unforeseen circumstances that necessitate a change. These components are updated with the new results and incorporated into the overall business plan. When this process is managed correctly, the company still achieves its main planning goals, even though the *way* it gets there changes.

Chapter 1

Why Plan Your Business?

OVERVIEW

The owner of a small sheet-metal fabrication company once told me, "Why plan? It only gets in the way of what would have happened anyway." That's a fatalistic notion often held by managers of small businesses. Too many believe that they're totally at the mercy of larger competitors. In fact, for many, exactly the opposite is true.

Think of the reasons for your company's success. You'll probably come up with a series of traits that are uniquely yours—characteristics that your larger competitors can't begin to duplicate. That's why you're in business.

Chapter 1 identifies the reasons for a written business plan. Of course, *you* may already believe in the idea. However, you may have to sell it to the others in your company. This ammunition may come in handy.

RECOGNIZING USES OF THE PLAN

For many of us who left corporate America in favor of a smaller work environment, the idea of drafting a business plan may seem offensive. After all, isn't frustration with all that busywork one of the reasons we left in the first place?

We all have an aversion to doing anything on our job that doesn't immediately help the situation we're now experiencing. However, isn't it also true that a little foresight and action *before* the fact can help eliminate many of the problems we face each day. Wouldn't it be nice to anticipate something like a price cut by your major competitor or a rise in the interest rate on your credit line? Of course it would. And with that anticipation comes an organized and effective response. *That's* what planning does. Additionally, we prepare a workable business plan to

- Determine where the company needs to go
- Communicate the direction and route to make the company hit its targets
- Forewarn of possible roadblocks along the way
- Formulate responses to contingencies
- Keep the business on track to reach its planned goals

Planning for Promotion of the Company

Many people associate a business plan with start-up companies. Often our first exposure to a business plan is for the purpose of convincing investors and lenders that we have a viable idea at which they should throw money. That's *not* what we're developing here.

Though the techniques may be similar, the purposes are entirely different. So are the results. Promotional plans are often untested, pie-in-the-sky theories of what someone thinks will work. The goals, objectives, and numbers are usually unproven. Detailed departmental plans for hitting targets are frequently hazy—if they exist at all. Promoters don't want to burden their investors with the mechanics of execution. That comes later, after the money is in the bank.

Think of a start-up's promotional plan as *concept-driven*. It's more general in nature. The presentation leaves many questions of practical execution unanswered. These plans are fine for their purpose. However, most aren't intended as a blueprint for running the company.

Planning for Operational Purposes

We're not creating a promotional plan for a new start-up company. Instead, by using this book, you create a practical realistic planning tool for your business. The emphasis is on integrating the *details* of what each department within the company does to help the firm reach its overall goals. We want to tell each person in the company the single most important thing they need to do—*must accomplish*—to contribute to the overall success of the business. Certainly this results-oriented attention to detail can (and probably should) be used for a start-up venture. However, the promoters are right—it would confuse outsiders not familiar with the inner workings of the company.

Our focus is on practical solutions to everyday business objectives. We design these to work in concert with one another. When they do, the company moves from where it is today to where its owners, investors and managers want it to be.

ESTABLISHING GOALS

Why establish goals? I've heard from colleagues who run other small businesses that they always seem to fall short of any goals they set for the company. There's almost a feeling of helplessness. Their companies are small and lack the resources needed to turn goals into reality.

Some wonder why they should spend time developing a business plan that *might* help the company make money over the next year or two—especially when they could be working on something else that's guaranteed to make money today. That's hard logic to refute, especially in a tight economy. Many small-business owners and entrepreneurs go after the quick buck. Those are the ones that don't last. Companies that lack a definite direction and the ability to stay on course eventually sink. It's the firms with vision and a plan to exploit that vision that become the stars.

If you don't set goals and then try to reach them, it's guaranteed that your firm will stay right where it is today. With changing technology, changing customer demands, and increasing sophistication, marching in place is business suicide. During the 1990s and as we approach the next century, no company has the luxury of conducting business as usual. If you stay where you are today, the rest of us will leave you in the dust.

Company Goals

Chapter 4 deals exclusively with the mechanics of setting meaningful overall company goals. These are the targets for change and transition that your firm must reach over the planning horizon—for our purposes, the next twelve months.

Company goals cover such major issues as

- Products offered • Customers targeted • Company image
- Competition • Levels of service • Product quality

Companywide goals established in the business plan move the company into the position where it needs to be.

Department Goals

Chapter 5 shows how to establish goals for individual departments. At very small companies, often that's for one person. No matter. Design department goals to connect with specific requirements of both the overall company goals and the goals of other departments in terms of product and timing. We make department goals in order to

- Assist other departments that depend on those specific results
- Achieve the overall company goals

A good example would be in the area of finance. Say the firm needs additional funds to buy the machinery needed to expand its manufacturing operation. This will generate the sales revenue needed to meet overall profit targets. Here are examples of specific department goals:

- Get additional funds.
- Purchase and take delivery of new machinery.
- Expand manufacturing.
- Generate added sales.
- Help attain the overall profit objectives.

Failure to reach of any one of these department goals could jeopardize reaching the overall company's target. Additionally, within every department, it's easy to identify exactly what that department must do to further the company's cause.

APPRAISING YOUR CURRENT POSITION

Chapter 3 deals with establishing your company's current position. The question here, however, is *why* do this? After all, most managers of small businesses are close enough to their everyday operation to know where they are, aren't they? Not necessarily. At least few take the time to think about where they are, then write it down so that others can judge its accuracy. We're talking about things like

- Market position • Company strengths and weaknesses

- Reputation • Industry viability • Technology • Product line
- Adequacy of capital • Capability and sufficiency of employees
- Sufficiency of plant, machinery, and equipment (the *infrastructure*)

Often the hardest part of starting a business plan is honestly determining your current position today. It's not always so obvious. Take the case of Domino's Pizza Corporation. What business is it in? Of course, it sells pizza. So does every one of its competitors. The Domino's planners decided that differentiating Domino's product based on higher quality was too hard a sell. Besides, it wasn't necessary.

So what business is Domino's *really* in? The convenience industry. Its pizza isn't any better or worse than most of the competition. However, the niche Domino's chose for itself in its plan was the business of selling convenience. For a while it had that entire market to itself.

Another example is that of a payroll processing service. Its current position is that of providing financial convenience to its clients. The company performs a task that other companies would rather not do. While assessing the current position, someone came up with the bright idea of expanding the services offered. After all, financial convenience extends beyond simply doing the payroll. Why not add bookkeeping, tracking and collecting receivables, and personnel consulting?

See how the planning process not only answers a lot of questions you may not have thought about for some time, but *prompts* questions that may turn into opportunities? That's the kind of penetrating thought that goes into assessing your firm's current position.

TARGETING YOUR BUSINESS

Why plan your business? How about giving your company something to shoot for? Goals are something everyone needs in order to do better than he or she would have otherwise. We all get satisfaction by aiming for a target, then hitting it. It's even better if we're part of a collective effort—a team—that succeeds in reaching a set of common goals.

Communicating Targets

Preparing a viable business plan communicates the company's specific goals and objectives to every member of the company. It sets down in black and white each person's mission, what's expected of him or her, the timing of specific results, and how they will affect the company.

Additionally, by studying the business plan, each person responsible for specific results can see not only how his or her performance affects others but how other departments will affect the person's own efforts. This is the only way to create a coordinated effort.

Fostering Creativity

It's interesting how establishing targets and the methods of attaining them increases the creativity of everyone who participates. Once the targets and methods are on paper for all to see, it's surprising how new and innovative approaches surface. Routes to a target cast in stone for years are suddenly open to question. Perhaps the way you've always done it really isn't the best way. Maybe a new way has emerged. Perhaps an employee recently learned something that gets the job done better, faster, and cheaper.

All you have to do is ask for help from those in a position to know. That's how creating a business plan fosters creativity. It also brings us to the next reason for creating targets.

Participating in the Plan

Ever notice how those who are in on a decision from the start have a special commitment to it? They *own* that decision. Their reputation is suddenly on the line. Often they'll make it work through pure stubbornness. They don't want to fail or be proven wrong.

Developing targets jointly with those charged with reaching them creates the same pride of ownership. If you are an owner or a manager reading this, make sure you really *listen* to those whose input you ask for. You want to achieve three things from targeting the company's goals using a joint effort:

- Better, more viable targets that get the firm where it needs to go
- A different insight into problem solving from someone with a different perspective and background from your own
- Pride of ownership through participation

I guarantee that business plans developed with the able help of those responsible for implementing them are far more likely to succeed than those handed down from the ivory tower with no input from the real workers.

Singing from the Same Sheet of Music

We need a set of written targets in the business plan to communicate to all concerned where we're going and how we're getting there. Without that, we risk misunderstanding some critical assignment. Companies with written business plans are that much closer to 100 percent certainty that everyone understands the targets, the timing, and what specific individuals must do to help the effort.

COMMUNICATING WITH OUTSIDERS

Business plans are important to lenders, investors, and partners. They want to understand what management intends to do with their money and the company in which they have a financial stake.

Probably of most interest to lenders and investors is the financial section of the business plan. They're looking for confirmation that

- The company has enough money to do the things necessary to provide the expected return.
- The cash flow generated by the company is sufficient to service the debt.

Lenders often use certain benchmarks to assess a company's financial viability and the lending risk they've undertaken. These are usually in the form of financial ratios. Quite likely your lending covenant lists specific financial ratios that the company promises not to fall below. Lenders view breach of these ratios as a serious violation of the lending contract that could result in the loan being called.

So the business plan should address these covenants and restrictions. The financial plan we create provides a separate schedule of the financial ratios most commonly used in lending covenants to make it easy for you to see that the company remains in compliance.

Of equal importance, the monthly monitoring mechanism we'll set up tracks these important indicators and tells you when you're getting close to having a problem. At that point it's usually best to bring your lender in on what's happening at the firm. At least it lets the lender know that you are in control and weren't surprised. Further, it gives you time to formulate an organized response to correct the problem.

Often partners—especially limited partners—don't have daily contact with the company. They aren't as familiar with the day-to-day operations as the employees and the general partner(s). They are passive investors. This being the case, the business plan must demonstrate to them

- What the plan expects the company to achieve
- Projections for the cash available for partner distribution
- What the risk of failure is

The business plan should walk these partners, passive investors, and lenders through the logic associated with particular management strategies and objectives. It should answer questions like

- What will meeting each target do to achieve the overall objectives?
- How will specific targets help other departments do what they must to promote the overall objectives?
- What happens if we miss specific targets or don't achieve them on time?

Anyone preparing a solid business plan should answer these same questions, not just those making a presentation to the money people.

TARGETING SPECIFIC REQUIREMENTS

Have you ever seen a business plan *without* specific and detailed targets and deadlines for critical areas of the company? Did the plan work? If it did, this success was probably more a matter of luck than of anything management did to proactively cause it to happen.

Your business is too important to trust to luck. You'll stand a much better chance of controlling the course you chart for your company and reaching your plan objectives if you have specific goals for each key area of your company. That's why we'll spend so much time determining what's important and identifying what each department must do to cause the overall plan to succeed.

Let's assume for the moment that your business plan has identified the major objectives the firm needs to achieve over the next year or so. These probably include things such as

- The industry in which the company wishes to compete
- Profit or some sort of profit index such as return on capital or return on investment
- Types of customers the company needs to attract
- Level of service provided
- Controls management needs to exert over the company

Now, the question is, How are we going to do all these great things? The answers provide the road map for executing, monitoring, and making midcourse corrections in your business plan.

That's *why* we generate such a detailed business plan. However, the question you're probably waiting to ask is, *how* do we do it? Like this: We take each part of the plan and identify every department that's critical to its success. Then we go into each department and identify those specific things the people must do to bring the department to the point where it fulfills its role in the overall plan.

It's usually best if we can keep the number of targets for each department as small as possible. Ideally, we'd like to be able to say to each employee, *Here is the single thing you need to do—even if you don't achieve anything else all year—to make your department a success.* With such tight focus and minimal distractions, the chances of success are usually greater.

Let's move on to the specific departments and identify the planning targets we need from them.

Projecting Sales

Once most small businesses figure out where they want to go and what their objectives are, they turn to the sales department. That's probably because businesses, particularly small ones, are usually sales-driven. Start-ups, however, are often an exception. For the first year or more, some bio-technology and computer companies don't sell anything. They're just trying to get their technology established and maybe patented so that they can begin selling something at some future point in time.

An example of this was Genentech. For at least the first year after going public, it didn't sell anything. Yet its stock was among the most actively traded. Investors placed their money on products that might sell *someday*. Its business plan was driven by *technology* and *engineering*, not by sales.

For most of us, the business plan is still sales-driven. The question is, How much do we need to sell in order to meet the firm's revenue goals? Probably the best way to answer it is to generate a monthly sales budget by product. Using this, we can predict what comes in (in the form of revenue) and what needs to go out (in the form of vendor payments).

If the business plan includes entering a new market or developing a new product, these come into the sales plan. There are costs associated with new product development. Certainly entering a new market requires advertising expenditures and market research.

Once again, we usually schedule these costs by month. We want this level of detail because so much of what the rest of the company must do depends on this sales budget.

Manufacturing Plan

The manufacturing department needs to know how many units to make in order to have enough available to meet sales demand. Indeed, this department plan must *anticipate* that of the marketing and sales department. For manufacturing and production, the levels of sales for each month represent a due date. From there they'll work backwards to identify such things as:

- Machinery and equipment required
- Raw materials purchasing schedules
- Inventory storage requirements
- Production schedules
- Labor schedules and overtime or temporaries, if any

See how this begins to fall into place. There's nothing magic about the business plan we're going to create. It's all just a matter of determining where we want to go, then working backwards to identify what we must do to get there.

Financial Plan

The financial person (or people) must determine the cash requirements associated with the sales projections. Among these are

- Scheduled vendor payments for the raw materials
- Salaries and wages
- Purchase of additional machinery and equipment
- Collection of receivables and the resulting cash inflow
- Arrangement for additional working capital financing, if necessary

Additional Purchases

If you intend to reposition the company by launching a new product or entering a new market, there's a chance that you'll need to buy additional equipment. If these are durable goods (things that last for more than a year), they're called *capital equipment.*

This part of the business plan identifies what, when, and how much the company needs in additional purchases of capital equipment to execute the plan. If we're aware of this in the beginning, we can arrange for things like

- Advance purchase commitment discounts
- Training our people to use the new equipment
- Alternatives to outright purchase, such as leasing
- Possible financing of the purchases
- Expansion of lines of credit to assist with the cash outflow

Suddenly everyone in the firm begins thinking in a coordinated fashion. That's one of the benefits of creating a business plan. Opportunities like those just listed for capital purchases begin to pop up with just a little advance thought.

People

Probably the most important part of any business plan is the human aspect. Money we can always get—and from a number of different sources. The same goes for machinery and equipment. However, people are unique, and this is especially important for high-tech businesses. For some of the genetic engineering companies and those firms now converting technology formerly used in the defense industry to peacetime applications, only a handful of qualified experts exist in the world.

So the people aspect of the business plan is of great importance to certain types of companies. We'll talk more about planning for labor expense in Chapter 12. However, for now we need the business plan to identify any shortfall in specific expertise necessary to execute each part of the plan.

That's not always easy. There are people's egos to contend with. There's also the unknown if you're embarking on a new venture for which there's little history. All of us have a tendency to say, I can do that. By the time someone has proven that he or she can't, it's often too late.

Carefully think through the people aspect of your plan. Take into honest consideration what present staff realistically can and cannot do. This is a big reason for creating a business plan. It takes time to find the right people. A solid business plan identifies the knowledge and expertise required in various parts of the company. If we develop the people plan carefully, we'll have plenty of time to find the people we need, get them aboard, and familiarize them with the firm. When it's time for them to perform their critical jobs, they can hit the ground running.

Motivating People

Another part of our people plan is the all-important motivational aspect: How do we get our people to execute the business plan and move the firm to where it needs to go? This part of the business plan forces us to think about what motivates our particular group of employees.

It's true that motivating forces differ for various types of companies and employees. What might work for employees at a dry cleaner won't be adequate for the design engineers at a computer peripheral manufacturing company.

Therefore, another reason why we plan our business is to identify and *communicate* to our employees

- Exactly what performance goals are expected of them
- Precisely what they can expect in return for hitting their targets

GUARANTEED RESULTS

Control the outcome. That's a tall order. Certainly the plan will encounter unforeseen problems (as well as opportunities). However, part of the business plan we're going to create for your company takes these into consideration.

More important, by the time we begin implementing the plan, we'll have already worked out several viable contingency plans. Just like an airplane pilot who has trained for emergency procedures until they're automatic, we've already got the response charted because we've anticipated the contingency happening.

Of course, we can't predict every circumstance. We don't even try. However, chances are that those things we haven't specifically addressed as possible threats to our business plan are variations on some theme that we *did* anticipate. Further, we've already rehearsed controlled responses to these contingencies. Our response is orderly and well thought out, and it correctly addresses what really needs doing.

That's how we can guarantee the outcome. Just because we discover a roadblock barring our original route to our targets doesn't mean we can't take an alternative route.

Remember what that owner of the small sheet metal fabrication company told me: "Why plan? It only gets in the way of what would have happened anyway." That fatalistic idea doesn't stand up to a well-devised business plan that considers what might happen to divert our course and deals with it before a crisis occurs.

The way we guarantee results is by determining that we're going to succeed no matter what. We expect hazards. Nevertheless, we'll deal with them, get around them, and continue with our mission. Business plans that provide ready-made solutions for specific contingencies gain a lot of support from the people charged with their implementation.

They make believers out of people like that sheet-metal mogul who thought he was at the mercy of whatever the forces out there chose to do to his company. Suddenly the business plan changes from a set of goals and targets we *hope* to reach, to a blueprint for success.

Updating the Plan

As the plan gets implemented, chances are we'll want to update it. Many companies choose to do this on a structured basis about halfway through the planning year. They take a look at each part of the business plan to see how things are tracking. The more astute managers, however, are aware of progress toward their goals each month. This is especially true for companies where there's some sort of financial incentive for successfully reaching planned targets.

Why do we update the plan? For the same reasons we created the plan in the first place:

- To ensure communication of the targets and due dates
- To demonstrate how each goal and subgoal will be reached
- To ensure coordination of those parts of the plan that deviated from their original course

Responding to Changes

When we update the plan, we incorporate changes that have already occurred. From there we can adjust the next part of the business plan to still take us to our original destination. It's like taking a second look at the map after we've reached a detour.

A scheduled plan update tells us something else, too. When the market or environment changes, if you update the business plan, you'll also know the impact of doing nothing. Not responding is always an option. The business plan and its updates allow us to avoid a reflex panic reaction to an outside influence.

Updates also answer the critics who accuse planners of crystal-ball gazing (and therefore wasting their time). Rather than looking twelve months into the future, we're only looking six months or less—until the scheduled plan update. That's much more accurate for planning purposes.

AVOIDING ANALYSIS PARALYSIS

Our description of the process and the reasons for preparing and executing a business plan may appear excessively detailed at this point. It's true that the business plan we're preparing considers every part of the company and how each contributes to achieving the overall goals. In that respect the plan is extremely detailed. However, within each department we want the plan to cover no more detail than absolutely necessary.

The more detail included, the more chance for error and confusion. Furthermore, unnecessarily detailed forecasts usually don't increase the accuracy of the plan. People tend to get caught up in the numbers to the point of *analysis paralysis*.

We can always do more research or dig deeper into revenue and cost projections. It's better to aim a little higher than risk wasting time generating data that's of little use. We can always get more detail. However, the effort expended generating something that's of no help can never be recovered.

Pegging the Level of Detail

As we go along, you'll get a feel for how much detailed information is appropriate for your company. The rules we'll follow create a business plan that's

- Precise enough for everyone to be able to identify his or her goals and how they fit into achieving the company's overall objectives
- Detailed enough to produce quantitative milestones that we'll use to track progress along the way

PROVIDING CONTROL

Business plans provide a healthy degree of management control over the company. That's especially important for companies—such as limited partnerships—that don't involve the majority of owners in daily operations. A quick look at the monthly income statement that compares actual performance with the plan tells partners how their company is doing compared with how it should be doing at that point in time.

Delegating Responsibility

Small businesses have a habit of growing as they become more successful. With the help of an effective business plan, your firm may experience this happy event. However, as small companies expand, they often outgrow their original management.

A company where the president makes every single decision (because it's his or her money on the line) soon grows into a nightmare for employees. Backlogs develop as people wait for the owner/president to respond to requests for decisions. People become resentful of not being given even the most minor authority. Commitment to the work declines because management views employees as brain-dead automatons.

Sound familiar? The business plan can prevent this from happening entirely. It all depends on how well senior management delegates authority.

Promoting Commitment

Smart managers who are at least reasonably sensitive to human needs realize that everyone wants the boss's trust. Delegating the authority to get the job done—whatever authority it requires—proves management's trust. Even if your company is large enough that only the department heads are able to help prepare the business plan, there's still plenty of room to delegate authority down the line.

Take, for example, the production schedule on the shop floor. The business plan specifies the production schedule needed to meet the sales plan. An autocratic owner would *tell* the shop manager exactly what needs doing. "Come to me if you have any problems," he or she would probably say.

A better solution is to explain the production needs to the shop manager, then stop. The shop manager's job is to make sure the goods are available in the finished goods inventory and ready for shipment when the sales plan needs them. Chances are that shop manager knows more about how to get the job done than the firm's owner anyway.

Astute owners delegate this responsibility for production to the shop manager, then let him or her do the job. People who are entrusted with that authority and believe their boss has confidence in them usually break their backs trying to be successful.

Delegating Authority

Along with responsibility must come the authority to make whatever decisions are necessary to get the job done. Say, for example, that someone must authorize overtime during a particular production run. The authoritarian style often requires approval from top management to incur such an expense. However, delegating the responsibility without granting the authority to act really amounts to only a transparent window dressing. Your employees can see through it as clearly as they can see out their window.

Maintaining Accountability

So, how do you delegate this authority and still maintain a level of comfort that the job is getting done? That's where the business plan helps. Managers who understand how to help their employees succeed can delegate creating the target benchmarks used for evaluating the plan progress.

It's these periodic determinants of performance that management uses to gain a level of comfort that each part of the plan is proceeding the way it should.

But what about that overtime expense? It's one thing to meet production goals, but not at any cost. Don't forget that there's still a profit target dictated by gross margin benchmarks. There's no reason to avoid making the shop manager responsible for production costs as well. Essentially, we make the manager responsible for meeting the production targets and accountable for the costs incurred to do it.

So, now you've delegated not only the *amount* of production, but the *cost* of production as well. Further, you've identified exactly the person who should have the authority over those things. The business plan should provide periodic benchmarks for each of the things we've delegated. There's nothing wrong with letting the shop manager know that your expectations include not only the amount of production but cost as well. However, it's meaningless to make someone responsible and accountable for anything without giving that person the complete authority to get the job done.

OUTGROWING MANAGEMENT

One of the most common reasons that a once-successful small business goes down the tubes is that the company outgrows its original management. It usually happens that management maintained a death grip on the entire decision-making structure of the company. The employees can't grow. This stifles creativity. They can't breathe. Soon the firm begins to die of asphyxiation.

Sometimes it takes a brush with bankruptcy to open the owner's eyes. The brilliant ones hire a professional manager, someone skilled at motivating people and running a business. That's what happened at Apple Computer. The board ousted the two founders, Steve Wozniak and Steve Jobs, in favor of a professional president. Of course that's a blow to someone's ego. After all, the founder nurtured the company from a seedling. They fed the firm contracts and clients and agonized over every sneeze the young company experienced during its growth.

Nevertheless, there comes a time when every company needs less of the very special technical expertise provided by its founder. The viewpoint of management must change at some point in time to that of a more seasoned executive in order to prosper.

The business plan provides a forum for management change. Often, astute owners can see the type of management style that's needed. The really smart ones can look introspectively and ask themselves if they still have the tools and skills to lead the company where it needs to go. If the answer is no (or yes, but let's get some additional help), it's better if the change begins as their own idea.

CONCLUSION

Have I convinced you? Do you have enough ammunition to persuade the doubters in your company that creating a viable business plan is something worthwhile? If not, you might look more deeply at why you're meeting resistance. In some cases managers are afraid of goals. They have a fear of failing. Sometimes managers are just plain lazy. They can foresee a never-ending cycle of increased targets.

We call their reaction *sandbagging*. That's when a manager deliberately low-balls estimates of what the department can achieve. The thinking goes something like this: *If I tell them what we can really do, then we'll have to break our backs even more the next time. Instead, we'll lower this estimate, hit the target, and allow management to raise it to where it should have been in the first place.*

This behavior has to do with a lack of management trust, commitment to success, and participation in creating the business plan. Sandbagging is a symptom of management's failure. If you notice your managers sandbagging their targets, look at the method used to create the business plan.

Chapter 2 deals with the structure of the business plan.

Chapter 2

Structuring Your Business Plan

OVERVIEW

Think of your business plan as a production line. What goes in at the start are raw material and unfinished assemblies. In our case, the raw materials include:

- Talent and initiative from your employees • Capital
- Market position • The company's creditworthiness
- The firm's earning capacity
- Assessment of changes in the marketplace

The unfinished assemblies include ideas and concepts that people want to try. These are the most valuable parts of the plan. They can take the company where it needs to go.

As with most assembly lines, what goes in at the front end probably doesn't resemble the completed product. The planning process refines, changes, and adopts these original input items. It uses them all. During this process, we'll

- Assess all your firm's resources: financial, technological, and human, to name a few.
- Identify where your company needs to go in order to prosper.
- Sometimes work backwards from a target to determine what specific departmental goals are needed.

In the end we'll have a workable business plan that's far more than just a written document. We'll understand the changes in property, plant, equipment, management, technology, financial structure, and capital resources needed to reach our targets. Everyone responsible for executing the business plan will know what's expected of him or her and when it's due. We'll establish milestones where we need coordination between different departments to accomplish a particular goal. We'll be able to see progress toward those intermediate goals—definite, *quantified* progress, reported regularly. We'll make midcourse changes in time to avoid jeopardizing the larger goals.

The structure of this business plan is like nothing you've seen before. This one is a nuts-and-bolts, how-to-get-it-done-without-fail tool kit. We're going to grab your company and take it where it needs to go. You won't find much of the theoretical *strategizing* so many other planning books carry on about. That's fine for larger companies that can wait five years or more for results.

Instead, what happens to your company during the next twelve months concerns us. If you can hit your short-range targets year after year, the longer term will take care of itself. Chapter 2 introduces the planning structure we'll employ for your company. It identifies the various techniques and methods used in the process. By the end you'll have an idea of how each part of the planning process builds on what went before. Further, you'll understand how the business plan ties all the various functions in your business tie together.

ACTION PLANNING

The way we structure this process, the *action* of planning is just as important as the written product (sometimes more so). The planning structure builds relationships between departments that did not exist before. The design and implementation of departmental goals cements communication between people and their departments. The need for coordination between efforts that appeared unrelated becomes obvious.

A successful business plan requires the cooperation of each department in the company. Don't worry about resistance. There are some specific things we'll do to ensure the commitment of even the most diehard antiplanners.

Demanding Results

Our orientation in this action plan is results-driven. That's probably not a foreign concept for most small-business owners and managers. Their very survival depends on results—usually daily. But there's a twist. The results we're demanding come from your employees. These are the people responsible for implementing the business plan. For the company to prosper for any length of time, the *group* must commit to the plan's success. The *group* must understand the single thing that each person must do above all else to make the company successfully hit its targets.

Finally, the *group* must be the body that evaluates its own performance and rewards or punishes its members. Peer influence is far more persuasive than any single reward offered by a manager. It's made even more potent when the group becomes a *team* seeking a set of common goals.

Of course we'll demand results. Those results are concrete targets—mostly quantifiable, but always clearly understood by everyone involved. Assign specific individuals responsibility for attaining these results. Their commitment comes from their participation in establishing worthwhile goals that they're responsible for reaching.

Let's walk through the structure of this hands-on, no-excuses way to hammer out and execute a business plan.

ASSESSING YOUR CURRENT POSITION

This probably requires the most soul-searching you've done in some time. We want an honest appraisal of your company's present status. Include each aspect of the company you deem critical to its success. Consider such things as

- Products • Distribution channels • Market share and influence
- Customer loyalty • Technological innovations and advantages
- Management talent • Employee capabilities
- Manufacturing capacity and equipment • Competition • Pricing

The role of each of these attributes in furthering our goals does not concern us now. Indeed, we haven't established our goals yet. Instead, we want an honest appraisal of where we stand today.

Using this information and comparing it with the company's goals—once we establish them—we will see a gap emerging between where we are and where we want to be. It's that gap that much of our business plan deals with. Closing that gap is our goal.

IDENTIFICATION OF COMPANY GOALS

From the beginning we'll work to create clearly defined goals for your business plan. These goals begin at the top of the company and work their way down. Some are longer range—twelve-month time horizons. Other subgoals needed to reach the larger targets are intermediate range—say six months. Some are just three months out or even less. These are usually extremely critical things that *must* happen before work can proceed on the next step of a larger goal.

Unlike those of some planning exercises you may have experienced, our goals are brutally precise. They are the product of the firm's planners recognizing the specific targets the company must meet during the next twelve months if it is to prosper. It's easier for those who implement the plan to communicate precise goals rather than fuzzy, broad goals.

That's just what we want—clarity. Since our time frame is short, there's no room for anyone wasting time doing something that doesn't specifically help us get where we want to go. To this end, there are two questions we ask when establishing company goals:

- Where do we want to go in terms of products, customers, profits, return on investment?
- What changes do we have to make in each department to get us there?

Differences from Larger Companies

The business planning needs of small companies are very different from those of their larger counterparts. First of all, small firms lack the resources and influence of large companies. Second, smaller companies worry more about survival today than conquering the world tomorrow. That's why our approach deliberately omits

- Statements of philosophy and the *mission* of the company
- Creation of a strategic plan that's consistent with management's philosophy

These are of little use to us in guiding the company over the next year to a specific end point. Now, this isn't to say that we should stick our heads in the sand and ignore a longer-term look at our future. However, that activity is probably better done once we've gotten the firm under control and understand how to make short-term changes that enhance profitability. Certainly, if this is your first planning exercise, the approach we're using gets tangible results using real targets that are achievable. It's comparable to walking before trying to run.

Attainable Goals

Have you ever seen people give up before they start because the task intimidated them? That's something we don't want to have happen here. Recognize that there may be too large a gap between the goals you come up with and the firm's current position. There may come a time when you say, There's no way we can accomplish all that this year.

It takes a smart manager to recognize that the chasm is too wide to jump in a single leap. Instead, he or she must reassess the goals, and maybe scale them back. A somewhat less ambitious set of targets results. However, they are realistic targets that everyone believes in. The outcome is greater commitment and higher probability of success than if you tried to ram unnecessarily burdensome goals down everyone's throat.

The trick to setting attainable goals is to strike a balance between targets that represent a realistic reach and those that are so far out that they'll certainly cause failure. On the one hand, we've identified something worth shooting for, and we'll reward our team appropriately. On the other hand, people view impossible goals as negative even when they are sweetened with better rewards. People would rather have a reasonable chance of receiving a bucket that's 90 percent full than no chance of receiving one that's overflowing.

RECOGNIZING FACTORS CRITICAL TO PLAN SUCCESS

Once you've identified your current position and arrived at the targets for your company, it's time to figure out how to bridge the gap between the two. The technicians call this process *reverse engineering*. In essence, we're taking the end result and working backwards to determine the steps we need to get there.

In Chapters 4 and 5, "Setting Company Goals" and "Setting Department Goals," you'll learn how to identify those intermediate steps that begin to build a bridge over the capability gap.

Analyzing Success Factors

You'll find that your business plan leaves the foggy world of strategies and mission philosophy very quickly. Instead, what makes the company move toward specific goals interests us.

Let's say that your firm's overriding target for the next year is to reach a 10 percent return on capital. There's nothing wrong with that goal. It's quantifiable. There's no question how to determine whether you've reached it (amount available for owner distribution / capital = return on capital). Even better, we can track progress toward it each month. Now, here's where the factors needed to reach this target begin to emerge.

Let's say that two things need to happen if we are to reach our 10 percent target:

- Sales must increase by $1,000,000.
- Production costs must decrease by $500,000.

The plan separates factors critical to each of these targets into a series of sub-goals. In our example, the plan might spread the sales increase over several different products and among the quotas of different members of the sales staff. To decrease production costs, the firm might have to acquire some new machinery. Outright purchase would require more capital. That would take us in the wrong direction. Instead, the answer might be to lease the equipment. There are many other possible sales enhancements and production cost cutting measures, but you get the idea.

See how concrete solutions begin to appear once we know exactly where we want to go? The road map to get there isn't difficult to create. Each step of the way we've identified specific targets and goals that we must meet by a certain time and assigned to certain people as their responsibility.

Analyzing success factors is an exercise that consists of merely working back from a definite goal to see just how you're going to accomplish it.

COMPILING DEPARTMENTAL PLANS

Consider overall company goals as the top level. Then department goals fall into the second tier. They provide the detailed blueprint for accomplishing specific actions in a time-phased manner that coordinates the company's effort to reach a larger goal.

Setting Goals by Department

We want to coordinate the company's business plan among departments. When actions and results in one department are important for another, we must make sure these departments are communicating throughout the design and implementation of the plan.

This isn't always as easy as you might think. Not all department managers have the company's best interests at heart. It's human nature to think of yourself first. Some might view new ideas coming out of the business plan as

- Unwieldy • Too convoluted
- Untested and untried, and therefore a waste of time
- Threatening to jobs or the status quo
- Ignorant of the experience of those who weren't consulted

Of these five, the last is the most deadly. Take special care in choosing those who participate in the design and implementation of your business plan. Some people can't wait to punish others for thinking they know more about the thing that person knows best. It's a matter of ego. How many times in your career have you heard someone say, "I could have told them it wouldn't work. They should have asked me first before wasting all that time and money." Some people deliberately set out to prove they're right.

Part of the participative planning process is to create the feeling that what's good for the company is good for each department. Our objective is to change the focus from each department working at its jobs autonomously (us versus them). Many companies limp along like this. Their employees focus on their own tasks as the beginning and end of their responsibility.

For your business plan to succeed on the level we're talking about, each department must become part of a larger team. Suddenly employees' success depends more on how the company as a whole succeeds than on what they contributed by themselves. That's the way the company distributes rewards, too—based on the team's success.

Marketing

The marketing department's goals are sometimes difficult to quantify. Nevertheless, the results of its efforts are quantifiable; we see them in the sales numbers. We can make the marketing segment clear by reverse-engineering the target into a set of action steps to reach it. When you're thinking about the targets your marketing department must hit to achieve the firm's overall goals, consider things like

- Company image • Perception of the customer
- Identification of product benefits • Introduction of new products
- Support of the sales force

The marketing plan has slightly loftier objectives than many other parts of our business plan. For example, say the firm needs to introduce a new product— one that's completely different from anything the firm is known for. Part of the marketing plan is to reposition the company so that it has sufficient credibility in the new product's field.

Once we have determined the marketing objective, establishing the advertising and promotional efforts the company needs to accomplish its goal becomes a more mechanical process.

Admittedly, marketing objectives are sometimes fuzzier than some of the goals you'll find in other departments. But with a little thought, you should be able to attach some solid targets and indicators of progress.

Sales

It's relatively easy to determine targets and goals in the sales department. Indeed, with the exception of finance, few departments live and die by the numbers as does Sales. If one of your goals involves revenue or profit, chances are that some of the departmental subgoals to get you there include the sales department.

Further, goals and quotas are familiar to the sales force and its management. That's how the company pays them. This shouldn't be an uphill battle. One thing you'll probably have to do, however, is make sure the compensation is appropriate for what the sales force is being asked to do. That's only fair. If the sales force is responsible in some significant way for helping the company achieve its overall business plan, then it should participate in the rewards to an equally significant extent.

Establishing sales goals involves some thought as to the customers and various markets involved. Often, the plan identifies types of customers or even specific customers. At the sales department's disposal is an arsenal of resources.

One such resource might be a change in the credit approval criteria. In some industries, obtaining trade credit may be a pain for customers. As a result, the company may lose business just because it hasn't made it easy for the customer to buy. One of the strategies in the sales plan might be changes that help make purchasing the firm's products easier.

Another thing many companies use as a sales tool is the kind of sophisticated order entry system now available for desktop computers. Some of these modern automated systems have a computer interface not only with the inventory control system but also with accounts receivable. The speed and accuracy with which customers can place an order (or inquire about an order already placed) suddenly comes out of the dark ages. Not only can the order taker tell instantly if the item is in stock, he or she can put it on back order if it isn't. Even better, some systems suggest already approved substitutes. The result is that many sales that might have been lost to competition because of unavailability are locked in.

Further, with the customer's balance owed available to the order taker, an instant credit decision can be made at the time of order. There's no waiting for approvals to grind through a manual system. Another of the books in the Adams Business Advisors series, *Accounting for the New Business*, tells in detail how to establish a modern order entry system at your business.

Operations

The operations department or division probably includes

- Manufacturing • Quality control • Shipping • Receiving
- Warehouse and inventory

Practically speaking, many of the goals associated with operations involve cost-cutting measures and improved production processes. However, some of the most successful firms have launched new products based on manufacturing technology. The disposable contact lens is a good example. A whole new submarket in disposable lenses opened up for contact lens wearers because new production processes brought manufacturing costs down. With the exception of an occasional enhanced polymer coating, disposable lenses themselves are almost identical to regular extended wear lenses. But now they can be marketed as a throw-away. The customer has less expensive lenses, and the manufacturers make a greater profit because they sell more lenses at the same or higher margins.

Some companies give specific operational targets to the quality control department. Its business is numbers. Therefore, quantifying performance targets and monitoring them is nothing new. However, QC usually acts as the referee. The real improvement comes from other operational departments, such as production, warehouse picking, and packing. These departments need to work closely with QC to monitor how the plan is working.

Another focus of the operations plan might be the manufacturing department itself. Often reaching cost or production targets necessitates the rearrangement or complete revamping of the production line. This can be a major undertaking. Not only does it require teardown and reengineering of existing facilities, it probably includes acquiring some new equipment as well. This schedule dictates the timing of capital equipment purchases. From that falls out another scheduled cash outflow of which the finance department must be aware.

Often outside specialists are invited in to assist. Additionally, and probably most significantly, production is completely stopped during the entire effort. Such a major undertaking can be one of the most significant events in the entire business plan. It affects almost every other department in the company. If this phase is not executed as planned, it has a domino effect on the rest of the company.

Surplus manufacturing or warehouse capacity can be another aspect of operations. Though not nearly so potentially disruptive as adding to or reorganizing the production facility, the impacts can be great. They mostly have to do with other parts of the firm that can possibly convert and use the facilities being vacated by the production department. This allows for expansion elsewhere in the company without additional facilities overhead costs. Without the business plan, this opportunity might never have come to light because the two departments might never have considered such a swap.

If the answer is to get out of unneeded facilities entirely, plans need to be made to either sublease or sell the property. Either way it will affect the company's cash flow and property tax liability.

People

This is where much assistance can be given the rest of the company. Often a capability gap can be bridged by hiring the right people. If you're lucky, the knowledge and background of these special people will improve departments beyond those in which they work.

Another aspect of the human component is salaries. If your shop is unionized, reaching labor expense targets may not be entirely in your hands. However, one of the benefits of creating a business plan is its ability to assist in dealing with those contingencies that always seem to occur. The behavior of your union during negotiations is one of those contingencies that can be anticipated. A logical response can be worked out before the situation becomes a crisis. Maybe it can even help avert a strike.

Even in companies that do not have to worry about a union, salaries are often used as targets in the cost containment sections of business plans.

Purchases

These are the purchases of additional capital equipment needed to bridge the gap between your current manufacturing capacity and what the plan says it should be. Perhaps your firm needs to upgrade its assembly line to meet both production targets and cost reduction goals. Goals in the business plan for these purchases specify things such as

- Price • Terms • Timing • Capability

These are among the most critical of many companies' goals. Problems with delivery, engineering, or installation (to name a few) can send a well-thought-out business plan into a tailspin. That's why we include communication and tracking of individual departments' milestones as part of the overall plan implementation. If something happens to any critical component—purchasing of capital goods included—there are things we can do, given enough time, to reduce the impact.

Not only is the schedule for these additional purchases important for the manufacturing department and any other areas in the company that depend on delivery dates, but it's also vital for the finance department. Generally such special purchases of costly equipment require provisions out of the ordinary. If the company is buying the equipment outright, the controller must coordinate a large outflow of funds with the cash flow plan. Leases and some other forms of financing usually require a deposit. Additionally, both the company and the lender must negotiate and approve the financing commitments.

Financial

The financial subplan really doesn't have many targets of its own, with the exception perhaps of arranging for borrowing facilities. Instead, it's affected by almost every other department's plan. The sales targets, for example, are what drives the balance of accounts receivable. The finance department is usually responsible for A/R collections. Therefore, part of the financial plan must be a formulated response to managing, accounting for, collecting, and financing the projected receivables.

The manufacturing and production plan affects accounts payable to a large degree. Someone has to pay for the raw materials and subassemblies the company needs to buy in order to produce the goods the sales and marketing departments plan to sell. If the funds don't come out of cash flow from cash sales and collection of accounts receivable, the finance department must plan to arrange an interim line of credit.

Often one of the points incorporated into the financial plan is adjusting the aging of accounts payable. If the industry standard or custom is a greater age than that which the company normally uses, then an opportunity may exist. However, to take advantage of that opportunity, the plan must coordinate the effort of those who do the firm's purchasing and those who make decisions regarding payment of bills. Certainly, the business planning effort brings something like this to light and provides a structured forum to make sure it gets done. Then it creates a mechanism to follow its progress to make sure all is going as we expected.

When we get to Chapter 13, "Creating the Financial Plan," we'll identify just how to incorporate all these financial variables into an understandable and useful plan. However, while we're still on the plan structure, it's important to understand the various relationships each department has with the others. Nowhere is this more apparent than in finance.

The working capital required to run the firm (current assets – current liabilities = working capital) is the responsibility of the finance department. You must have enough cash available to pay your current bills while you wait for customers to pay what they owe your company. Changes in the subplans of any of these areas will cause working capital requirements to change:

- *Credit limit and/or credit policy:* Changes receivables balance and sometimes the type of customer along with payment habits and risk of bad debt.

- *Inventory purchase terms:* Changes the due date and trade discount percentage of the materials bought for production. This causes cash outflow requirements to change.

- *Order quantities and required safety stock of inventory:* Changes the amount of inventory on hand, which alters scheduled cash outflow.

- *Collection effort expended on receivables:* Changes the speed of cash collection.

The finance department prepares its subplan based on what the other departments say they're going to do. Smart financial planners use *indices* to track the performance of specific segments in the financial plan. These are nothing more than quick computations, usually in the form of ratios or comparisons, that tell how a critical item is doing.

For example, the flow of inventory out of the company is a primary concern of the financial controller. A good index is the inventory turnover ratio (cost of goods sold / average inventory balance = inventory turnover). It gives a quick indication of how the sales plan is proceeding and how accurately the company has gauged product demand.

Another indicator used in tracking progress toward collection targets is the turnover of accounts receivable (credit sales / average receivables balance = A/R turnover). This gives the controller an idea of how fast the company collects its receivables. If the firm is collecting too slowly, this index tells you so at a glance.

Some astute financial managers link the speed of collections with the pay rate of accounts payable. Ideally, the turnover of receivables should be at least equal to or (even better) faster than the company's turnover of its payables. In this happy circumstance, the firm's vendors are financing its receivables, since it collects from its customers *before* it has to pay for the goods it sold. Nice if you can do it. With proper financial planning and enough attention paid to the other departments in the company, you can at least come closer to the ideal than you would have otherwise.

IDENTIFYING CASH CAPABILITY

A huge determinant of many small-business profit plans is the amount of cash available for implementing all these great ideas. Certainly we want to be aware of such a real-world constraint, but not to such an extent that it completely stifles creativity. The more imaginative and successful entrepreneurs I know never let a little thing like money stand in the way of getting a really good concept off the ground.

Further, money is always available to finance ideas that show promise. A solid track record of past success identifies such projects. Then, a logical, detailed business plan for use as a blueprint for executing the idea lends credibility to the project.

Using the Business Plan to Determine Cash Capability

One of the spin-offs from developing a detailed business plan is the structure it provides to computation of the firm's ability to generate needed cash. Simply stated, cash capability is *the amount of money now in the bank, available from lenders and generated from operations during the accounting period.* If you want an equation, here it is:

Disposable cash currently on hand *plus* any cash investments maturing during the accounting period *plus* collection of existing and anticipated receivables *plus* available lines of credit *less* payment of existing and anticipated payables *equals* cash capability

Of course, we get many of these numbers from the business plan. Uses of cash capability estimates include

- Determination of additional capital purchases, if needed
- Determination of additional inventory purchases, if necessary
- Estimation of disposable cash (excluding available lines of credit) at the end of the accounting period—this usually catches at least the passing interest of partners and investors
- Identification of the cash position at the end of plan implementation

COST ACCOUNTING

Your company's cost accounting system (if you have one—service companies generally don't) provides a good monitor of manufacturing and production costs. The cost system establishes standards for things like

- Purchase prices of raw materials • Hourly labor rates
- Amount of labor used for production
- Amount of material used for production • Reject rate
- Rework costs

These provide benchmarks for use in monitoring production efficiency.

The cost system often gets its standards from the production and manufacturing department's detailed business plan. Just like any other department, it identifies the requirements and works backwards to figure out how to do it. If one planning requirement involves a manufacturing cost reduction, then Production may rework its cost standards to make it happen.

Enter these standards into the cost system as targets. That's what the plan tracks actual production costs against—usually every day and often several times during the day for large, expensive production runs.

Cost accounting systems are very good at pointing out specific types of cost variances in particular items produced. Use them to pinpoint a production cost that's over established standards. Then take corrective action *before* it does irreversible damage to the business plan.

IMPLEMENTING THE PLAN

After all those responsible for the business plan have reached a consensus on goals and timing, it's time to execute the plan. Sounds simple, doesn't it? All we have to do is what we said we were going to do in the plan. But it doesn't always work that way.

I've seen small businesses spend time creating a workable plan, only to have their managers go back to their departments and conduct business the same old way, almost as if nothing like creating a business plan that would change the course of the company ever took place. Some people just don't seem to make the connection between planned action and *real* action. That's why we structure into the plan effort a separate section to ensure proper execution.

Monitoring Results

Very shortly after we've completed the business plan—probably within the first week of the implementation phase, we begin monitoring results. We do this for two reasons:

- To get the monitoring mechanism up and running
- To make sure the plan is not being ignored by key sections of the company

Within the plan structure, the monitoring mechanism is among the most important components. It makes no sense to spend your valuable time determining the best course of action to take, right down to the amount of raw material inventory to purchase and when to pay for it, then go off and hope for the best. We said at the beginning, this is a *hands-on, how-to-get-it-done-without-fail tool kit*. Simply hoping for the best doesn't cut it.

One of the things we're going to hammer at as we discuss each component of the business plan is how we can watch over the results to be sure we aren't wandering off course. For most departments this is easy enough. A weekly or monthly report that shows actual results compared to those in the plan is sufficient.

However, we design the monitoring mechanism not only for upper-level managers, but for those on the firing line as well. It makes more sense to give those responsible for hitting specific targets immediate feedback on how they're doing. After all, if they've really taken the responsibility for hitting these targets seriously, they'll demand that kind of feedback.

This isn't an involved, expensive, time-consuming management information system. Few small businesses could afford one even if they needed it—which most don't. Instead, the emphasis is on simplicity. We want the monitoring mechanism to get our people the information they need when they need it, to tell them what changes they need to make.

An example of such a simple monitoring mechanism could be in the accounts receivable department. Let's say one target is to reduce the average time it takes to collect receivables by three days. However, there's a problem with sending out sales invoices. Sometimes there's as much as a five-day backlog between the sale date and the day the firm renders invoices.

The monitoring mechanism that helps the receivables person watch this might be an invoice processing backlog report. All we want to know is how long it is taking to send out invoices. If they don't go out the same day as the sale, this is a problem for the person responsible for receivables collection. With this information, the implementation team can make informed decisions on how to fix the problem. Indeed, a written report may not even be necessary. All it may take is a well-placed question to get the answer.

Assessing Results

Our implementation plan will have a definite structure. In that sense, the company conducts a monthly review of the plan's progress. The plan monitoring mechanism provides those responsible for successful implementation of each area with an unbiased assessment of their progress. We want this done with the plan implementation team as a group. That's how we keep open the channels of communication. It's also how we maintain peer pressure.

Agenda of assessment meetings

These meetings shouldn't take very long—an hour or so at the most. Some managers may complain that they don't have an hour to spare. This isn't a spare hour. It's part of their job. Performance as employees depends on their successfully implementing their part of the business plan. That kind of blunt explanation of the plan's importance and the seriousness with which we treat it should get everybody's attention. If some people still don't get it, we can always find others who do.

Here are the items we want to accomplish during each assessment meeting:

- Review of actual performance indicators compared to plan
- Discussion and explanation of any deviations
- Solutions to bring deviations back on track
- Minor adjustments to plan to monitor implementation of solutions
- Problems coordinating efforts of different departments
- Anticipated problems during the next thirty days and longer
- Restatement of financial incentives the team is working for

Free-flowing meetings that have no agenda tend to run longer than they need to and don't accomplish their objectives. That's why we structure the progress assessment meetings. The meeting is important. The time of those involved is valuable. There is something significant to accomplish.

A structured agenda expresses these facts. It leaves no doubt as to who presents what and when. Nor does it allow for deferment of subjects that might be sensitive. *Postponement* of sensitive discussions might place achieving the plan at risk.

If someone is embarrassed because they stumbled, then so be it. However, be sure to teach the group how to pick up its victims and dust them off. We want commitment to results without excuses. We don't want to alienate valuable members.

Making Midcourse Changes

You wouldn't expect the captain of a ship to consult the compass once at the beginning of a voyage and not look again until he thought the ship should be in port. The same goes for implementing a business plan. At least once during the implementation cycle, the planning team needs to reassess where it has taken the company. Usually the plan requires some midcourse changes, if for no other reason than that unforeseen opportunities may have sprung up that should be exploited.

Again, structure this gathering with a definite agenda. Cover all the things that the regular progress assessment meetings cover, but on a larger scale. If the midcourse correction meeting takes place halfway through the planning year, then address year-to-date results.

Additionally, this is the forum in which to make larger changes to the plan. Maybe the company's goals have proven unrealistic or perhaps the team sees a way to go well beyond what it thought it could. Often midcourse corrections result in significant changes to goals, or at least to how the company reaches its goals.

The meeting maintains the timeliness of the business plan. Few people take seriously goals that don't recognize changes that have occurred since they were first established. By now it should be obvious that everyone involved in creating and implementing the business plan must take midcourse corrections seriously.

What we hope to get out of the midcourse changes is a guiding hand for the business plan as well as an updating. The company will have learned a great deal about interdepartmental cooperation since the plan was first created. This new-found coordination may create some operational shortcuts by which some departments can help others reach their goals.

By now you know that business planning is not some unstructured, amorphous activity done in a vacuum. Instead, we establish a definite method and a set of specific procedures for each department in your company to follow. The result is a coordinated and timely road map to take the firm from its starting point today to the destination management feels will make it prosper most one year from now.

Along the way we'll identify specific road signs to watch for that mark our progress. When we need to make small changes, the implementation team can execute them with a minimum of disruption. At least once along the way we'll take a look at our year-to-date progress. We expect to make some significant changes at that time. Once again, we structure the process so that it is predictable. There are no surprises with the results and no excuses for missing your target.

Now, let's determine our starting point. Chapter 3 answers the question, Where is the company today?

Chapter 3

Where Is the Company Today?

OVERVIEW

Chapter 2 introduced the *capability gap* between where the firm is at present and where it needs to be according to management's business plan. It's closing this gap that sets the business plan in motion. The first step is to identify the starting point.

That's what assessment of your company's current position accomplishes. Chapter 3 focuses on specific aspects of the company—aspects that are critical to gaining a clear picture of not only where the company is today, but what resources are available right now to help close the gap between our beginning and end points.

Additionally, gaining an understanding of your firm's strengths unmasks its weaknesses at the same time. We want to know where the company needs to shore itself up.

This is an honest representation of three things:

- The state of each critical element of the company
- Specific strengths that will help the firm execute its business plan
- Specific weaknesses that could jeopardize the success of the plan

We're looking for the facts here. Anything less than a realistic, unbiased point of view won't help our mission. So, when you're asking these tough questions of yourself or your employees, don't sugar-coat the answers. Make it clear that the truth may hurt. Honest answers may point directly at certain individuals' failings. However, you should also make it clear that this is the first step toward those same people becoming the new superstars.

PURPOSE OF ASSESSING CURRENT POSITION

What's the first thing most of us do before starting on a journey to a place we've never been before? We take out a map and figure out where we are now. Then we trace a path to our destination. Finally, we plan a route that includes stops, detours, and all the little things that ensure successful arrival at our destination.

The first step, figuring out where we are now, is nothing more than assessing our current position. However, it's a little more complicated because there are several aspects of the company to consider. Our current position, for example, includes a clear idea of the business we're *really* in and the technology we employ in our manufacturing operation. Our employees' capabilities have a large impact on where we are today.

The finished product of this chapter will be a written assessment of your company's present market position. It will identify the strengths and weaknesses of your products, manufacturing facilities, managers, and staff. We'll evaluate the company's financial structure and borrowing capacities. In short, this chapter identifies everything you need in order to determine the gap between your current position and where your business plan says you should be in one year.

WHAT BUSINESS ARE YOU IN?

Let's start with the single most basic question every business planner asks: *What business are we in?* Before you answer too quickly, think about it. In Chapter 1 we discussed the real business of Domino's Pizza Corporation as providing a convenience service, not just selling pizza.

Here's another example. Have you ever seen those traveling petting zoos that set up in shopping malls? What's their business? Animal attractions? No. Advertising for the mall? You're getting closer. How about all those parents who drop their kids off at the petting zoo and scoot away to do their shopping? Isn't the zoo really in the child care business?

Now, would the addition of rare (and expensive) baby Peruvian llamas add enough value for the zoo to charge the malls a higher fee? Probably not. How about adding certain safety measures, or maybe washing the animals so they smell nicer? Why not hire a zoologist to give kiddy lectures on the animals? Suddenly the zoo company is catering to its real line of business. Now the company can raise its fees because it has something the competition hasn't thought of—yet.

Accurate identification of the real business you are in goes a long way toward defining that gap between your starting point today and your planned goals. Here are some questions to help you further.

1. *Where do you make most of your revenue?* People buy the particular products or services you provide. What are they? Why do they buy from you? Can they get it anywhere else?

2. *What is it that your company does best?* Looking inside your company, identify the one thing it does better than anything else. Next, look outside your firm: What do you do better than anyone else who does the same thing? What is your company known for, and why do people come to you rather than your competitors? Maybe your firm's reputation depends more on something associated with the products it sells—like their delivery—than to the actual goods. Domino's Pizza and its fast home delivery differentiated it from everyone else. McDonald's hamburgers grew first from the speed of its product delivery, then later from its quality.

3. *What do you provide that your competitors don't?* We want to know how your customers perceive your company as being different from your competitors. It's not necessarily so important *what* you actually provide

over and above your competition. What really matters is what your customers *think* you provide. After all, any salesperson will tell you that perception is reality.

4. *What need do you meet? Whose need do you meet?* People make purchases to satisfy some need. What need do your company's products satisfy? Whose need is it? Don't get stuck just on products or services. Get down to the most basic need level. Remember the petting zoo. The real customers were parents. The need was temporary child care. This question should also help you answer the next one.

5. *What markets does your company serve? What customers within these markets do you sell to?*

With some thought, these five questions will help you identify without a doubt the true business of your company.

APPRAISING MARKET POSITION

Large companies often hire armies of consultants and market researchers to figure this one out. Small businesses don't have that luxury, nor do they need it. Most owners and managers of small companies are close enough to their end customers to have a feel for their company's market position. Here are the factors you'll want to consider when evaluating your current market position.

Pricing

Where does your firm stack up in terms of pricing? Are you the market leader? A follower? Do you have something unique that allows you to employ a different pricing structure from the rest of the market? Are your prices generally at the high, middle, or low end of the market?

Quality

Along with durability, the features of a product often dictate its perceived quality in the marketplace. Styling has a lot to do with perceived quality as well. If a product is sleek and appears to be able to do the job, the marketplace views it as high-quality.

Depending on your customers' reasons for buying from you, quality may have less to do with your products than with something else your firm does. Perhaps it's your extensive inventory of replacement parts. Maybe it's high-quality service technicians. Look for the real reasons for the assessment of your company's *quality quotient* when evaluating market position.

Service

If service is an essential part of your product, then chances are it should figure into an assessment of market position. Companies whose customers perceive them as being good servicers may enjoy a higher market position than those whose customers do not.

Sales Volume

If you're speaking in terms of raw numbers, sales volume defines market position. This may be difficult for a small business to assess, however. If you have ready access to information on sales volume in revenue dollars or units sold, use it in your current position assessment. However, keep in mind that few business plans base any meaningful goals on being number one in sales. That's relevant only when linked with a larger target that actually does something useful for the company rather than its owner's ego.

Technological Leadership

So much of industry has to do with technology. Products that employ state-of-the-art improvements usually enjoy a higher market position than those that do not. This is particularly true in businesses in which technology changes rapidly and customers demand the latest innovations.

If you are in such a high-tech industry, it's probably important to include this aspect in your assessment of your current market position. Chances are that technology will have something to do with reaching your firm's planning goals. You need to understand what technological gap (if any) exists between current and required capabilities.

Advertising

Often market position is at least partly a function of advertising. Your business plan may require a certain improvement in market position. If advertising plays an important role in this, then assessment of your programs is probably a significant factor in determining present market position.

APPRAISING PRODUCTS

Whether you provide hard products or services to your customers, their current position figures prominently in what your company needs to do to accomplish its planned goals. Perhaps you need to add some products or delete others. Maybe certain products no longer meet customer needs and require redesign.

This can be a difficult part of the current position assessment. Often small-business owners closely involve themselves with product development. There's an emotional attachment there. Sometimes they cannot conceive of any improvements that can (or should) be made to their "baby." Here are some points to assist in current product assessment.

What Do We Really Provide?

Remember Domino's and the petting zoo. What both firms provided to their customers wasn't exactly what it appeared to be. Look closely at *why* your customers buy your products. It's often these motives that tell what the company really provides.

What's Coming Up?

If you are in an industry that's moving, chances are that you have either entirely new products or changes to existing ones already on the drawing board. They are a big part of your current position assessment. You may change, cancel, or accelerate these products depending on where the business plan takes the firm. Cancellation of some U.S. weapons systems after the end of the cold war is a good example. Assessment of America's current position revealed changes that could free funds for use in reaching other goals.

How Do These Products Meet the Need?

Try thinking of your products from two points of view:

- That of a customer trying to fulfill a need
- That of someone with a choice of the different products on the market

Now, how do your products currently meet the need? Don't think of this question as demeaning to your company's products. You must accurately assess where you are today in the important process of meeting customer demand. This answer will almost certainly be vital if the business plan targets meeting consumer needs as one of its goals.

Compare Your Products against the Competition's

The question is simple: How do your products measure up to those of your competition in terms of

- Price • Quality and durability • Meeting customer needs
- Technological advancement • Features

The list goes on and changes for almost every type of company. But you get the idea. Small-business plans often require specific sales levels to meet profit targets. We can't set these levels without an accurate assessment of how our own products compete against those of our competition.

Service Company Questions

Many small businesses sell services rather than hard products. Here are some additional current position assessment questions for the services you sell.

Name five customers that buy from you and why

This should point out some of your service's strengths. Additionally, it will probably prompt additional questions regarding the type of customer your company attracts. That comes later in this chapter.

Name five customers that don't buy from you and why

If you can name them, you're already familiar with these customers. Maybe you've tried to do business with them and failed. Maybe you've kicked them out of your firm. However, if these are customers who all seem to avoid your company for the same reason, it's probably important for your assessment of the current product position. We want to know what it is about your firm that's presently repelling this type of customer.

APPRAISING DISTRIBUTION CHANNELS

How do you get your product to your customers? For some companies, the distribution channel *is* the selling point of the product. Our example of the pizza delivery company comes to mind. It correctly determined that quality (within reason) wasn't the primary issue. The customer based his or her purchase decision on speed and delivery.

Many companies have several channels of distribution. Some use a combination of wholesalers, jobbers, retailers, and often mail order.

I have a friend who owns a large commercial bakery (she's an heiress who started the business just for something to do). The company began as a retail operation selling bread, rolls, and muffins. Soon it expanded into private-label production using proprietary recipes designed for a huge chain of specialty grocery stores. The bakery added yet a third channel of distribution when it developed its own brand name and began marketing directly to other retail chains.

Today my heiress friend leads a life that would have impressed even her zillionaire father. Her operation has three major channels of distribution. Her production kitchens run three shifts six days a week. She barely has time to get her nails done (some things never change), and the Junior League and Garden Club have both fallen by the wayside. Her business grosses over $8 million a year.

What Distribution Channel Grosses the Most?

Probably the main question regarding channels of distribution is which one generates the most revenue (revenue, not profit). This should tell you one of two things:

- The way most of your customers prefer your product
- Where you're concentrating most of your marketing effort

Many companies find that the distribution channel that presently generates the most gross revenue isn't necessarily the one that *they* would prefer.

What Distribution Channel Nets the Most?

This is the real money question. Often the channel that grosses the most *isn't* the one that nets the most. It doesn't make sense to break your back selling huge volumes through one distribution channel, only to realize that the channel is so expensive to maintain that it eats up much of your profit. Better to sell less but through a high-profit channel of distribution that allows you to keep the fruits of your labor.

That's the kind of issue and gaps that assessment of your current position points out.

Describe Each Distribution Channel Step by Step

Now, what steps can you eliminate? Product distribution is expensive. It costs money and takes up valuable management time. If you can streamline, bypass, or otherwise remove any links in the process, you are ahead of the game. Sometimes companies can create more profitable lines simply by altering an existing distribution channel. Think about it. Profit improvement through adjusting one or more distribution channels may help bridge the gap between your current position and the planned end point.

Identify the Changes Your Competition Has Made

Distribution can be a great marketing tool as well as a key to profit improvement. Are your competitors doing something that looks promising? How are their methods different from yours? What do you think these new wrinkles have done to their profit? How can you use this knowledge?

Imitation is the sincerest form of flattery. To the extent that we can go to school on the competition without risking our own money to see the outcome, we're better off.

What Changes Have You Made Lately?

The process of identifying your channels of distribution should include what you've learned from past changes. Determine what changes you've made that have improved gross revenue and net profit and what haven't. This gives you some idea of the latitude you have to make changes (if necessary) to your company's channels of distribution.

Another related question you might consider is, Why was the change you made effective or ineffective? We want to emulate the successes and learn from the mistakes.

COMPETITIVE EDGE

Every company has at least some sort of competitive edge. The accountants call this goodwill. It's an intangible asset that sets your company apart from the competition. Often competitive edge is as much a function of consumers' perception created by an effective advertising campaign as of any real difference. We don't really care which causes our customers to buy. All we care is *that* they buy. Remember, *perception is reality*. However, we do want to understand the reasons for the purchase. Small businesses can benefit from these lessons taught by the marketing types.

Here are some of the things many companies say give them their competitive edge. Use these as a starting point to figure out what makes your company successful.

Technology

Depending on your industry, technology may be a factor in assessing your competitive edge. This doesn't just mean the technology your product offers to customers and end users. Production technology can also be a huge contributor to your competitive edge if it lowers production costs and therefore allows you to undercut the competition's prices without sacrificing your profit margin.

Quality

Whether the perception of quality is real or something your advertising campaign has created, it's still a competitive edge. Unfortunately, *any* customer perception is difficult to assess without a costly opinion survey. If you can reasonably assess the perceived quality of your products, then use this as part of your current position assessment.

Absent that, you can get a good indication of your products' or services' actual quality just by comparing them with the competition. Be honest and try to put yourself in the shoes of your customer or end user. Now ask yourself, Is the quality of this item a competitive edge for my company?

Customer Familiarity and Loyalty

Often companies have a competitive edge simply from customer loyalty to a product with which they're familiar. Arm & Hammer baking soda is a good example. Who actually *thinks* about which baking soda is better? Most go with the familiar yellow and red box they have used for years and that they saw on their mother's shelf and their grandmother's shelf. That's why this product has enjoyed a competitive edge for so many years.

Does your product have customer loyalty that gives it what amounts to the franchise Arm & Hammer's customers have given it? You're fortunate if it does.

I know of one bank consulting company that has such loyalty. It comes not from its customers but from the bank regulators. Troubled institutions break their backs trying to please the regulators. It's almost a done deal when these authorities suggest that the bank hire this particular consultant. Unfortunately, the poor bank directors wonder just who those consultants were working for when the government later sues them using information generated by these consultants and paid for by the bank.

Packaging

What is it about your company's packaging that gives it a competitive edge? Is the present packaging a drawback? In the case of Arm & Hammer baking soda, the company used its super-familiar yellow and red packaging for other products. Air freshener is one of them. It even contains some of the company's baking soda.

Convenience packaging can be a big advantage. If your competitors' packages are easier to use than yours, all other things being equal, your firm may be at a competitive disadvantage. These are the types of things you should consider when evaluating the competitive position of your packaging.

Customers

Assessment of your customer base is a big part of determining the overall current position of your firm. The more you know about your customers and the reasons they buy your products, the better you can evaluate your firm's present strengths and weaknesses. Here are some questions to prompt you.

Are your products purchased by any particular age group?

If so, is this the age group you're really targeting? If you have a loyal customer base in a particular age group, can you capitalize on this to transfer other products into it?

Are your products purchased by a particular ethnic segment?

Is this an appropriate group for your product? Sometimes, products associated primarily with one ethnic group cannot realistically transfer to another group. The Afrosheen line of hair care products enjoyed a successful run marketed primarily to African-Americans. Could the company have realistically expected to cross-market to other ethnic groups? Probably not.

On the other hand, some "ethnic" products do enjoy a tremendous cross-cultural marketing potential. Most consumers associate typically Japanese products with high quality. They are not difficult to market to other groups who value technological excellence and high quality.

Are your products purchased by a particular gender?

You might view this as an elementary question with an obvious answer. However, if you're experiencing a revenue gap in your firm's current sales capabilities, you might explore marketing to the opposite gender.

Are your products sold primarily in a specific geographic region?

If so, can we transfer the success in one area to another? Here's a wonderful example: A client of mine manufactures ladies' gloves. The firm sells most of its gloves in cold-weather climates—naturally. However, in probing further into the firm's current position, we asked the question, What do people do for gloves when they're moving from a warm climate to one that's cold? Of course they have to buy gloves. Now all we had to do was figure out where there was a warm climate with large numbers of people constantly moving back to a colder climate. Hawaii! Tourists coming from cold weather, especially from Japan during the winter months, want to buy gloves. Now sale of these gloves in Hawaii accounts for a nice portion of the business.

What income group buys your products?

This question is more for a retail company. However, those manufacturers that sell to wholesalers might twist it a little to ask about the financial stability of their customers. Regardless, we really want to know the financial resources of our customers.

Follow-on questions might relate to how significant a purchase this product is for such a customer. This relates to issues of *price elasticity* (the sensitivity of demand to changes in price—products that are not very sensitive are *price-inelastic*).

Are your sales tied to the purchase of another product?

Often sales of one product prompt the need for purchase of others. If you have any such products, but currently don't supply the follow-on, there might be an opportunity. At any rate, recognize the issue in your assessment of current position.

PRICING

The pricing of your products can provide insight into your competitive position. You need to determine if your company is usually the price leader in the area or a follower. Does your firm have certain products that it must market in an extremely price-competitive environment? Do customers perceive little difference between your products and those of your competitors? Under those conditions, you probably can't change prices much without also changing the demand for your products.

Customer loyalty has an influence on your ability to change prices as well. With some types of customers, a change in price really doesn't affect demand. These people are so loyal that they'll buy your product regardless (within reason).

Another determinant of price sensitivity is brand recognition. If your products have a trusted and recognized brand name or packaging, you may be able to alter prices without too much change in demand.

Assessing Price Sensitivity

One of the factors in determining your current overall position is your product price sensitivity. All the reasons above dictate the relative ease with which you may change prices without affecting demand:

- Customer loyalty • Differences between competitive products
- Brand recognition • Packaging • Uniqueness

We want a gauge of the sensitivity of your pricing. This information will probably come in handy as we work through the plan to identify possible increases in gross margins required to achieve specific profit targets.

Identifying Your Position on the Price Curve

Most products follow some sort of price curve. The high-quality end of the market usually has the highest prices. Demand influences features, technology, styling, and popularity. As these things fall off, so does the price. Companies that have all these features in their products should be at the top of the price range. If they're not, they'll try to exploit the marketing feature of high quality/low price. Consumers want to believe that such seemingly mutually exclusive goals can coexist.

You need to identify where you are on the price curve in relation to your position on the demand curve. If there's a true disparity, you want to know about it. The disparity may be between the features and uniqueness of your product and the price you charge. Maybe you should be charging more. Alternatively, perhaps you'll find that you can charge less, sell more, and increase overall revenue. It depends on the flexibility in your production costs.

ADVERTISING

One of the reasons for your current position is your company's advertising. You need to assess the current state of your promotion efforts, not only for your products but for your company. In markets where there's little difference between actual products, competitors often try to create a perceived difference between the companies that make them. The theory is that the more favorable knowledge a customer has about the company, the more inclined that customer will be to buy its products. That's one of the reasons companies advertise their participation in charitable causes. They are simply promoting an image of community involvement.

Types of Advertising

Let's not forget identifying the way you advertise. Compare that to the way your competitors advertise. Determine which is most effective, not only in terms of generating customers but also in terms of being cost effective.

A frequently used index is advertising dollars spent per sales revenue. Naturally, the lower the index, the better. Additionally, there's a linkage between the type of advertising and the target market you're trying to reach. Your current position assessment may reveal that the target market doesn't respond to your advertising methods.

Endorsing Products

What are the results of a group or individual endorsing your product? Is it effective? Is the endorser appropriate? Does the endorser command credibility with the target market? Is this the type of image that will sell your products?

Endorsements are expensive. Their effectiveness is transient. Professional athletes are a good (and bad) example. Their fame is fleeting. When they fall, you don't want to be associated with failure or a has-been. Their credibility comes and goes with each game. The worst case is to depend on a specific image (such as wholesomeness), then discover a shady past or a present occurrence that casts a pall on your company.

If your company uses endorsers, definitely include an evaluation of them in your assessment of current position.

PRODUCT AVAILABILITY

This can often be a problem in small companies. You can't sell something you don't have on hand. Lately the computer market seems mired in availability problems. Consequently, customers go to alternative sources—competitors. These may provide an acceptable substitute. Even worse, once-loyal customers may decide they like your competitor better.

If product availability hasn't been a problem before, but you expect it to be in the future, this belongs in your current position assessment. Chances are that your competitors are in the same boat. If not, then you may be at a distinct disadvantage. Your business plan needs to address that issue.

PRODUCT FEATURES

Here's where an honest assessment can be most valuable. What features do your products have that distinguish them from the competition? This is one of the reasons your customers buy. It's not the only reason—issues of price, loyalty, and company image are somewhere in the mix too—but features are right up there.

Here is a short list of product features:

- Technology employed and available from the product • Styling
- Color • Enhancements over the competition • Availability
- Price discounts for bulk purchases
- Purchase terms—trade discounts or time payment
- Selection of options • Durability • Service availability
- Technical support and engineering assistance
- Interchangeable parts with other products • Training for users

We need to know the market position of your company's products. From there we can correctly adjust these features to help the products meet their goals in the business plan.

Service

Many manufactured products are so complex that customers expect to need some sort of service. They want assurance from the firm that sold them the product. At issue are questions of

- Stability and longevity of the seller
- Technical competence of the service personnel
- Speed of service
- Geographic proximity of service centers
- Cost of service
- Frequency of service needs

The way your company approaches service may determine its competitive niche. That's why an honest assessment of your firm's service capabilities is a necessary part of the current position analysis.

APPRAISING COMPETITION

It would be nice if we all knew as much about our competitors as we do about ourselves. That's not possible, nor is it really necessary. However, we do need to know something about them if we intend to compete effectively. Here are some of the things that should go into assessing their current position as it relates to your own.

Products

These are the most obvious things we need to assess. Ask how your competitors' products stack up against your own. Use the same criteria you used when evaluating your own products: styling, color, technology, etc.

If you are aware of any new products ready for immediate introduction, you'll want to throw those into the analysis as well.

Organization

What are your competitors' organizations like? Do they have the ability to make fast and accurate decisions? How will they respond to changes you make? Are their managers competent? Are they leaders or followers? How are they capitalized? Do you think they're going to be around for a while?

Stability

Often customers choose one contractor over another for a long-term project because of its stability. How do your competitors stack up to your own stability? Are they transient? What's their history? If they've been around for a hundred years and there's no reason to suspect anything's wrong, then they are probably stable.

It may be that assessment of your stability compared to that of your competition reveals an advantage. It's nice to be able to put something so important into your sales and marketing arsenal—especially if you're selling a durable good that *will* require servicing someday.

ASSESSING OPERATIONS

This part of the analysis requires an introspective look at your company. How does the firm do things? Is it efficient? Review the production line. Look at the efficiency of the manufacturing equipment. Do production methods employ the latest that current technology has to offer? If not, would expenditure of the funds to bring the operation up to date contribute a sufficient return to justify the expense?

Take a look at the property, plant, and equipment. Is it adequate? Does your warehouse provide sufficient space now? What would happen if you expanded inventory? Would you have a place to store it? Is the warehouse security sufficient for the products being stored there? Often businesses change the types of things they keep on hand over the years. However, their storage facilities sometimes aren't updated along with them.

Is your firm's infrastructure adequate? This is a catch-all term for such things as

- The accounting system • The payroll system • The mail room
- Banking relationships • The computer system • Offices
- The employee benefits package, including insurance, salaries, and working environment

If product development and engineering are important to your company, you should include these departments in your assessment. Appraise the qualifications of your product development and engineering staffs. Maybe their skills require upgrading as part of the business plan. Tie their track record to their products' success in the marketplace.

Another operations issue involves capital equipment already committed. What does the equipment already purchased but not yet installed do for your competitive position? Is it something you can use in the business plan?

ASSESSING STAFF

This is often difficult for many owners. Nevertheless, you're not in the business of giving jobs away. Step away from any emotional attachment to these people you might have and look at them as employees. Now, assess your employee base using the following criteria:

- Management talent and depth • Employee abilities and depth
- Experience • Background
- Commitment to the company and its plan
- Special qualifications important to the company
- Cost of these talents compared with what's currently available on the open market

The labor pool concerns companies. Identify the capabilities of your firm's labor pool. Are you near a university that can provide you with qualified engineers? Are you in a field that uses specially qualified individuals (such as those coming out of the armed services)? If so, are you near a facility where such people gather (such as a military base)?

APPRAISING FINANCIAL RESOURCES

If an army runs on its stomach, a company runs on its bank account. This is one of the most crucial parts of the current position assessment. By now we've already identified the characteristics of the accounting department. We understand the money that's already committed for additional purchases of inventory and equipment.

Now we want to identify the money sources available to the firm. Here are the main areas on which this current position assessment should concentrate.

Working Capital

Earlier we defined working capital as current assets less current liabilities. This is the amount of money it takes to run the company through a single business cycle. What is your current level of working capital? You may find an opportunity to reduce it by collecting more receivables than you put on. Or perhaps your inventory is greater than you need.

Conversely, your working capital may be surprisingly low. If that's the case and you don't have the ability to generate more money, the business plan will have a large constraint before it starts.

Sources of Capital

What sources of additional funds does your firm have? Are the owners or partners willing to come up with additional capital if necessary? How about stockholders? If you don't have stockholders right now, what are the prospects of floating a placement of stock if you need to raise additional capital?

Alternatively, a private bond placement is slightly less risky to an investor because it provides a guaranteed minimum return in the form of twice-a-year interest payments.

In any case, your current position financial assessment should include a realistic look at your company's ability to generate additional capital if necessary.

Borrowing Capacity

Is your company bankable? How do you determine just how much you can borrow? A quick chat with your banker might shed some light. Additionally, you should compute the key financial indicators that describe the financial status of your company from the most current balance sheet. These include

- Current ratio: current assets / current liabilities
- Quick ratio: quick assets / current liabilities
- Debt/equity ratio: debt / owners' equity
- Return on equity: (net income – preferred dividends) / common stockholders' equity
- Return on assets: income before interest and taxes / total assets

- Interest earned: income before interest and taxes / (interest + preferred dividends)

If some of these ratios appear out of whack, they may affect your firm's ability to get lenders to extend credit. If that's the case, you need to know this at the start of the planning exercise.

Chapter 4 takes the first step in generating your business plan—setting company goals.

Chapter 4

Setting Company Goals

OVERVIEW

Chapter 4 demonstrates how to develop goals that are effective, specific, and achievable. These are the criteria we'll be working with in judging the goals we establish throughout this chapter. Once we've nailed down our goals, we will have answered most questions regarding

- *What* the goal is • *How* it ties into the company's overall objectives
- *When* the goal needs to be accomplished
- *What other goals* depend on the target being hit
- *Who* is responsible for meeting the goal

Many small-business owners and managers believe they're at the mercy of larger competitors. In some cases that's true. However, more often we see small businesses compete effectively because they've created a unique niche for themselves. Producing such a niche doesn't happen by accident. The company shapes it by hitting specific goals and targets.

Goal setting takes some thought. In Chapter 3 we identified our current position. If we know that and understand our present capabilities we're able to identify where we want the company to go. Unlike those of some planning exercises you may have participated in before, our goals are specific. You may have already guessed that from the short list above of the questions these goals address.

Our approach to goal setting for a small business is not really one of strategy. That's too foggy. Instead, we want to identify those solid targets that *will* take the company from where it is today to a specific place by a definite time. *That's* our goal for Chapter 4.

SETTING OVERALL GOALS

Most small businesses have short-term goals associated with profitability, cash flow, and return on the owners' investment. These are the types of goals we'll be working with. They are specific and quantifiable. When met, they make the company prosper.

Of course, a small business can't use short-term financial goals exclusively as it evolves throughout its life. At some point we need to formulate some strategic goals so that the company can branch out and expand. However, that's not the stage we're at in this book. Earlier we said that small-business planners need to walk before they run. We design our planning goals to get the firm under control and learn how to drive it from one point to another.

Setting the Number of Goals

There should be as few overall company goals as possible. We don't want to confuse people. Nor do we want to have so many targets for people to hit that they lose track of which one is the highest priority. When we get down to the department level for goal setting, our objective is to communicate to each person that single thing—even if its only thing done all year—they must do to help the firm reach its overall goal.

That kind of focus should go up the ladder as well. Overall company goals must be very few in number. It's best if you can select that *single objective* that causes the company to perform as its owners and management intend.

Criteria for Overall Company Goals

There are four things we demand of the overall company goals established in the business plan:

- They truly get the company where it wants to be.
- Each department's tasks can be clearly defined.
- Progress along the way is measurable.
- Success of one goal does not mean failure of another.

Specifying Overall Company Goals

The first step in identifying company goals is to figure out where the firm needs to go. Owners and managers must determine why they are in business. For most enterprises the answer is simple: to earn a living and a profit on investment in the company. Unless you're independently wealthy without your company's net worth and are just looking for a hobby, that's probably close to your goal as well.

Therefore, getting the company where it needs to be most likely has something to do with profits and return on invested capital.

Stating Goals

The best goals are those whose meaning everyone understands. They are specific and leave no doubt as to the company's position after achieving its goals. Further, we don't want any complicated formulas to determine whether a goal was actually achieved. This inhibits assessing progress toward the goal along the way.

We want to keep the number of overall goals small. It usually turns out that financial goals are the ones that really count to small-business enterprises. After all, there's only one reason the owners keep the business—to make money.

Using financial goals, the rest of what the company must do to achieve them pretty much falls into place. For example, let's consider an increase in overall profits of 10 percent ($250,000) for this year as a primary financial target. Here's how we derive a few of the other subgoals that will make this goal happen:

1. Sales must rise by $1.2 million.
2. Gross margins must rise by 1.5 percent.
3. Warehouse space must expand by 2500 square feet.
4. Working capital line of credit must increase by $300,000.

Assign these four subgoals to specific departments. Other targets to achieve *them* fall into place as well. Continuing with our example, here's how the target of raising gross margins by 1.5 percent cascades down to the production line:

1. Reduce negative material usage variance by 10 percent within the first quarter and maintain that new efficiency level through year-end.
2. Reduce negative labor variance caused by unscheduled machinery downtime by 5 percent.
3. Upgrade production machines 1 and 2 to reduce downtime by 25 percent and improve material and labor usage by 5 percent each by the end of January.

Of course there are many other things that would come out of this cascade of goals. Chapter 5, "Setting Department Goals," details this. The point is, we're developing a logical approach by starting at the *target* and working backwards to determine what needs doing and when.

Characteristics of Goals

Business plan goals are short. They tell just two things: *what* and *when.* They tell them exactly. Here is a list of characteristics of the most effective overall company goals:

- Clear • Precise • Short • Divisible among departments
- Achievable • Can be monitored along the way • Motivating
- Consider other departments' needs and timing
- Acknowledge external realities (like creditworthiness)

The company's needs and its timing do not confuse those charged with creating a plan to achieve the company's goals. They understand the exact steps needed to hit the stated targets. That's what we mean when we describe an effective goal as being *divisible.* Everyone understands all the components necessary to make the overall goal work.

Quantifying Goals

Two more characteristics of effective goals are their quantification and definite deadlines for reaching them. Here are two examples of effective overall financial goals:

- Return 12 percent on invested capital by fiscal-year end.
- Provide owners with $200,000 for discretionary distribution by fiscal year-end.

Notice the deadlines. Every goal needs to have a due date. Without it, there's no target to hit. Now, take a look at two goals that are not effective:

- Increase investment capital.
- Pay company stockholders a dividend.

What's wrong with these? Certainly, increasing investment capital could be a good goal for a start-up company or one that is looking to expand and is in need of additional funds. If the company is family-run, there's nothing wrong with paying the family/stockholders a dividend above their regular salaries.

However, there's no goal to shoot for, no target to hit. How much investment capital is needed? When? What kind of dividend will the company pay? How much and to whom? When?

If the goal is worth aiming for, it's worth identifying exactly what yardstick we'll use when considering whether we are successful. Additionally, the goal must provide a starting point for the departments responsible for reaching the goal. They must identify the tasks they need to accomplish and when.

Identifying Intended Results

Overall business goals need to clearly communicate the expected end results. That's why we said earlier that the most effective goals were quantifiable. Of those, at least at the top level of a small business over the short term, financially oriented goals are probably what really matter to the owners.

Establishing Intermediate Targets

Not only must an effective overall company goal establish the end point, it must also place milestones to hit along the way. We want to be able to track our progress. If the firm requires a correction before we reach our targets, we need to know when and how to make it.

Further, a change in one goal of the business plan is likely to affect at least some other part of the overall plan. Milestones help us to trace the effects mid-course changes in one part of the plan have on the rest of the plan.

Chapter 15, "Establishing Benchmarks," deals extensively with the methods used to select progress indicators. However, before we leave the topic now, let's say something about the motivation potential of being able to identify intended results—not only at the end, but at the intermediate milestones.

People like feedback. When you're working on achieving a complicated companywide goal that has many subgoals at the department level, feedback is a necessity. Benchmarks and milestones along the way help keep the plan implementers on track.

The first book I ever wrote was *How to Fire Your Boss* (Berkeley, 1991). Before I began writing, I asked the editor if she'd like to see the first few chapters to be sure we were on the right track. "No," she said. "I'll tell you how you did when I see the finished manuscript." While drafting those 700 manuscript pages, I had nightmares of receiving a call after it was done saying, "Chris, this isn't at all what we had in mind." Fortunately everything worked out. But imagine the anxiety and potential for error that could have been eliminated had the project manager allowed for periodic review and the possibility for midcourse corrections.

There's a feeling of confidence in seeing a landmark you were expecting halfway through a long journey. You know you aren't lost. It helps motivate you to press on. Further, when you reach intermediate milestones it is a good time to give an intermediate performance reward.

PRIORITIZING GOALS

Focus is the hallmark of a good business plan. The goals are few, they are precise, and their priorities are clear. Remember, at the departmental level of a small business, we want to communicate to each employee, This is the single thing, if you do nothing else, that you absolutely must accomplish. That can be done only if the top-level overall company goals were carefully prioritized and that priority clearly communicated. When that happens, the business plan has a better than average chance of succeeding.

The priorities established in setting the overall goals of the company must be coordinated. For example, goals involving increased profits require more sales. The firm must develop the new product before the added sales can materialize.

Then, as we get further into the logistics of the plan, we'll find other subgoals like additional warehouse space to house the new products once we place them in finished goods inventory.

See how the process of establishing overall company goals requires coordination of priorities? Of course, to make the exercise all the more exciting, there are usually *conflicting priorities*. It almost always seems that at least two critical targets must be hit simultaneously for the plan to move on, or that we cannot achieve either of two goals without meeting the other first—almost like the circular reference you may have found in the last computer spreadsheet you did.

Here's an example. Let's say that one of your goals for the next year requires expansion of accounts receivable. You're going to sell more product (another goal), and, naturally, the company will have more receivables on the books. Now, expanding accounts receivable requires more working capital. So another goal is to increase the working capital line of credit at the bank. However, the bank is an asset-based lender. It wants to secure their loan with your assets. The asset it's chosen in your company's case is—you guessed it—accounts receivable.

We face a question of priorities. On the one hand, we need the receivables on the books to collateralize an increase in our line of credit. On the other hand, we must have the increased credit line before we can get the receivables on the books. The two goals appear mutually exclusive—you can't have one without first having the other.

That's what we mean by prioritizing goals. When you have two or more goals that seem to conflict with one another, identify which is the more important. There will be targets and goals your company would like to hit but for a variety of reasons may not be able to during the planning period.

It's better to understand these logistical limitations at the outset than risk surprise (and a dilemma) after it's too late to do anything about it.

Arranging Your Plan

When you prioritize and coordinate the targets and goals for your company, a natural arrangement should appear. Roadblocks like the receivables and LOC above become evident. Chances are the goals you come up with in the beginning are not the same as those that you'll stick with through the entire process of creating your business plan.

This crucial arrangement of goals begins in the first stage when you establish those goals you *think* the firm needs to achieve to take it where you want to be at the end of the planning period—usually within twelve months. The next stage is to establish all the subgoals and targets needed along the way to achieve the overall goals. This involves the individual departments.

The third stage is to rethink the first stage, overall goals, in light of the practical limitations brought out in analyzing just how the firm is going to execute the plan. There's nothing wrong with rethinking overall goals. Out of this process come definite company goals that we *can* achieve considering the real-world technical limitations of the company.

Recognizing the Critical Path

Engineers use a technique for project scheduling called the *critical path method*. Simply stated, it's a time line of all the things needed to get from a starting point to a targeted end point. Along the way there are subgoals and smaller projects that feed into the larger targets. The route winds around but eventually a definite order of targets becomes clear.

That's the critical path—the order of projects required for the process to move from step 1 to step 2 to step 3 and on to the end. Ancillary steps occur along the way, but their timing isn't really critical to maintaining overall progress to the ultimate goal.

Part of prioritizing your goals involves determining which targets to hit first, second, third, and so forth in order to keep implementation of the plan moving forward. There will be some that the firm absolutely must reach before anything else can happen. Chances are that something like the engineer's critical path will result.

TIMING

When you determine your final few most essential overall company goals, don't forget to include the deadlines. Timing doesn't only add dimension and a target end point to each goal. It also provides a definite milestone on which other parts of the plan can count for the things *they* need.

Timing the Domino Effect

The timing of the various goals is similar to a line of dominos. As we reach one goal, it sets up what we need to reach the next goal. The same thing happens for the next goal and the next. Soon one goal falls, causing the next to fall and the next. That's what we want.

Similarly, however, if one domino doesn't fall, it won't topple the one after it and the whole process stops dead. Failure to reach a critical goal (one on the critical path) could have consequences for one or more goals scheduled to occur later.

An example is the goal of increasing profit margins by 2 percent beginning on January 31 and extending through year-end. Let's say to do that we must install a new piece of machinery by January 15. The company must train its production people to use the new machine efficiently for the next two weeks. By January 31 the machine must be functioning and reducing production labor costs as planned.

That's the timing the controller is counting on to reduce the manufacturing department's payroll expense. The controller probably has several other subgoals that depend on the timing of that cost reduction. If it fails to materialize, these other goals may be in jeopardy.

Reviewing Progress

Monitoring the company's progress toward its goals periodically ensures that we're aware of any risk of not hitting critical targets. If it looks as if there's a possibility of delay or a shortfall in expectations, we should see it far enough in advance to do something about it. It's at this point that the contingency plans come into play.

WHO SETS THE GOALS?

Many small-business owners think that since it's their money on the line, they should be the ones who set the overall company direction. The part about it being their money is right. However, the only way a manager can succeed is by motivating and leading employees.

Of course, it would be tough to convince owners that they don't have the right to set overall company direction. Nor would we try. That's where management turns from a science into an art. One of the best ways of persuading someone that a particular goal or target is worthwhile and possible is by listening to what he or she has to say about it.

The role of the owner/strategist becomes one of facilitating the creation of a set of achievable targets that accomplish three things:

- It meets the owner's requirements.
- It gives the people responsible for hitting the targets a say in their destiny.
- It motivates everyone to succeed.

Participating with the Implementers

Probably the most important characteristic of effective goal setting is support from those responsible for achieving the targets. That support most often comes from a participative effort.

To reach any overall goals, your company must work as a team. That requires commitment from everyone responsible for a critical section of the business plan. People like being consulted when it comes to decisions regarding their time and performance expectations.

The surest way to irritate people and make them resent their role in the plan is to try ramming it down their throats. You have a good indication that this is happening when you hear complaints about targets being set by people who aren't close enough to the department being targeted. The people who work there may object that the planners haven't considered all sorts of things that are certain to make it impossible to reach the targets already set.

What they're really saying is that they want the courtesy of being consulted. People work best when they have a feeling that they can exercise at least some degree of control over their job and environment. Without that participation, people don't feel they're being competently led (and they're right). Instead, they are being pushed into making a commitment that they had no say in creating. The risk to the company is no commitment to the plan.

That's why business plans fail. They were created in an ivory tower without the participation of those responsible for making them work. They treat these important people as nameless, faceless pawns, existing solely to do management's bidding.

When you establish your company's overall goals and the specific department goals, make sure that the people responsible for achieving the plan participate in creating the goals, targets, deadlines, *and* rewards for success.

Without that kind of participation, you're trying to create the business plan in a vacuum. The people closer to the firing line have insight into the ways the company can more easily move from its current position to achieve the overall goals. We want their knowledge of how to coordinate various parts of the company in reaching the company's overall goal.

Equally as important, we want their commitment to the plan's success. They need to have a feeling of ownership of the goals and targets. As every small-business investor knows, owners have only themselves to blame if something goes wrong.

Linking Participation with Responsibility

How committed will your shop foremen be to a set of production volume and cost targets that they had no say in establishing? Further, if they didn't participate in creating the goals, chances are they had no say in the resources needed to achieve them either.

This means that a naive owner has unilaterally demanded that subordinates be made responsible for doing a job when they had no say-so in establishing the boundaries. To compound the error, management forgot to ask which tools they needed to help them succeed.

What's the likelihood of failure? Probably better than 50/50. We see this all the time in small businesses. I sometimes wonder if managers thinks their employees are magicians, and that just ordering that a target be reached, means it can be reached.

Adjusting attitude

After having seen such dictatorial goal setting, one can see the flaw in management's attitude. Giving someone a target to hit without the tools necessary to succeed carries an implicit statement about management's outlook toward its subordinates' work ethic:

> They are not working up to their capacity. All it takes to
> reach the goal is trying harder.

Goals set using such an attitude will fail. Management cannot foist responsibility on subordinates without first eliciting from them a commitment to success. There is no *ownership* of the goal.

In establishing responsibility for reaching the targets of a business plan the rule seems to be

> If I didn't help establish the target or the path to reaching
> that target, then I'm not responsible.

Managing Expectations

The depth of employee backgrounds is often thin at small businesses. Nevertheless, owners establish a set of expectations by making someone responsible for reaching targets needed to bring the company closer to its overall goals.

The expectations are that the person responsible will do whatever it takes to reach those targets. Management expects a certain amount of resourcefulness and self-reliance. If subordinates don't provide guidance in establishing goals in the first place, how can we expect them to demonstrate the resourcefulness needed to succeed?

Successfully targeting the company's overall goals begins with the expectation that all of those involved in the effort agree on three things:

- The actual goals and targets
- The company's ability to achieve them
- The methods used to succeed

Managing the expectations of both owners and subordinates when setting overall company goals involves two points of view: subordinates' expectations and management's expectations.

Subordinates' expectations

Subordinates have every right to demand that management sincerely listen to their opinions and recommendations when setting company targets. How often have you seen company executives merely make a show of wanting to hear what subordinates have to say? Their attitude seems to be, This is an exercise to make them feel more committed. The owners believe they know what's best for the company. They don't really think there's anything the subordinates can add. They're just going through the motions because they think it's expected.

Nothing constructive comes out of such goal-setting sessions. Indeed, most subordinates I know who have participated in such shams are inwardly laughing at management. They know their input really isn't needed.

So, how do we correct this problem? The solution is simple: Owners and management must *sincerely* desire help in setting company goals from those who will be responsible for hitting those goals. It's a matter of attitude. It's also a matter of

- Listening carefully
- Considering the background and special experience with the inner workings of the company that subordinates have
- Avoiding a predisposed set of targets and ways to reach them that are already cast in stone
- Being aware of subordinates' own needs and goals
- Allowing yourself to be persuaded by someone with a better idea

Management expectations

Participation and expectations are a two-way street. Management has every right to expect employees to actively and sincerely participate in the direction the company takes. Further, no one expects management to abdicate its authority. After all, it *is* the owner's money on the line. There must be someone in control.

The owners and management retain veto power. The key to participative goal setting is to exercise that veto power with consideration and awareness of the human factors involved. Management has a right to expect sincere participation without unreasonable objections or ill-considered proposals.

The idea is to generate a feeling that owners, managers, and subordinates are a team. The business plan contains a set of goals containing the common objectives of the owners and those responsible for executing the plan.

If it's done right, the goals benefit all concerned. Further, if all concerned parties participated, there's a mutual commitment to the goals. Chances are that the parties discovered and fixed problems associated with the actual execution of the plan during the goal-setting exercise. *That's* the kind of feedback and participation we're talking about.

Specifying Company Objectives

We stated before that the most effective goals are those that are clear and precise. We don't want any question as to where the goal will take us or when we've reached it. To ensure that clarity, the best goals are the simplest. Here are four rules that should help you peg your objectives:

1. *State the desired results,* not how to get the results—that comes later, in the departmental goals. Instead, simply say what you want the company to achieve.
2. *State the time frame* in which the goals are to be met.
3. *Structure the goal* to include an action verb and the subject on which the verb acts. An example would be, "increase owner's return by $ _____ to a level of _____ percent by _____."

4. *Stress clarity* by avoiding the used of jargon, acronyms, or complicated performance formulas. This holds especially true when establishing the rewards.

Identifying the Goal's Audience

Overall company goals are global in nature. That is, they affect the company as a whole. A good test is to ask, to whom does this goal matter? The answer should be that it matters to those most important to the company. That's usually the owners, investors, partners, and lenders.

Such people view the company from a more macro perspective. They probably don't care that the controller's goal is to reduce accounts receivable balances to forty-five days. However, they do care about how such a goal can help the company hit an overall goal such as increasing shareholder return by 12 percent.

The most important goals are those that the company needs to achieve in order to satisfy its owners and investors. Not necessarily just for this year. We said earlier that our purpose here is to take the business from point A to point B over the next twelve months. It still is. However, as in chess strategy, we're also looking to set up the firm for the *next* move after we've achieved these goals.

So, the most important goals are those

- That are most important to our audience
- That get the company where it needs to go in this plan
- That set up the company for the next moves in subsequent plans

An example would be introducing a new product that is needed this year to satisfy the firm's profit objectives. However, this new product also serves as a live test for next year's plan. If it achieves its goals, management may intend to introduce an entire line of products built around this one. Further, by entering a new market with this particular new product, the company has started to break down whatever barriers to entry may be present.

That's how we use short-term business planning not only to satisfy today's goals but also to position the firm for next year's plan as well.

Setting Measurable Objectives

Earlier we identified the best goals as those that we can quantitatively measure. Financial goals typically fit that category. So do production goals and sales volume. Other, more strategy-oriented goals such as market share and target markets aren't quite so easy to measure. Besides, more often, you'll find that achieving something like a specific market share is more of a *tactic* for reaching another, more measurable goal, such as a profit of $1 million.

Growing as a Goal

Many owners of small businesses list growth as one of their primary objectives. They equate growth and being the biggest with profits. Sometimes that's true. However, more frequently we find that the only difference between a Fortune 100 company and one with sales of just $5 million or less is the size of management's headaches. Often the profit margin of the small firm is larger.

Still, growth is something many owners insist on incorporating into their business plans. They need to add, however, the additional targets of profit margin and return on the owners capital. With the inclusion of those two targets, growth becomes more of a tactic that's needed to achieve something more tangible and useful to an owner: money.

Growth rate index

If you're going to use growth as a goal, there's a method for mathematically determining the most realistic growth rate for your company. Beyond that number, the chances of achieving the goal are unlikely. Figure 4.1 illustrates the computation of the growth rate index.

A targeted growth rate of more than 24 percent for this company would not be an effective goal. The chances of the firm's actually reaching such a target beyond the growth rate index would be small.

ESTABLISHING GOALS THAT WORK

Goals that work are those that have the most chance of being reached. They are also those that, when achieved, take the company where it needs to go. That's why careful selection of overall company goals is so important. It's like saying, Be careful what you wish for—you may get it. We want to make sure that our goals are indeed beneficial to the company.

Working goals are also those for which we're able to gain the commitment and enthusiasm of those charged with implementing the business plan. We call goals that don't generate such commitment *dysfunctional*. They don't match the goals and objectives needed to reach the company's overall targets. There can be a number of reasons for dysfunctional goals:

- Not allowing participation in goal setting by employees
- Assigning goals that are clearly beyond employees' ability to reach—they've failed before they start
- Not matching achievement of the goal with the reward for success
- Not providing the authority needed to execute the responsibility

Stay away from dysfunctional goals. Our overall company goals should meet not only the firm's needs and those of its principals, but also the personal needs and ambitions of the people charged with hitting these targets.

Goal Incongruance

This is a fancy term for saying that departments and the individuals who run them oppose the overall company goals. Employees view such incompatibility as a zero-sum game—if the firm wins, they lose. An example would be shutting down an unprofitable plant. Those employees charged with meeting this goal will probably lose their jobs. If the company hasn't already made provision for transfers, chances are that plant shutdown will be very costly and will probably take longer than anyone ever anticipated.

Figure 4-1
Computation of Growth Rate Index

Assumptions

Net income	$900,000
+ interest expense	50,000
= Net income before interest expense but after taxes	$950,000

Net assets employed at beginning of year:	
Total assets	$5,000,000
- Cash	100,000
- Short-term investments	250,000
- Current liabilities except short-term debt	1,500,000
= Net assets employed at beginning of year	$3,150,000

Dividends paid	450,000
Target debt/equity ratio	60.0%
Target deferred taxes to equity ratio	10.0%

Computation

Net income before interest expense but after taxes	$950,000
÷ Net assets employed at beginning of year	3,150,000
X Earnings paid out as dividends	450,000
÷ Net income	900,000
= Fraction of earnings paid out as dividends	50%
X Reciprocal	50%
= Subtotal #1 [(NIBT/NA) X reciprocal]	15.1%
Computation of subtotal #2:	
Target debt/equity ratio	60.0%
+ Target deferred taxes to equity ratio	10.0%
+ 1	100.0%
= Subtotal #2	170.0%
Computation of subtotal #3:	
Interest expense	50,000
÷ Net income before interest expense but after taxes	950,000
= Interest expense as % of NI before interest but after taxes	5.3%
Reciprocal of Subtotal #3	94.7%

Growth Rate Index:

Subtotal #1	15.1%
X Subtotal #2	170.0%
X Subtotal #3	94.7%
= GRI	24.3%

Another cause of goal incongruity is judging employee performance solely on their achieving very narrow goals rather than contributing to the overall success of the group. Employees will do whatever it takes to meet *their* goals and ignore what that effort may do to other departments. They become overly protective of themselves and their departments. Sometimes war breaks out between departments. The concept of being a team player goes out the window.

Sometimes such incongruence causes employees to circumvent procedures. They may deliberately sabotage other departments' efforts if doing so enhances their own likelihood of success. We also see a tendency of people to protect their own backsides. If it looks as if they may fail, they often blamed this failure on someone else's failure to do a job that was critical to the project's success.

If the manufacturing department establishes incongruent goals, another aberration can occur. If the department produces more than is required or if its costs come in less than targeted, it may not report either success. Instead, it retains the difference between actual performance and the goal for the next planning period, when its luck might run out.

A last example of goal incongruity comes from the finance department. Say that generation of additional cash flow is a goal. The person responsible for payment of the accounts payable is important to the success of that goal. That person takes the goal seriously and simply stops paying vendors. Yes, this action achieves the goal for this planning period. However, it damages the firm's ability to conduct business in the future.

BRIDGING THE CAPABILITY GAP

In Chapter 3 we learned how to identify the firm's present position. In this chapter we identified the goals and targets for the overall company. Now there must be a bridge between them. We build the bridge by working backwards to find out what actions are needed to meet specific overall targets.

This process usually results in adjusting the priorities of the firm's overall goals. We sometimes find that the gap is just too big for us to build a single bridge during the current planning horizon. We may elect to build two smaller ones. However, the *ultimate* goal doesn't change—just the timing.

IDENTIFYING WHAT COULD GO WRONG

Expect things to go wrong. During the execution of every plan, deviations occur. Events, circumstances, and people's capabilities often prove different from what we originally thought. That's all right.

The mark of an effective plan is its flexibility. When things don't go right, a detailed business plan can identify the impacts on other overall company goals. Chances are that we use the plan to reroute some of the critical elements so that we successfully reach our most important targets.

The best way to judge what could go wrong is to take your most critical company goals and develop contingencies for problems. The problems should be along the lines of

- Shortfall in meeting the target
- Delay in achieving the goal

- Unanticipated costs • Unforeseen response by competitors
- Lower than expected profits

Ask what happens to the rest of the firm's goals if something goes wrong with one of the goals. The key is to determine how your firm can react to such contingencies without going too far astray from the original business plan. The purpose of anticipating these contingencies is to form an orderly response that minimizes their overall effects on the company.

An example is the finance department's borrowing targets. Often success in growing a company requires access to additional working capital funds. Most companies have primary lenders—those they count on during good times. However, the smart ones also have standby lenders willing to step in to fill the breach in case something adverse happens. There may even be standby borrowing agreements already in place. Of course, these lenders are likely to charge a higher rate because need for their participation by definition places them at greater risk. However, the plan can still go forward—it'll just be a little more costly in terms of interest expense.

Planning for Contingencies

We want to avoid—to the extent we are able—establishing company goals that are so tight and dependent on one another that failure of one goal invalidates the entire plan. We can plan for contingencies once we identify those few critical goals. We can assess what would happen to the other parts of our business plan if we experienced a shortfall or delay in achieving a particular target. This is a form of contingency planning. From the beginning we want to plan for alternative actions if we miss specific targets.

Remember, the purpose of our business plan is to take the firm from where it is today to another point. The overall goals don't change just because we didn't hit one of the targets along the way. A resourceful and committed implementation team will find another way to reach the ultimate goal.

Chapter 5 demonstrates how to create the departmental plans that act as the blueprint for the overall goals of the company. We'll continue working backwards from the overall goals to the starting point of what each department needs to do to fulfill its part of each companywide goal.

Chapter 5

Setting Department Goals

Overview

Chapter 5 demonstrates how to establish specific goals for each department—goals that work together to get the company where it must go. We'll concentrate on focusing employees' attention on the single thing each of them must do to help the firm achieve its main goal. The intent is to demonstrate how to identify those goals in each department that flow upward, moving the company closer to its overall objectives.

Setting Departmental Goals

The key to creating effective department goals is to make sure there's a linkage with the goals of the overall company. Department goals really become the blueprint for the plan implementation. Just as engineers read their blueprints and construction drawings to determine what steps to take next, employees use the departmental goals the same way.

Setting department goals is really a process of reverse engineering. We know what the answer needs to be. The goals established for the overall company get us there. Now each department needs to determine where its capabilities fit into reaching those objectives. Once that's determined, it's simply a matter of working backwards to identify the specific targets of each department. The result is the identification of those goals that contribute the most to achieving the company's overall goals.

Setting department goals requires the identification of these three things:

- *What* specific action needs to be done by each department
- *Who* in each department is responsible for reaching these goals
- *When* each target must be reached

The question is really one of mechanics. The most difficult part of the process is identifying what goals each department needs to meet in order to get the whole company to the end point its business plan has mapped out.

Getting There

Once we've arrived at the firm's overall goals, the department goals usually fall into place as a result. Here are some questions for each department to ask and actions to take in order to get the process rolling

How can this department help?

Every department needs to understand exactly what it must do to help implement the goals of the overall business plan. As for the company as a whole, the trick is to keep the number of targets for each department as small as possible. We're looking for the single most important thing that each department can do to help meet the company's most important overall targets.

Identifying the alternatives

For every problem, there are a number of different routes by which we can arrive at the same solution. Some are more efficient; others, more timely; still others, less costly. The departments evaluate the various courses of action available to reach their targets.

At this point there's a need for communication *between* departments. It may be that one option, while making little difference to the department that executes it, could have a huge impact on another department.

It's that coordination among the different departments in the company that makes the difference between an implementation *team* and simply a group of individuals acting strictly in their own self-interest.

As long as you're considering the different options available, here are some more questions to think about:

1. How do the different alternatives match up with the company's resources?

2. Is there one option that clearly offers a path of least resistance?

3. Which option makes the best use of company strengths? By doing so, does it also reduce the risk of failure?

4. Is there one option that places the firm or at least another department in a better future position?

Prioritizing goals

For many departments, there are several things they need to do to help propel the company toward achieving its overall goals. Then it becomes an exercise of arranging priorities. Still, we want to come up with as few targets as possible arranged in order of importance for each department.

The criteria should be along the lines of, Which department goals would do the most damage to the successful implementation of the overall business plan if we failed to reach them?

What is the biggest obstacle to reaching this target?

For every goal, there seems to be something standing between your present position and the target. What is it? Is this roadblock serious? How will you get around it? Does it present a serious risk to successful achievement of the goal?

Once you've identified these obstacles, you should separate the problem into smaller, more manageable projects. Often separating something that appears insurmountable into a series of smaller objectives makes its less intimidating.

Are there any external variables to consider?

Remember what we keep stressing about not working in a vacuum. Look outside the company to see if there's anything looming on the horizon that could present a threat to the department's achieving its goals. If we're talking about the finance department, there's always something out there. It could be an anticipated rise in interest rates. Alternatively, the possibility exists of a credit crunch forestalling the addition of more financing and it might even preclude rolling over current loans.

If the production department is at issue, consider potential environmental restrictions that might add tremendously to the cost of disposing of toxic effluents coming out of the facility.

Even the sales department is not immune to outside influences. For example, say that your company constructed and sold up-scale homes in an area where the aerospace/defense industry employed a significant part of the population. The market at first turns flat, then tumbles as this industry experiences massive layoffs as a result of congressional cutbacks in defense.

What internal variables do you need to consider?

Be aware of how the goals and targets of different departments affect one another. For example, say that your firm has two manufacturing divisions. One produces the products used on the assembly line of the other. What happens if the business plan calls for divestiture of the division that produces the product used by the other division? Suddenly that division has to find an alternative supplier. Even if it can still buy from the old division, now under new ownership, what will the cost of the assemblies be?

Depending on the influence of one department's goals on another, there can be adjustments in the timing and nature of the goals. In the divestiture example, once we identify this conflict, we can include a possible solution in the sale agreement for the manufacturing division. The agreement could stipulate availability of the assemblies at a stated price for a certain period of time. This would protect the goals of the assembly division from material changes by the goals of another department.

What milestones can we put into the goals?

We want the ability to monitor each department's progress toward its goals. Consider the progress milestones from the beginning of each department's goals. Perhaps to better control the progress toward a particularly critical goal, we need to separate it into smaller targets. We also do this to more accurately monitor progress toward the goal.

Knowing when you've reached the goal

If you've done a good job in identifying your goals, you probably don't need to ask this question. It's obvious when you've reached the target. If there is a good tracking mechanism at work, everyone watching sees the department approaching its goal, and it comes as no surprise when it finally happens.

One big help is establishing a quantitative target in the beginning. Then monitor performance right up to reaching the target. This also communicates the progress of one department to the other departments that depend on certain goals being reached. If there's a risk, everyone connected with the business plan needs to be aware of it. Chances are other departments can do something to help, or at least figure out a way to minimize the damage to them.

SALES AND MARKETING

The sales and marketing departments drive most small businesses. They need a certain level of *throughput* in order to be profitable. That's what the sales and marketing department provides the volume of goods going out the door.

Most of the critical departments in the company depend on sales targets being met. For example, the production and manufacturing department needs to know how may units to produce and when. The finance department needs to know the sales volume that's expected to roll into accounts receivable. From this it will determine such critical financial goals as the working capital required to run the firm and the financing necessary to sustain the sales targets.

Translating Company Goals into Sales and Marketing Targets

If the overall company goals involve levels of profitability and return to owners, chances are there's a direct correlation between those targets and sales volume. Some of the things the sales and marketing department needs to consider when formulating its targets include

- Target markets • Target customers
- Advertising and promotional efforts
- Product changes and enhancements • Customer service
- Credit sales limits
- Efficiency of the order entry process and system

Here is a list of sales goals used to actually translate the overall company's plans for profit, return on investment, and growth into action oriented quantitative targets. The business plan should include the sales and marketing targets right after the overall company's goals. Most of the other departments will need them in formulating their own plans.

Sales volume targets

Increase the annual number of units sold to 250,000. We can tie this target directly to the overall growth targets.

Sales price targets

Raise the sales price on all products by 5 percent beginning in January. Such a goal directly addresses the firm's overall profit targets. Additionally, the company coordinates it with the goals of the production department, which controls the other half of the profit equation, cost of goods sold.

Credit criteria

Relax the credit criteria to allow for the added sales volume. This is more of a strategic goal. It needs careful coordination with the finance department to define an exact plan for adjusting the credit criteria that has the desired effects without throwing accounts receivable out of whack. This part of the sales plan must include exact targets concerning issues such as

- Customer risk assessment   • Customer net worth
- Sales history to the customer
- Maximum line of credit extended under specific credit situations

Product enhancements

Install enhancements A, B, and C in the product line by March 15 to meet second-, third-, and fourth-quarter sales targets. The company needs to do something in order to both increase its sales volume and raise its price at the same time. These are usually mutually exclusive events. The enhancements targeted will make the product more desirable, allowing the company to charge a higher price and increase sales at the same time. Specify the timing of when to bring these enhancements to market as well. This places boundaries around the engineering, testing, and promotional programs needed for the enhancements.

Purpose of the Sales and Marketing Goals

We want to design the sales and marketing goals so that they communicate four things to the rest of the firm:

- Performance of the sales effort, stated in mathematical terms
- Timing of the sales targets   • Methods used to get there
- Impact of sales goals on other departments

Of these four items, the last is probably of most interest—at least to the rest of the firm. Once we've established a concrete sales and marketing plan, everyone knows what the team expects of his or her department. That's true in most small businesses.

This continues the concept of reverse-engineering our business plan. The sales and marketing goals took the overall company objectives and worked backwards to determine the level of sales revenue that would accomplish those goals. Now the rest of the firm sees the sales targets and also works backwards to identify the targets they must hit to make the sales goals happen.

Sales Revenue Projection

Often the most widely used tool that comes out of the sales and marketing plan is a projection of sales revenue. This simple schedule seems to condense the needs of the other departments into the most usable volume and timing estimates. Figure 5-1 demonstrates a simple sales projection.

Figure 5-1
Sales Projection

	Month 1	Month 2	Month 3	Total
Machine #1				
Units sold	200	230	250	3,380
Average price	$15.00	$15.50	$16.00	$11.38
Total revenue this product	$3,000	$3,565	$4,000	$38,448
Machine #2				
Units sold	300	400	500	6,150
Average price	$21.00	$23.00	$25.00	$17.00
Total revenue this product	$6,300	$9,200	$12,500	$104,550
Machine #3				
Units sold	650	700	750	9,300
Average price	$12.50	$12.50	$12.50	$12.50
Total revenue this product	$8,125	$8,750	$9,375	$116,250
Total sales budget:				
Units sold	1,150	1,330	1,500	18,830
Total revenue	$17,425	$21,515	$25,875	$256,065

This sales projection cuts off after the third month in the interest of space. In practice, it would show each month of the entire planning horizon. That's how the production and finance departments know what to expect and when. Additionally, having each month plotted out in terms of targets allows the company to track the sales department's actual performance against its plan. If results begin to fall short of the goals, those responsible for implementation of the overall company's plan need to know about it. So do the various departments affected by the sales and marketing plan.

We don't want unsalable inventory overstock. Further, maintaining working capital credit lines that end up not being needed is expensive. If the sales don't materialize, then accounts receivable won't be at a level that requires the additional financing.

MANUFACTURING

The manufacturing and production departments coordinate their goals in part with targets set forth in the sales and marketing plan. Manufacturing is responsible for making sure the finished goods inventory is adequate to meet the sales projections. Questions answered by the manufacturing plan include

- What products need shipping? • How many of each product?
- When are the shipments scheduled?

- What material, labor, and supplies are needed to manufacture this product mix on schedule?
- How long a lead time do we need to produce the inventory?
- Who is responsible, and what does that person need to do?

Additionally, both sales pricing and production costs directly affect the manufacturing targets. The company needs to maintain a specific level of gross profit margin. The computation of gross margin is

$$Gross\ margin\ =\ \frac{(\text{sales price} - \text{cost of goods sold})}{\text{sales price}}$$

If the sales department has targeted a higher selling price, then that takes some of the pressure to maintain the profit margin off Production. However, a more usual case would be to target the profit margins to *rise above* what the improvements in sales price alone caused. To achieve this target, Production would have to actually *reduce* its manufacturing costs.

Included in the production and manufacturing targets are all those ingredients that go toward creating the company's products on time and within the cost targets. These include

- Facilities • Manufacturing equipment • Labor • Quality
- Production volume • Inventory

Facilities

Production facilities have a direct effect on the company's volume capability as well as on the cost of production. It's certainly true that modern production facilities that employ the latest in technology run more efficiently. That translates into lower production costs.

If the production department needs to lower its manufacturing costs in order to help the company meet overall profit targets, then its facilities must be up to the task. In fact, upgrading production facilities by a specified time could be one of the production department's major targets early in the plan's implementation.

If that's the case, then the engineers must identify the facility layout and equipment needed. Additionally, the financial people must figure out a way to pay for it.

Another feature of production facilities is their physical location. Many such facilities require proximity to shipping points. For your company, that may mean easy access to truck or rail terminals, airports, or ocean shipping terminals. This need not be just to get the finished product to customers easily. Often *receiving* raw material or assembly inventory by the right transport method allows for more frequent, less costly deliveries and, therefore, less working capital tied up before the materials are placed into work in process.

Facility changeover

If the production department goals call for altering existing manufacturing facilities, then the business plan must include downtime to accomplish the task. Facilities changeover disrupts manufacturing operations. Therefore, adequate finished goods inventory must be on hand to avoid severe and costly stock-outs during that time.

Customers' facility changeover plans sometimes dismay suppliers. To them it means a likely interruption of their regular sales. If that's the case at your company, you may have some leverage in negotiating a lower price to avoid interrupting your vendor's shipping schedule. Of course, the cost of the alternative storage facilities required would partially offset the lowered cost. However, the price concession in exchange for the favor you're doing the vendor might further enhance your profit margins.

Facility closure

Alternatively, the production plan may call for closing down an existing facility. If that's the case, there will be either layoffs of personnel or reassignment to your company's remaining facilities. In any case, there will be some costs associated with the shutdown. There will also be some savings to include in the financial part of the business plan.

There may even be an opportunity to sublease or sell the unneeded facility if you own it. This could free up substantial capital that's probably needed elsewhere in the business plan.

Manufacturing Equipment

Just like facilities, manufacturing equipment has a lot to do with production efficiency. The more easily your product goes through the manufacturing process, the less costly it's likely to be. There's often a direct relation between efficiency and

- Labor used • Materials used • Quality control rejects
- Rework costs

Chances are that some of the production department's targets will have to do with manufacturing equipment. The cost of producing your company's products may need reduction. The four variables cited as bullet points above are all potential sources of savings.

It sometimes happens that certain types of manufacturing equipment don't need as much labor or material to produce the same product as their less efficient counterparts do. The latest generation of computer-controlled drill presses is a case in point.

The accuracy of these machines has reached the point where not only has the amount of labor needed been sharply reduced, but material wastage due to errors has been all but eliminated. Throughput of material has also increased. Further, the new equipment is proving more reliable than its predecessor, thus cutting down on idle labor time waiting for repairs and maintenance.

Acquiring production equipment

The manufacturing department may require several new pieces of costly equipment in order to meet its targeted output and costs. It may need to construct an additional production line to produce sufficient inventory to support the sales plan.

When you make the decision to place new equipment on-line, it's the business plan that provides the information conduit to the other departments. When the firm needs new or additional production equipment, the first such communication goes to the finance department. Someone has to pay for the equipment. Perhaps it's better to lease this type of equipment because of anticipated technological advances. If the seller also provides financing, the finance department is in the best position to know if there are more advantageous alternatives available.

Additionally, the financial plan should include anticipated production cost changes resulting from the new equipment.

Labor relations

The addition of new production equipment may allow the company to reduce the manufacturing workforce. That's good for the company. However, there may be provisions in the collective bargaining agreement (if your company is unionized) that limit the firm's ability to terminate employees.

Most small businesses won't risk a union strike for the sake of replacing a few production-line workers with a machine, regardless of how much faster or more cheaply the machine can do the work. Indeed, the possibility of experiencing some sort of organized job action is often one of the contingencies that the business plan addresses.

Quality Control

Most companies with a high-volume manufacturing operation monitor the quality of their output. Quality control (QC) rejects often figure into the cost reduction component of the manufacturing plan.

Rejecting raw materials

There are a variety of targets the manufacturing plan will use its quality control department to help hit. The first is the raw materials coming in from outside vendors. To the extent that the quality control department (or person) tracks the rejected raw materials, manufacturing time and money spent on units that are ultimately rejected are reduced.

One approach that many QC departments use is to monitor the rejects from various vendors. When they reach a specified point, the department removes that vendor from the bidder's list—at least until it has fixed the problem.

By instituting a raw material QC program, the manufacturing department can predict at least some progress toward hitting production volume and cost targets.

Intermediate QC inspection

Many firms have quality inspections of products at various stages while they are still in the WIP inventory. The theory is that if the problems are so bad, why waste any more time on a unit? Additionally, the cost of reworking a product while it's still in process is usually less than if we allowed it to continue and rejected it from finished goods inventory.

The manufacturing plan often addresses implementing the latest in QC techniques. The purpose is to lower overall manufacturing cost.

Overall QC programs

For many manufacturing operations, the overall image of the company's attention to quality goes a long way in making workers aware of quality control issues. A good example is the condition of the shop floor and the QC program that operates there. If an effective QC program is part of the manufacturing department's cost reduction target in its business plan, here are some questions to think about:

- Is the shop floor clean and free of material stacked up just anywhere?
- Is it well lighted, and does the layout promote an orderly flow of production through the facility?
- Is the QC program documented and reviewed so that everyone knows it's taken seriously?
- Are the QC personnel well trained and effective?
- Do production workers believe the firm is committed to its QC program, or is it viewed as only temporary?

Production Volume

Most manufacturing operations have definite targets for production volume. The sales plan determines these. Along with the raw production volume come goals such as

- Mix of products produced
- Timing for conversion from raw materials to finished goods
- Proper levels of safety stock

It may be that the production targets contained in the manufacturing plan require the use of new machinery or technology. If so, this needs to be communicated to both the person who does the purchasing and the finance department.

Assessing possible risks to fulfilling the production volume required is another part of the manufacturing plan. Potential labor strikes are only the most obvious risk. There could be such issues as

- Delay or shortages of raw materials and subassemblies
- Breakdown of key production machinery
- Governmental intervention for violations of pollution laws

If you see these or any of the many other risks to reaching production targets, be sure to address them in the manufacturing business plan. If they are a true possibility, then you should formulate a contingency plan in case they become reality.

We discussed earlier the possibility of lining up alternative sources of supply in case primary vendors experience adverse circumstances that keep them from making adequate and timely deliveries. The same holds true for your most important pieces of production equipment. If something happens to them, production might stop dead and fulfillment of the manufacturing department's targets might be at risk.

However, one possibility might be to arrange beforehand for the rental of replacement equipment. If the interruption of production is a real enough possibility, you may even want to contract for standby alternative production facilities. Many subcontractors are willing to commit (for a fee) some of their excess production capacity.

The point is that excuses for missing critical departmental targets are not acceptable—especially in the cold light of retrospect. Managers can predict most such adverse circumstances if they only think about what might happen and take the appropriate steps in case it does.

Allocating Indirect Costs

The manufacturing department needs to be aware of the indirect costs the accounting system is likely to allocate to the goods produced. Include these in the cost of goods sold. They then become an integral factor in gross profit margin targets.

Production departments

Every manufacturing entity allocates indirect costs differently. However, there are usually at least three major areas of the production department that allocate indirect costs. Be aware of them and definitely consider them in establishing production cost targets. These three sections are

- Special assembly • General assembly • Machining

Of course, there might be others depending on what your company produces. However, chances are they'll be variations of these three.

Service departments

Within most production sections there are certain overhead service departments. These provide essential services to the production line, but really cannot be allocated to any single product made. They usually include

- Manufacturing administration • Shop maintenance
- Industrial engineering • Production and inventory control
- Quality control

Types of indirect costs

There are many types of indirect costs that can get allocated to goods your firm produces. We can add some or all of them to both the production department and the associated service departments. Just be aware of them and be sure to include them when establishing cost targets.

Indirect labor:
  Supervision
  Other indirect
  Rework
Payroll costs:
  Vacation and holiday
  Overtime premium
  Pension contribution
  Group insurance
  Workers' compensation
  Payroll taxes
Miscellaneous variable costs:
  Power and other utilities
  Supplies
  Perishable tools
Fixed discretionary costs:
  Employee education
  Equipment rental
Fixed committed costs:
  Building and leasehold improvement depreciation
  Machinery and equipment depreciation
  Property taxes
  General facility insurance

Inventory

The manufacturing department's targets should include levels of inventory at different stages of the production and sales cycle. These are not just a function of the production required to meet sales targets. There's an art to maintaining the proper amount of inventory that both fulfills production requirements and keeps the consumption of working capital as low as possible. Chapter 10 covers calculation of the economic order quantity and the amount of safety stock needed.

FINANCE

The financial plan is more of a *reaction* to the other departments' plans. The purpose of a financial plan is to put in dollars and cents the financial impact of all the company's goals and targets. For many small businesses, the financial plan answers two important questions:

- How much do we need? • When do we need it?

These questions primarily concern cash flow. The cash flow plan is certainly a part of the financial plan—usually the final part. Cash flow pulls together every other part of the financial plan and identifies any surpluses or shortfalls.

Most small businesses include the following documents in their financial plans:

- Assumptions

- Projected financial statements, including balance sheet, income statement, statement of changes in financial condition, and statement of cash flows
- Accounts receivable collection schedule
- Accounts payable disbursement schedule
- Schedule of major purchases disbursements

Notice that most of these schedules depend at least in part on the targets of other departments. The receivables collection schedule is a good example.

Accounts Receivable and Collections

The A/R collection schedule depends on both the sales and credit/collections targets being hit. The person preparing the collection plan has to know

- When sales are scheduled to enter the receivables system throughout the year
- Anticipated aging of receivables before they are paid throughout the year

With this information, we can include cash receipts from the A/R system in the financial plan. This also provides a good monitoring mechanism when comparing the plan against actual performance in this key area.

Accounts Payable

Not only trade accounts payable but the payables resulting from inventory purchases go into this part of the financial plan. The person who targets the firm's A/P aging policy schedules the disbursements according to the manufacturing department's raw material and subassembly purchasing requirements.

The end product is a monthly A/P disbursement schedule that gets plugged into the projected financial statements.

PEOPLE

This is probably the most important part of any company's departmental business plan. Some firms call it the *human resources* plan. This is the part of the business plan that takes a hard look at just *who* is going to hit the targets specified for each department.

If the firm did a good job in assessing the people aspect of its current position, any gaps in the capabilities of the staff to reach the firm's goals should come out of the people plan. If areas of the firm need more technical expertise, the people plan should include it. If the manufacturing department targets increased efficiency and decreased labor needs resulting from installation of a new machine, that also needs consideration.

People Planning Goals

One of the missions of your human resources manager is to keep the labor force happy. This translates to providing competitive compensation and benefit packages. The people plan should probably include attention to these items:

- Salary and benefit survey of key positions to be sure the company isn't over- or underpaying
- Formalized timetable for regular employee performance and salary reviews
- Audit of statutory personnel compliance factors such as space requirements, safety, sanitary facilities, minimum wage
- Schedule of salary and wages paid each month throughout the planning horizon

The last item, salaries and wages paid, should include all scheduled performance and merit increases and anticipated bonus payments. Additionally, it should incorporate the costs of overtime, temporaries, and consultants if the individual departmental plans did not. This comprehensive labor payment schedule gets entered into the financial plan.

Chapter 6, "Identifying Capability Gaps," shows you how to bridge the gap between your current position and the company's targets.

Chapter 6

Identifying Capability Gaps

OVERVIEW

Chapter 6 builds a bridge between the current position identified in Chapter 3 and the company's goals established in Chapters 4 and 5. We've positioned ourselves to see both where the company is today and where it wants to go. However, between the two lies a gap—the *capability gap*.

This chapter demonstrates how to identify the capability gap. You'll see symptoms of it in the various departments of your company. A difference between where a company is today and where it wants to go is good. Everyone needs challenging goals. The key to dealing with a capability gap is to make it neither too small nor too large. Chapter 6 shows how to identify and manage the capability gap.

IDENTIFYING THE CAPABILITY GAP

Some small-business managers look at the gulf between their company's current position and where they want to be and see an impossible task. They can cite all sorts of reasons why the goals are too optimistic. Given half a chance, they'll convince not only themselves but their subordinates that the business plan won't work.

Sometimes they're correct. There are times to scale down goals. However, more often than not completing department goals already accomplished that task. The planning team does not determine these goals in a vacuum. The people understand their roles in achieving the targets set forth in the business plan.

Chances are that a good deal of negotiation took place to reconcile the ambition of the overall company goals and the realities of the department targets. Very few department managers commit to targets they don't have at least a reasonable chance of hitting.

Joint Ownership of the Plan

Insurmountable capability gaps result when two different groups set overall company goals and department goals. This is where small businesses have a leg up on their larger competitors. Small businesses don't have the luxury of large staffs that specialize in either the corporate plan or the departmental plans. Indeed, small businesses usually combine the efforts. Therefore, the same people are more likely to participate in both setting the overall plan *and* figuring out the departmental targets that make it happen.

This joint ownership of both the overall company goals and the departmental targets eliminates the we-versus-them mentality so often found at larger companies.

Competing Agendas

Large capability gaps sometimes arise when those who create the separate parts of the business plan have differing priorities. What's important to those who set the overall goals may not be on the agenda of the department heads.

A good example is a company that's trying to attract additional investors' capital. It links overall goals to such balance sheet goals as

- Changing financial ratios to meet investors' criteria
- Increasing cash flow • Reducing accounts receivable
- Lowering inventory investment

The company designed these targets to meet others' criteria of safety, liquidity, and yield for an investment they *may* consider making. However, to the operational departments, this agenda may not fit their concept of what's important.

The sales department, for example, probably sees a lower investment in inventory as a direct threat to commission income. After all, it can't make a sale if the product isn't available for shipment.

The manufacturing department also sees inventory cutbacks as a hindrance to an efficient-running production line. This divergence could create such a wide gap that Manufacturing views Corporate's goals as being foisted upon it. It takes no responsibility for working under conditions that unduly constrain it from doing its job.

People's attitudes and their competing agendas stretch the capability gap even wider. One group may say, "We know what's good for the company." Another group, the operational arm responsible for making the business plan happen, says "Oh, no, you don't." The gulf widens into a contest of wills. This dooms the business plan to failure.

Structural Capability Gap

Joint ownership and competing agendas create a *false* capability gap. It exists; there's no doubt about it. However, nothing structural in the company created it. People created it.

True capability gaps arise from a structural difference between the company's current capabilities and what the business plan requires. An example would be moving 20 percent of sales ($1.2 million) into the industrial safety market. If the company presently doesn't have any industrial safety products, then there's a *structural capability gap*. The company must bridge that gap. The steps might include

- Creating appropriate products
- Implementing a distribution channel
- Building brand name recognition
- Establishing a sales force in the target market

We design such operational goals to bridge this specific capability gap. They take the company from having no product to getting a material percentage of its total sales from that market.

The case of Pinkerton's

Pinkerton's name is synonymous with security services. The firm has several divisions dealing with various spin-off services. The company sells

- Commercial and personal security services • Investigative services
- Armored car services

Analysis of Pinkerton's capability gap might go something like this:

1. *Goal of the business plan:* Generate revenue from products rather than exclusively from labor-intensive services.
2. *Capability gap:* The company has no products, no engineering staff, and no manufacturing facility. Its sales force sells services, not products.

Bridging this capability gap requires a capital investment the company isn't prepared to make. Lack of capital further widens the capability gap. However, the firm isn't trading on one if its biggest assets—its name. It identifies an opportunity to license its name to companies that manufacture various types of products in the security and safety industry. In return it takes a royalty percentage on all sales.

Suddenly the company has eliminated the structural capability gap. This removes the need for a capital investment and for additional engineering and sales staff. Manufacturing facilities aren't necessary either.

The licensees manufacture the product quickly and without risk to Pinkerton's. Of course, the profit margin isn't the same as if the company had established its own manufacturing operation. However, the time span is years shorter. Further, the company doesn't suffer the expensive mistakes that are inevitable when entering a business that's foreign to management. Most important, the firm's capital isn't at risk in an unfamiliar business.

SIZING THE CAPABILITY GAP

There's a right size for the capability gap. If it's too small, there's no challenge. People who don't have to stretch may not take the business plan seriously. Further, underambition doesn't realize the company's true potential.

On the other hand, excessively challenging goals can create a gap the size of the Grand Canyon. Again, people may not take the plan seriously. They may think that those who created the company's overall goals plainly didn't have a handle on reality. Obvious structural gaps between what the company wants to do and the reality of what it *can* do make the architects of the business plan look as if they're out to lunch. No one takes the plan seriously, and its credibility suffers.

Right Sizing

The correct capability gap is one where

- A starting point can be seen.
- Changes can be specified.
- Milestones to track progress are identified.
- Resources needed to bridge the gap are available.
- Participants see a clearly defined goal.
- People believe the goal is reachable.

Notice that these are also some of the same elements we used in setting up the department plan.

Each department critical to the plan's success must clearly see these six items through the capability gap. Absence of any one of the six makes the gap seem insurmountable. These ingredients allow us to separate the various elements of the gap and address them individually. More often than not, separating a problem into its component parts makes it less intimidating. Further, it allows a sharing of responsibilities and the development of a cohesive project team.

The team approach is important to right-sizing the capability gap. Even in very small businesses, the power of a group addressing a problem exceeds that of just one individual. First, more ideas float around among a group of people. Secondly the more people addressing a common goal, the more resources converge on it.

The Pinkerton case is a good example. Bridging that capability gap required people from marketing, operations, personnel, and finance. Since the firm had no engineering or manufacturing capability, this important resource was omitted. It later turned out that Pinkerton's didn't need it. However, to get all the information, it used outside consultants in these areas. It determined the costs to create and manufacture a product line. It compiled revenue projections.

Everyone saw the gulf between the company's goal and reality. However, there was one marketing person who knew something about licensing and royalties. That's all it took. The rest of the group embellished the thought and ran with the idea. Eventually it became reality.

In this case, was the capability gap too large? Obviously not, since the company bridged it successfully. At first look it may have seemed too large. Nevertheless, the company had enough diverse people to separate the problem into its component parts. It turned out that the marketing part was the key.

This wasn't just luck. The process happens successfully all the time.

America's Space Effort

President John F. Kennedy identified history's greatest capability gap during a speech on May 25, 1961. There, he committed the country to putting a man on the moon before the decade was out. Experiments in space vehicles had begun just a few years before. The jet engine was still in its infancy. Now the president wanted a man on the moon in eight and a half years. The gulf between the target and current capability was over a million miles wide. This was the right size gap for the project team. Here's why.

Starting point

There was no clearer starting point than the one we had. The (then) Soviet Union was further along than America in space exploration with its Sputnik program. This country hadn't even developed the infrastructure needed to bridge the capability gap. There was a perceived need for this project. If nothing else, it was needed for our country's defense.

Clearly defined goal

Goals don't get much more clearly stated than what JFK said in 1961: "Landing a man on the moon and returning him safely to Earth." Equally important, just about everyone envisioned the goal. To make sure, NASA published hundreds of artists' renderings of just what achievement of the goal would look like.

Further, the camera that beamed Neil Armstrong's giant step for mankind back to Earth on July 20, 1969, told the world that America had achieved its goal. NASA managers determined the placement of that camera years in advance of that historic step.

Changes specified

One of the first things needed was a program manager. Enter NASA. From there emanated the advances in technology, materials, fuels, life support, aeronautical engineering, and astrophysics that were necessary to meet the goal. Brilliant managers created a structure designed to bridge this capability gap. They knew what needed doing. That's one of the scariest things to people facing a capability gap—they don't know what needs doing or even how to find out.

Resources needed to bridge the gap

The entire effort cost billions. However, the one person with enough clout to garner the necessary resources devised the plan. Further, those who could assist—Congress in this case—believed in the goals. They did what was necessary to make the required resources available.

Finally, a special group of men—the astronauts themselves—provided the single most important resource needed. NASA made much of these men with the *right stuff.* Their belief in the program and their undying commitment did much to garner further support and guarantee that the needed resources would be available. Their lives depended on it.

Milestones

Like every complicated project, this one used definite milestones. Each moved the effort a specified distance toward the end target. In this case, NASA used the famous Mercury, Gemini, and finally Apollo programs. Each program built on the knowledge achieved in the prior one.

Belief that the goal is reachable

The larger the capability gap, the harder the sell. It helps when credible and influential people in the company give the project their support.

Gaining support is most difficult in the early stages. There may be a scarcity of resources or technology. Perhaps the firm's personnel need enhancement. After the company successfully hits the first few milestones, the *perceived* capability gap narrows.

ITEMIZING THE CAPABILITY GAP

The best way to identify a cleft between the company's overall goals and its present position is to look into the individual elements of the business plan. There, we identify the specific shortcomings of the firm. We also determine their seriousness.

Products

Sales generate revenue. Most small businesses orient their goals financially in some way. Therefore, revenue has a great deal to do with most capability gaps. Since products offered for sale determine incoming revenue, analysis of company products helps identify the capability gap.

The first question to answer is, What products does the company sell, and how do they promote attaining the overall business plan?

Take this answer from the information gained during the current position assessment. Chances are that if a capability gap exists, some of the problem lies in the current products. Perhaps there's not enough profit margin to meet financial goals. Maybe the market is shrinking. Perhaps there's a new technology that's replaced the company's product line.

Dentists in the United States have experienced shrinking demand for the last ten years. The cause is technology-related. The state of dental health care in America has never been better. Toothpastes, toothbrushes, rinses, and fluoride treatment have all worked to reduce the need for expensive dental procedures.

Paper manufacturers that produce computer paper have also seen a shrinking market for their pin-feed continuous-form products. Technology has made possible laser jet printers that use single sheets of regular office paper. Many companies have sharply reduced or eliminated entirely their demand for pin-feed products.

The gap between current product capabilities and targets the business plan must hit defines this part of the problem. Now we know two things:

- How far toward our goals current products can take us
- The distance any changes we make need to cover

Change existing products

What changes to its product line can a company realistically make? Are they sufficient to bridge the shortfall its existing products left? It may be that no matter what changes the company makes, they just aren't enough. The goals still remain out of reach. If that's truly the case, then the goals are unrealistic and need to be changed.

Add new products

New products create both blessings and nightmares. Their potential for added profits may bridge the capability gap. However, two things are *always* true about new products:

- They take longer to produce expected results.
- They're more expensive than anyone ever thought.

Few small businesses can design, manufacture, and bring to market a new product in *any* time frame. Yet bridging the capability gap in the time needed to implement a business plan (about one year) may create an unreasonable deadline.

Look carefully at bridging solutions that require a new product. Often there's an alternative. One would be a joint venture with another company farther along in the new product's development process. Alternatively, you could hire a firm that already makes this product to produce your own private-label product.

Both alternatives are more reliable than starting from scratch. Further, management more precisely controls the timing and costs.

Penetrating Market Barriers

Breaking into a new market may bridge part of the company's capability gap. As with any capability gap, there's a reason the market barrier exists. It may be the position the firm enjoys in the market. Maybe it's the company's market niche. Perhaps its image of quality or price creates a barrier to penetrating particular markets.

Entry barriers

Results from efforts at market penetration aren't nearly so precise as those from filling financial capability gaps or gaps bridged by engineering solutions. Take care not to overestimate results from penetrating a new market.

Entry barriers range from the types of advertising to product features. Breaking down entry barriers requires its own small-business plan. Identify such things as

- Expected sales
- Costs for any required product changes or enhancements
- Expenses, including marketing, sales, and promotion
- Time frames for each step of the process

It's much easier to penetrate a new market using an existing product than to develop a completely new product from scratch. The firm is playing the same tune, but to a new audience.

Contingencies

As with most remedies whose results are unpredictable, have a contingency plan ready. Many companies that depend on penetrating a new market to bridge their capability gap do two things:

- Discount the expected results.
- Develop alternatives in case market penetration proves more difficult than anticipated or takes more time.

Discounting results on the front end never hurts. If you're wrong and the new market penetration moves ahead of the discounted schedule, this success provides a cushion for other solutions to different capability gaps that remain open.

Alternative courses of action always provide a feeling of comfort. That's especially true when dealing with something as unstable as customer demand—particularly customers new to your company.

A good example happened at the credit card operation of one of New York's major money center banks. The business plan called for bridging a profit capability gap by penetrating a new market. The plan targeted recently graduated college students for aggressive promotion of the credit card. This population didn't meet the firm's credit-scoring criteria. Regardless, these were special cases and deserved special treatment.

The plan worked. It hit revenue targets on the nose. Kudos went to the astute marketing people who thought of penetrating this new and lucrative market. The business plan tracked perfectly for three months.

Then it became evident that these new customers had no problem using their new credit cards, but they did have difficulty paying their bills. The delinquencies and default rates among this new market segment were one-third greater than those for the bank's average customers.

The capability gap closed at one end (revenue) but opened (collection costs and default expense) at another. Fortunately, the finance department had provided for this contingency in *its* part of the business plan.

Capital

Money often figures in the capability gaps of small businesses. Companies that begin life undercapitalized seem to constantly run up against capital constraints. Many times the business plan gets completed. All revenue and expense targets appear achievable. The latest in assembly line technology controls production costs. However, there's not enough cash coming in during the three-month down season to meet the payroll.

In this case, working capital produces a capability gap. However, this could just as easily have come from

- Funds available to purchase production equipment
- Cash flow sufficient to service existing debt
- Capitalization to meet lenders' minimums

There are many other symptoms of a capital gap. The good news is that we can bridge it. The planning process nails down availability, timing, and costs. Problems in securing financing arise at the beginning. This isn't true of other capability gaps, such as sales.

Additionally, there are always many sources of capital available to qualified companies. Some of them are

- Existing partners or investors
- New partners or investors
- Newly issued stock or bonds
- Lending institutions

- Private venture firms
- Venture capital funds from investment houses

Manufacturing

Capability gaps most common to the manufacturing department involve

- Volume • Costs • Quality

Failure to meet the target for any of these three has a domino effect through the rest of the company.

Volume

Failure to bridge a gap between current production capacity and that targeted in the department's goals causes sales revenue to fall short. Conversely, excessive obsolete inventory may create a working capital gap in the finance department. Bridging that gap may depend on the production and sales departments converting the inventory to cash.

Costs

There may be a gap between planned costs incurred for the necessary production levels and those at which Manufacturing currently can produce. Often technological constraints dictate production costs. Advanced production equipment often bridges this gap. Robotics provides a solution to many production cost problems. Computer-aided designs bridge another gap. Additionally, the computer-assisted manufacturing equipment now commonly found on many shop floors lowers production costs and increases throughput. Sometimes the solution is to move the operation offshore to a less expensive labor market.

Often the repair or replacement of worn-out production machinery lowers manufacturing costs by

- Reducing unscheduled maintenance
- Lowering labor costs for a unit of production • Cutting QC rejects
- Reducing rework costs

Quality

Often the bridge one department builds to span its own capability gap creates a gap for the production department. This happens when there's a gap between current sales and plan goals. The sales solution may call for entry into a new market. However, this market requires products of a different quality standard than those the production department currently puts out.

That creates a new capability gap. The sales department has solved *its* problem, but produced one for another department. Bridging the quality gap might require Manufacturing to reengineer its line, or perhaps change product design. Whatever the solution, Manufacturing assesses it from the standpoint of

- Achievability • Timeliness • Cost-effectiveness
- Impact on the rest of its work

People

By this point we've identified capability gaps in products, markets, capital, and manufacturing. Chances are that we've identified at least an initial plan to bridge those gaps. However, the driving force behind any actions that successfully bridge the capability gap is the people that make it happen.

People allow capability gaps to occur. It may happen unconsciously. Often people just aren't aware of what's going on outside the company. They fail to respond to competitors' strategies. The funding to quickly bring more cost-effective production technology into the company may be absent. Perhaps the person in charge of that department didn't make a strong enough case to get the equipment on the funding priority list.

Whatever the reason, *people* are responsible. People's capabilities create gaps in where they're able to take the firm. That's one of the reasons for winning and losing political campaigns. People believe that one candidate isn't capable of leading them where they need to go.

Companies are much the same. People have limitations. For some, the problem is their education; for others, the background and experience they bring to the job. For example, bridging the capability gap may require targeting an entirely new market—say travel-related businesses. However, the present marketing director knows only aerospace companies. Further, the incumbent refuses to learn anything about the new target market. We need change to provide the skills necessary to bridge the capability gap.

We see other examples in the senior executive positions of financial institutions. The chairs, presidents, and many senior VPs appear to be great managers while everything goes smoothly. Then things turn sour and the Federal Reserve auditors appear on the scene. The same executives the Fed had just a year ago applauded for their brilliance are suddenly incompetent. Indeed, in many cases the Fed sues these executives for their misdoings. Never mind the praise the Fed auditors had heaped on them only recently.

The lesson the Fed has taught us is this: The tougher the economic climate, the more likely it is that there will be a *management capability gap.*

Assessing employee requirements

Identifying the capability gaps in a company's employee pool requires insight into

- Technical capabilities • Management skills • Leadership
- Commitment

When you did the current position assessment, these employee attributes probably surfaced. Now, however, you're in a position to identify what's needed to get the various departments where they need to go. The difference between your labor pool's current position and the abilities required is the employee capability gap.

Small businesses know their people much better than their larger counterparts. Chances are that since you have fewer employees, you can recite the education and technical backgrounds of everyone needed to bridge each capability gap we've identified. Small businesses are in a position to accurately judge employee leadership capabilities and commitment to making the business plan work.

Since top management is closer to the situation, and to each employee, assessments are usually more accurate at small companies.

Solutions

Replacing a current employee with someone whose technical background precisely mirrors what's needed is always an alternative. However, bridging employee capability gaps doesn't always involve changing horses. There are other solutions.

Consultants can fill temporary capability gaps. They furnish the experience and technical qualifications needed for a short period of time. If you need people whose skills are less specific than those of a consultant, temporary employees are a possible solution.

If the capability gap isn't urgent and if incumbents are able to learn, you can always train them. Education and training in the specific skills that will bridge the capability gap are preferable to firing someone.

Over time people gather much knowledge of the company. They absorb the corporate culture. Strong personalities partly shape the company's attitude and work ethic.

Terminating valued employees can be wrenching to small businesses. Survivors of such purges wonder about the firm's allegiance to *them*. You may have bridged one capability gap only to find that the disruption created another.

President Reagan created such a situation when he fired the striking air traffic controllers. This solved the issue of increased pay and benefits. However, it opened the issue of the nation's capacity to control its air traffic. Suddenly the FAA had a huge capability gap in its ability to staff its air traffic control facilities with trained personnel.

Changing executives

Leadership from the top requires both vision and an organized capacity to act on that vision. Boards of directors often determine that present management cannot bridge the capability gap during tough economic times. General Motors, American Express Corporation, and Sunbeam are just three examples of companies whose boards judged current management not up to the task. These companies all suffered purges at the top.

What's interesting is investors' reactions. More often than not, it's favorable. Announcement of these changes caused each of the three stocks to rise. Lenders and major investors often request (or demand) a seat on the board so that they can influence the policy of the company in which they have a stake. By doing this, they're monitoring any capability gap between where the company needs to go and present management's ability to take it there.

BRIDGING THE CAPABILITY GAP

Many of the things a department comes up with when targeting its goals are a stretch. Perhaps the capacity to fulfill a necessary goal doesn't yet exist in the company. That information needs to come out at the very start.

Once we know the shortfall between the department's current position and the required end point, we can begin figuring out how to bridge the gap. Maybe the production department needs a more modern assembly line. The resulting cost reductions will provide the improvements in gross margin called for in the overall profit goals.

Perhaps the company lacks capital and the creditworthiness to borrow it. The finance department has to bridge this money gap. One solution could be raising more investment capital. Another might be improving its bank relations and cleaning up its balance sheet.

Bridging the capability gap at the department level involves assembling all those things needed in order to get the department's contribution to the overall plan in place. If these things aren't in the firm at the present time, then management must determine how to get them. If a department needs more technical expertise, then it needs to figure out the timing and costs of additional training and people.

Once we've determined department goals, the projected results flow up to the overall company plan. Chances are that the departments have come up with some new information. Perhaps the cost to bridge this capability gap is so great that it throws off some other part of the business plan. Maybe the timing is such that there's now a problem with another aspect of the overall targeted goals. Whatever the issue, you need to resolve it in the overall plan. Any required adjustments then take into account this new information.

That's what we mean by not working in a vacuum. The departments are consciously working to accomplish the company's overall business plan. They're also aware of the impacts of their own actions on other departments. It's up to top management to ensure that participation in the design and implementation of the company's business plan flows from the top level on down.

Figure 6-1 structures a department-by-department analysis of the steps needed to bridge the capability gap.

Targeting Results

The best way to build a bridge spanning the capability gap is first to quantify that gap. Once you've determined the capabilities of a particular department and the shortfall between that and present reality, you've won half the battle. Now you're in position to determine *how* to go about bridging the gap.

A good example is that of a three-store chain of stationery outlets. The business plan called for a specified return to its partners. The problem was that the chain had already saturated its market. It had even brought in several of the larger businesses in the area as corporate clients.

All partners agreed that there was a gap between what the partners needed the chain to produce and what it was capable of producing. This revenue gap

Figure 6-1
Bridging the Capability Gap

Department	Present Capability	Planned Requirements	Capability Gap to Be Bridged
Sales & marketing			
Product demand			
Competition			
Pricing			
Service			
Customers			
Advertising & promotion			
Production			
Machinery & equipment			
Labor			
Union problems			
Facilities			
Distribution			
Shipping			
Control			
People			
Capabilities			
Experience			
Salary structure			
Legal compliance			
Inventory			
Storage facilities			
Security			
Material handling equipment			
Finance			
Creditworthiness			
Capital availability			
Accounting systems			

amounted to $250,000. The bridge over this gorge came in the form of a new product line—computer printers. For many businesses, computer printers have exceeded the level of the staff's expertise. The stationery store partners became experts at fonts, interfaces, driver software—even the gauge of the cable required for running long distances between the printer and computer. Not only did they sell the products, they installed, and serviced them as well.

Revenue from this new line of business steadily grew over the planning period. Eventually, the chain bridged the revenue gap. More important, the profit generated from this venture gave the partners the kind of return they needed to prosper in their business.

Faulty bridges

Beware of building a bridge that doesn't quite reach the target. I know of an art dealer in New York who needed to expand her customer base beyond her firm's regular customers. One solution seemed to be exhibiting a different line of artists. This was supposed to get a different type of customer.

The problem was that this bridge over the firm's revenue capability gap failed to enhance the company's current image. Instead, the existing customer base seemed to deteriorate, since the gallery no longer showed what these customers wanted to see.

Another solution was to establish a separate marketing department. Its task was to expand the firm's sphere of influence. This helped, but proved too slow in generating the necessary revenues.

Instead, the firm needed a larger bridge, one that could generate an entirely new type of customer—customers the gallery could count on to support its growth plans. The solution came in the form of a new division. Rather than *sell* art, this division *leased* it to corporations. The owner staffed this division with an art expert, an interior designer, and a leasing expert. Not only did the division lease what turned out to be very expensive art, it brokered the pieces as well when the clients decided to buy it.

This bridge over the revenue capability gap generated revenue from two places:

- Regular cash flow from leasing payments
- Scattered payments (often quite large) from art brokerage fees

Tie-in with Departmental Plans

Once the capability gap for each department is identified, bridging it is incorporated into the departments' operational plans. Bridging the gap *becomes* the departmental plan. We've identified the *single thing*—if the department does nothing else—that each must achieve if the company is to succeed in implementing its business plan.

Often, bridging the capability gap causes departments to rearrange their priorities. It brings to light goals and targets that may not have been at the top of the *must do* list. Further, and equally as important, it identifies those impossible-to-bridge gaps.

Evaluating the Impossible

Some things just aren't possible for companies during the current planning horizon. This doesn't mean they'll never get there, just that it may take a little longer—perhaps several planning horizons. There's nothing wrong with that. Indeed, it's at that point that we switch from the purely *tactical* plan we're creating here to a more *strategic* plan.

The firm breaks down the ultimate goal into intermediate goals, reaches one, and then moves on to the next goal and then the next. Finally it arrives at the end point originally targeted. It achieves what might once have been an impossible target.

So, how do we evaluate seemingly impossible gaps in the company's ability to fulfill the business plan? Separate the bridge into its component parts. Workout specialists do this for distressed companies. There's nothing magic about it. Here are the steps:

1. Identify the most critical capability gaps.
2. Determine those that appear impossible to bridge.
3. Recognize the reasons for these insurmountable obstacles.
4. Plot the time and resources needed to convert the impossible to the possible.
5. Identify changes to the overall company plan necessary to provide the time and resources needed.

"With this analysis," says noted educator and counselor Janet Conolly Berens of Missoula, Montana, "It's called choices." We've determined a course of action to accomplish the "impossible." We've identified the resources and time required to reach that goal.

Now comes the question, Do we really want to spend the time and resources necessary to accomplish this goal? If the answer is yes, then we incorporate it immediately into the business plan. If it's no, then other goals move up on the priority list.

Chapter 7, "Writing the Business Plan," discusses the actual written document. Its utility comes not only in what it says today, but in both its initial creation and our ability to refer to it as the plan unfolds.

Chapter 7

Writing the Business Plan

OVERVIEW

The *process* of business planning provides at least three-quarters of the benefit. However, the process needs a *product*—the written business plan. Business planning is ongoing. By definition, as soon as it's done, it begins aging. The market changes. Competition responds to different strategies. We all become smarter about different ways to implement the written business plan. Soon, the plan we drafted just six months ago becomes obsolete. Nevertheless, that doesn't make the written plan any less useful. Further, the written document provides a base from which to revise the plan.

The written business plan provides a means of communicating four things to the entire company:

- Where the firm is headed • Precisely how it intends to get there
- What signs of progress to watch for along the way
- What's expected of each department to help the company succeed

It leaves nothing to guess. Every goal and target, each milestone and benchmark appears in black and white. So does the responsibility assigned to each department.

Chapter 7 describes what goes into the various sections of the written business plan. The objective isn't to draft a pretty document that gathers dust on a shelf after completion. Rather, we're more interested in generating a tool that will be used throughout the entire planning process—from implementation to mid-course corrections and into the next plan.

Additionally, we'll cover each of the sections of the business plan. Chapter 7 shows what goes into the most useful small-business plans. We'll emphasize clarity and specifics. The style is brief with the intent to communicate two key things:

- Where we're going • How we'll get there

Earlier we described how to identify the capability gap for the company as a whole and for each department. Now we'll demonstrate how the written business plan bridges those gaps.

CONTENT OF THE BUSINESS PLAN

The components of our business plan consolidate the ideas and objectives voiced during the planning process. However, instead of merely having these ideas in mind, the written plan lays out specific actions to implement them. Most plans for small businesses use schedules to communicate goals and targets. They don't use volumes of written text.

Instead, our written business plan targets specific departments. It describes what they need to accomplish, often using numbers. Then the plan schedules milestones against which we monitor progress toward our goals.

Each area of the company comes under the plan's scrutiny. Most likely you'll see a separate section for each major department. Figure 7-1 shows an outline of a typical business plan.

Cover Sheet

This may sound superfluous. However, for companies with different business segments or several stand-alone operating divisions, a cover sheet helps identify the enterprise we're talking about. Additionally the cover sheet should identify the year that the business plan covers.

One other thing: Bind your business plan together, even if you use nothing more than a three-ring binder. People must be able to take it with them and refer back to it frequently without its falling apart.

Table of Contents

Make this as detailed as needed to let you get to the precise topic you want without having to page through the entire plan. Figure 7-1 is a start. Alternatively, some companies add index tabs in the document itself to make finding the major topics easier.

OVERALL COMPANY PLAN

The first section of your written business plan describes the company's overall goals. Many plans start right off by defining specific quantitative targets for the company. Take these from the work done in Chapter 3, "Where Is the Company Today?" and Chapter 4, "Setting Company Goals."

Developing a Logical Progression

The overall business plan isn't just a list of goals. Instead, it provides the *reasons* why it's important for the company to move in the plan's direction. The most effective plans develop a logical progression for this movement that goes like this:

- Assessment of current position
- Identification of reasons to move from the current position
- Clear definition of where the plan is taking the company
- Overview of how to get there

You're right if you think this sounds like a bit of a sales job. The company's officers and planning team (if you use one) must sell themselves on the direction of their business plan. If they can't do that, they won't be able to sell anyone

Figure 7-1
Plan Contents

Business Plan Contents

Cover
Table of contents
Overall company plan
      Current position
      Goals and targets
      Capability gaps
      Bridges
      Schedule of milestones
Marketing and sales
      Unit sales schedules
      Gross revenues from sales schedule
      Marketing programs: projected results and costs
      Schedule of milestones
Operations
      Manufacturing plan
      Shipping
      Warehouse
      Inventory
      Service
      Administration
      Schedule of milestones
Major purchases
      Schedule of items required
      Timing
      Costs
      Analysis and justification
      Schedule of milestones
People
      Requirements to bridge capability gaps
      Current salary schedule
      Scheduled increases
      Net salary schedule
      Insurance and other benefits
      Recruiting plan
      Layoff, furlough, or plant closure plan
      Schedule of milestones
Finance
      Assumptions
      Projected financial statements
      Schedule of loans
      Borrowing and payback schedules
      Schedule of milestones

else—not their employees and not the bankers and investors who are asked to finance the plan.

Further, the logical progression clarifies management's thought process. Those who read the business plan see the justification for moving the company from point A to point B. Now, if you are an owner, you may think you don't need to justify your actions to anyone. That's true only in the sense that you have veto power over others' suggestions. Sometimes even that's not true if the financial part of the plan assumes that the firm borrows money from its banker.

Finally, the overall business plan serves as an executive summary of all the other parts. This is a good place to pull together the departments' goals and objectives required to get the company where the plan says it should be.

Defining Overall Company Objectives

Each department bases its goals and targets on this part of the plan. The more specific the firm's overall goals, the easier it is for each department to create its own plan. Many firms include their overall goals in quantitative form. These might include

- Profit targets • Return on capital invested • Growth rates

From this point, it makes sense to summarize the performance needed from each department to accomplish these goals. This summary answers such questions as

- What do we as a company and each department do best?
- What major targets must each department hit for the plan to succeed?
- Where do the firm and each department fall short of the plan goals?
- How are we going to bridge that gap?

Overview of Key Objectives

The overall company plan does not tell how each department intends to hit its individual goals. It doesn't list each department's detailed goals either. That level of detail comes in the departmental sections that follow.

Instead, the overview of key objectives uses the major department targets to support the plan's overall logic. We want readers to understand our tactics. We also want the plan to convince readers of its probable success. We don't want them mired in excessive detail.

From this point, the individual departments expand on exactly how they're going to hit their key objectives. From this flow the detailed departmental subplans.

Timing

Even in the overall plan, it's necessary to establish benchmarks and milestones we expect to hit along the way. These provide intermediate targets for the overall plan. An effective method of presenting the milestones is to use a time line. Include on the time line each department's major goals. This serves almost as a master calendar for implementation of the business plan.

MARKETING PLAN

For many small-business plans, revenue drives everything that comes later. That's why we often include the revenue-generating sections toward the front of the business plan. That's most likely the point from which we develop other departmental plans. Usually we generate revenue from the marketing and sales plan. However, in some start-up companies, the only cash inflow comes from investors' capital. This was true of Genentech for several years. If that happens to be your situation, put the finance and operations parts first.

Providing Answers

The marketing and sales plan gives direction to the rest of the company's requirements. The operations group must manufacture, store, and ship the goods sold. Finance needs to pay for the process and manage cash inflow and outflow. Personnel needs to staff at the activity level specified by the company's sales. The marketing and sales plan must answer these questions clearly for the rest of the company.

Supporting the Sales Projections

The marketing plan supports the sales projections. It should explain exactly how the company intends to generate the sales figures. Logically, the company needs to do something to *cause* sales to occur. That's why we've placed the marketing plan ahead of the sales plan. Here are some marketing issues that help justify the sales projections.

Promotional plans

Sales don't just happen—especially plans for aggressive sales. The company causes customers to buy. It does this by using promotional plans. If your sales projections depart from historical trends, then there must be something in your promotional plan to cause that. Communicate that departure in the marketing plan. Identify what makes this campaign different from its predecessors.

Advertising plans also come under this heading. Identify what media the firm intends using. What trade shows, fixtures, and booths does the plan include? Does the increased sales schedule correspond with these promotional efforts? If not, then the sales plan isn't tied to the marketing plan.

Defining the market

Unless your business plan indicates business as usual, chances are that the marketing plan calls for entering a new market. Identify that market. Answer questions like

- Who makes up this new market? • What is the competition?
- Why buy from you?
- What factors are important to these new buyers?
- How do your products meet this demand sufficiently to support the planned sales levels?
- Why is this sales projection realistic?
- What contingencies has the plan included?

Sound like tough questions? It's better that we address them in the marketing and sales plan—at the front end—rather than try explaining any revenue shortfalls later.

Method

We want to know what combination of sales tactics the company intends using. The marketing and sales plan not only identifies the results of these methods, but must also schedule out the costs. Marketing methods might include combinations of

- Direct sales
- Increases or decreases in the size of the sales force
- Brokers
- Consignment arrangements

The promotional methods that small businesses employ include media coverage and event sponsorship. Even if it's only sponsoring a charitable event for the local Rotary Club, that's part of the marketing method. The firm expects to get some sort of return on that expenditure. If not, then (from a profit-planning perspective) why do it?

Price promotions also fall into the marketing plan. Both the sales volume projections and the revenue projections must include the effects of such promotions. We don't want the finance department expecting the firm to generate one level of revenue from a targeted sales volume, only to find out that we used a price discount to hit that sales volume level.

Include price changes in the marketing plan as well. Some companies spend advertising money to beef up product recognition, then increase prices at the same time. Theoretically, demand stays the same but profit (net of advertising cost) increases.

Promoting the company's image is another method that doesn't necessarily benefit direct sales. Many companies use this as the beginning of a very concentrated product promotion. For example, let's say the company's marketing plan targets upscale consumers of hair care products. An image campaign might promote the company's philosophy regarding purity of products, its concern for the environment—whatever it thinks means something to the target market. Once it has delivered that message, the ads directly pitching the particular product hit.

Tracking cost versus benefit

Marketing costs can quickly get out of control if we don't first identify them in the business plan. This section of the plan tells three things about each marketing tactic:

- What we're going to do
- What we're going to achieve in terms of unit sales and revenue
- How much it will cost

When we schedule out the revenue benefits and costs, everyone knows *when* both events are supposed to happen. The marketing department tracks the results of each campaign against the costs. As soon as one method or tactic fails to meet its expectations in terms of cost versus benefit, we terminate it and try something else.

SALES PLAN

The sales projection schedules communicate precisely unit volume and sales revenue. They derive from the marketing plan. Most firms begin with a monthly projection of units sold. The sales department usually supports this with sub-schedules illustrating

- Product mix sold • Pricing schedules • Sales revenue

Often, companies with more than one product separate sales volume by product. That way everyone can see how actual performance tracks against the plan. Additionally, it's easy to track the return on each program if the firm runs separate marketing campaigns for each product. That's how we make marketing decisions using the precision of a rifle rather than the shotgun approach.

Coordinating the Sales Forecast with Marketing Programs

We want the sales forecast to *evolve* as a result of the various marketing programs. That way, the company gets used to demanding a performance return (in terms of sales) for marketing dollars spent. The marketing program schedule should correspond to changes in forecast sales volume.

It's a matter of cause and effect. *That's* the type of coordination of the marketing and sales plans that we want.

Pricing Decisions

The sales projection must also include the effects of changes in demand caused by pricing decisions. Of course, the marketing plan may attempt to mitigate the impact on demand that a price increase may have.

However, there's a process by which the sales projection evolves from these two influences. The sales part of the business plan both identifies circumstances and quantifies their effects. The net results may appear flat. Nevertheless, those reading the plan should clearly see that both events went into the sales equation. That way no one fears that we forgot something important.

Seasonality

Many firms have ups and downs in their sales volume throughout the year. Seasonality plays an important part in the financial plan's cash flow projections. The sales volume and revenue schedules *must* include fluctuations for seasonality.

Sales Commission Expense

The sales plan carries few expenses. Instead, we concentrate these in the marketing plan. However, many sales organizations promote products to their own sales force. Securities brokerage firms are famous for this tactic. The sales force receives a commission incentive in the form of a premium to push a particular product.

When planning such programs, be sure sales projections include the impact on commission expense.

OPERATIONS PLAN

For most small businesses, Operations forms the backbone of the business plan. From the marketing and sales sections we know how much of what the company intends to sell. Now, the operations section describes how to provide those things. This section pulls together all the different parts of the company that create, ship, and service the products it sells.

Production

The manufacturing plan provides the key to the more detailed production schedule. It tells us how much of each product to manufacture and when we'll need it. Derive the production schedule by working backwards from the sales unit volume plan. Here are nine items that most written manufacturing plans include:

- Units produced and timing of production
- Engineering necessary for the plant, production line, and other facilities
- Quality control • Distribution
- Investment in manufacturing equipment
- Projected machinery downtime for both preventive maintenance and emergency repairs
- Labor force required • Training • Raw materials required

Of course, your written plan may not require all these items. Choose the ones that are relevant and leave out those that aren't.

The most useful production schedules contain the most detail. Companies that do high-volume manufacturing but keep very small amounts of raw materials and assemblies in inventory might schedule production by the week. Certainly the production schedule should show each month at a minimum.

Scheduling Production

The production component of the business plan usually shows only *monthly* volume. However, within the production department itself, many companies schedule each month independently. The lead time required to make the products and receive raw materials dictates production schedule timing.

The production schedule is nothing more than a listing of the finished goods inventory that needs to be in the warehouse to meet the sales demand. Creation of the production plan works like the diagram in Figure 7-2:

Figure 7-2
Creative Flow of the Production Plan

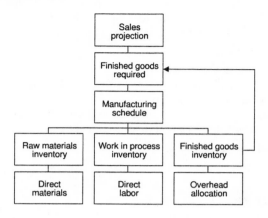

Notice that all production components come out of the initial manufacturing schedule. Further, we schedule changes in production as demands from the sales schedule dictate. That way, the business plan gets updated in all departments affected by changes in sales volume estimates. That's what we mean when we say the written business plan works backwards—backwards from the marketing and sales plan.

Inventory

As long as we have the sales and production schedules, we can project the various stages of inventory. Again, we start with the required finished goods inventory, derived from the sales schedule. That's the targeted end point for inventory. Now the operations plan identifies the resources needed to produce this volume of goods. Questions this part of the plan answers include

- How long does it take to convert work-in-process inventory to finished goods?
- What manufacturing components, such as direct and indirect labor, does WIP require?
- What overhead allocations take place to complete the cost of goods sold?
- What production rates are required? How do these compare with past rates?

At this point the inventory schedule identifies the various stages of WIP each month leading up to the necessary finished goods. Continuing to work backwards, the plan next identifies the raw materials inventory required. The written plan answers these questions:

- How much raw material does WIP require each month?
- What order quantities should we use for each inventory component?
- What safety stock do we need to ensure that we don't run out?

That's how the business plan formulates the purchasing schedule for the various components of raw material. The end result is a schedule of raw material and subassembly delivery dates for items required by the production system. Usually this schedule includes at least every month for the duration of the business plan.

Using this schedule, the purchasing people negotiate the various bulk deals offered the firm. Additionally, they line up backup vendors for vital materials to ensure availability.

Inventory Items in the Plan

The operations part of the business plan that deals with inventory should clearly answer some additional questions. These are assumptions that could change over the planning period. Changes in these assumptions alter the production plan.

Lead times

Identify the lead time it takes to get critical inventory items. We want to be sure the plan considers potential availability problems. Additionally, part of the inventory purchase schedule should consider the economic order quantity and the appropriate levels of safety stock. Chapter 10, "Creating the Operations Plan," gives both of these computations.

Purchase terms

The financial people preparing the cash flow plan need the terms of purchase for the inventory acquisition plan. Such coordination of different plan parts helps identify potential risks and opportunities. Perhaps the cash flow plan reveals an excess of cash at the time Production schedules delivery of a major inventory shipment. The planned purchase terms might then call for a deeper discount based on next day payment. That's an opportunity only careful preparation of the business plan and review by all departments can reveal.

Alternatively, a price discount Purchasing gets by ordering twice the normal shipment could require additional temporary warehouse space. The written operations plan communicates this to the rest of the company. Perhaps we can store the added inventory someplace other than the usual warehouse.

Planning for price changes

Inventory purchase schedules frequently include provisions for price escalation. If we know the items, quantities, and purchase times, an expert can develop a hedge strategy. Publicly traded commodities are a good example. Coordination of the inventory plan with a hedging strategy executed by the financial department could hold down prices that might otherwise rise out of control.

Cost of goods manufactured

The most effective production plans detail the cost of goods manufactured in their monthly production schedules. That way, we know nothing was left out. Often, one department pushes off to another department costs such as certain overhead allocations. If the receiving department does the same thing, we risk ignoring some major costs. Detailed production cost schedules provide a method of tracing those costs. Consider these production costs in your written business plan:

- Direct materials and components • Direct labor
- Indirect labor and supervisory salaries
- Maintenance and repair labor • Maintenance and repair parts
- Production supplies • Depreciation allocation
- Insurance allocation • Telephone • Power and other utilities
- Fuel • Rent

Planning for Obsolete Inventory

Many written business plans address specific problem issues. The business plan excels at formulating a clear path to problem solving. There's no better place to discuss getting rid of obsolete inventory and installing a program to ensure that the problem doesn't return. Even though it may not be a top priority for the plan, it can't hurt the company.

Organized Labor

Many companies include in their business plan a section dealing with an upcoming union contract negotiation. Naturally, this isn't something you share with an adversarial union prior to contract negotiations. However, the operations plan should address the contingencies of such a negotiation. The financial plan identifies the salaries and benefits assumptions used in formulating the business plan.

Further, that part of the business plan comes in handy when you determine how far you can go with the union before placing the business plan at risk.

Quality Assurance

Costs for maintaining a level of production quality vary as volume changes. However, the actual quality of finished goods rarely changes. Nevertheless, part of the written operations plan should address manufacturing quality control. Here are some of the things to consider.

Level of quality

Different products targeted to different markets have different quality levels. This shows up in engineering tolerances and the materials used. If that's the case for your company, the business plan should address these quality issues. There's usually some sort of plan to reach intended quality levels. Any less than that and the product won't measure up. Any more and the company needlessly incurs additional costs.

Quality assurance staff

Most quality assurance programs require people to maintain them. Further, these people may require special training. The plan should address the nature, timing, and cost of QC staffing.

QC testing equipment

If your quality program includes special testing equipment, be sure to include its cost. Further, some sophisticated manufacturers require specially built testing equipment. If that's the case, it's a good idea to identify the items, their costs, and the lead time needed to get them built.

Monitoring vendors

Some quality assurance programs begin with inspection of raw materials and subassemblies upon delivery. The company drops those vendors whose products don't conform to the company's quality standards. If that's part of your QC program, document it in the written business plan. Include the standards established for vendors. Also include the conditions under which the company drops vendors. That's how the plan monitors the success of the program.

Benchmark standards

Airtight business plans identify the company's performance standards. This is true of quality assurance programs as well. If possible, include in the plan the quality standards for each production inspection stage. Just like the rest of the business plan, this provides a target for those responsible. Additionally, it leaves no room for doubt concerning the expected performance standards.

Customer Service

Many companies include their customer service departments in the written business plan. These departments represent a significant cost center. Further, these companies' products often wouldn't be competitive without a customer service department. Even service-oriented companies, such as insurance and credit card firms, have customer service departments.

This is an expensive undertaking. One way to ensure that the costs don't get out of hand is to include targets and goals for them in the business plan. Some of the measurement targets to consider include

- Number of technical and field service staff
- Number of warranty service calls
- Average cost of warranty service calls
- Number of repeat service calls
- Number of customer complaints

Distribution

This cost center ties with both the production volume and sales components of the business plan. Sometimes companies promote their products with the shipping and handling costs included in the sales price, and sometimes not. Regardless, the business plan must identify that point.

If the company pays or in some way subsidizes the distribution costs, then this expense component becomes critical. Here are a few of the items to consider when writing the distribution plan:

- Mix of products sold—some are more expensive to ship than others
- Customer locations • Method of sale
- Number of items in each shipment • Method of distribution
- Packing materials • Warehouse picking costs
- Material handling equipment • Warehouse staff

Administration

Large companies often have such huge administrative costs that they include Administration as a separate division. That's not usually the case with most small businesses. They're small enough to include the administration component of the business plan under Operations.

If your company has several divisions, chances are that there's a corporate entity that oversees everything. That's its job. Somehow the plan must allocate the cost of this overhead among the revenue-producing divisions. This allocation increases the profit they must make. That's why overhead allocation is a constant source of irritation among division managers. They usually don't like the interference from the corporate entity. They don't enjoy paying for the privilege, either.

Make sure your written business plan identifies the administrative costs. Just as for any cost center, itemize these and project them for each month. However, the most important piece of information is the *allocation* of these costs to the various operating divisions. Include it in the division of financial projections.

MAJOR PURCHASES

Often the bridge over a capability gap requires the addition of equipment, enhancement of the plant, or other types of acquisitions. This section describes

- Exactly what the company needs • When the items are needed
- Their cost • How the firm will pay for them • Terms of payment

The company's major purchases are a significant part of the written operations plan.

The written major purchase plan should include a schedule for each purchase along with all the relevant financial information. The departments that need those purchases want to know the delivery date. The finance department needs to formulate plans for payment.

Another thing many major purchase plans include is the merits of each project. This short summary identifies the need for the project and its economic justification. Often the analysis includes

- Discounted cash flow back to present value • Return on investment

- Internal rate of return • Payback period

The written plan tracks the performance of each project. Specific individuals are responsible for its success.

PEOPLE

People help bridge capability gaps. This section of the plan demonstrates several things:

- What types of expertise are required • Where they're needed
- When they're needed
- How the company intends to attract these people
- Once they are in place, how the firm intends to retain them
- How the company manages the benefits system, such as health insurance
- How the company ensures that it provides necessary training
- How the company motivates employees

Additionally, this section includes all the salary expense schedules used in the financial plan.

Salaries

A detailed salary schedule is among the most important parts of the people plan. We want to project both the starting salaries and any scheduled increases. This provides a detailed look at the cash outflow associated with the company's employees.

Officers and directors

The salaries of officers and directors often include special payments, such as bonuses and contractual payments. Be sure to include these in the salary schedules.

Manufacturing salaries and wages

These often vary with manufacturing volume. In some companies, additional temporary people come in during peak periods and leave when production slacks off. Other companies work their permanent employees overtime to staff the heavy seasons. Be sure the written salary schedules include these fluctuations along with the higher wage rates.

Some companies pay based in part on the number of pieces a production line employee produces. If that's the case with your company, be sure to include the changes and their computation in the written business plan. That way there's no question how the plan generated these costs.

Technical Expertise

Here's another bridge over the capability gap. If the need for additional technical resources is permanent, the people plan should include provision for the new hires. If it's only temporary, perhaps the needy department can get away with a consultant. In that case, the expense belongs in the department's plan, not in the people plan.

Perhaps there's a way to inject the needed technical expertise into the current employee base. Training to enhance someone's capabilities is almost always preferable to hiring an outsider.

FINANCE

This part of the business plan communicates in dollars and cents the income sources and their use throughout the plan period. The financial schedules become the part of the plan most often referred to as implementation unfolds. We judge performance milestones using these schedules. They also control the incentives that motivate people and ensure the plan's success.

Financial Forecast

The financial forecast has four components:

- Financial position—projected balance sheet
- Operating plan—projected income statement • Cash flow
- Assumptions

The financial position identifies the projected assets, liabilities, and owners' equity during each month of the business plan. The major purchases plan must tie with the assets part. Additionally, the projected inventory balances at all three stages (raw materials, WIP, and finished goods) flow into the projected balance sheet.

The projected income statement incorporates all the income sources from the sales revenue plan. It includes all production costs along with the other expenses associated with running the firm. The result is the net income. It flows up to retained earnings in the owners' equity section of the projected balance sheet.

The cash flow projection is often the most critical financial schedule for small businesses. This answers the key questions, How much do we need and when do we need it? From this information flows the borrowing schedule.

Borrowing Schedule

Here the financial plan identifies the strategy for funding the business plan's cash requirements. Everything from working capital requirements to funding major asset purchases to payment of shareholders' dividends flows through the borrowing schedule.

The borrowing schedule identifies the various types of financing the company intends to use. It includes terms of repayment along with the projected interest payments. Additionally, many sophisticated companies identify the convenants and restrictions lenders are most likely to impose on the company.

The rest of the financial plan uses these benchmarks as minimum levels of performance against which to target the financial projections.

SPECIAL PROJECTS

Almost always, a business plan has at least one project that cuts across departmental boundaries. If you put this project in any single department's plan, you might overlook contributions from other areas of the company. New product development is a good example. Every department in the company contributes to the plan for development of a new product.

If your company has such a project—possibly to bridge an existing capability gap—include it in a separate section of the written business plan . However, make sure all the other department subplans include its impact on their department. Some companies like to separate their special projects from the rest of the firm's performance. Doing this allows the question, What does our performance look like both with this project and without it? So a sales forecast might look like this:

Subtotal sales + new product = total sales

Chapter 8 takes the first step at the department level—creating the sales plan.

Chapter 8

Creating the Sales Plan

OVERVIEW

Every morning as the sun peeks over the African veldt, an antelope awakens. It knows it must run faster than the fastest lion or be eaten. At the same time, a tiger opens its eyes. It knows it must outrun the slowest antelope or it will starve. It matters not whether you're an antelope or a tiger: When the sun comes up, you'd better be running.

The sales plan is the first step in getting your business plan up and running. Here we forecast the company's gross revenue. Chapter 8 shows you how to create the monthly sales plan. Production schedulers use it. So do the purchasers of raw material and subassemblies. The controller schedules collection of accounts receivable for cash flow purposes from the sales targets.

Though no book can tell you how much revenue to forecast, this one demonstrates a systematic method to help you arrive at those numbers. Equally as important, you can use the format and techniques offered to monitor progress toward your goals.

WORKING BACKWARDS FROM THE OVERALL PLAN

Chances are that at least some of your overall company goals involve profits or return on investment. The sales plan provides the revenue required to realize such financial goals. Therefore, we must identify those overall company goals that are *driven* by sales. We can easily spot such goals in the form of

- Profit levels • Growth rates
- Return on capital or owners' equity targets
- Market penetration for specific lines of business

Converting Overall Goals to Sales Targets

As long as we can identify a company goal and quantify it in terms of either unit sales or revenue, we can link it to specific sales goals. For example, say Poncho Enterprises' goal is to increase return on owners' equity to 15 percent by year-end. Compute return on owner's equity as follows:

$$\text{Return on owners' equity} = \frac{\text{Net income}}{\text{Owners' equity}}$$

Poncho and his investors worry about this number because the company competes with alternative investments of their capital. The return on their ownership in the company must at least equal or exceed that on alternative investments with equal risk. If it doesn't then staying in the investment doesn't make sense.

For Poncho's sales planner, the operative number is *net income*. Now we start working backwards. We know owners' equity. Let's assume there's no intent to change owners' equity during the planning period by injecting more capital. The only thing that changes owners' equity is net income going into retained earnings (one component of owners' equity). However, that won't happen until after the books are closed at year-end. Let's assume owners' equity remains at $3 million.

The net income that provides a return of 15 percent on $3 million is $450,000. We found this number as follows:

$$\frac{\text{Targeted net income}}{\$3,000,000} = 15\%$$

$$\text{Targeted net income} = \$3,000,000 \times 15\%$$
$$\text{Targeted net income} = \$450,000$$

Grossing up sales revenue

Grossing up is business planning jargon for the process of starting with a net number, then projecting upward to the gross number. In our case, we now know Poncho's planned net income. From past history, we can assume that the company's operating costs run about $1 million. This includes all overhead items. Additionally, gross margin (net sales less cost of goods sold) has run about 45 percent for the last five years. We also assume 5 percent for sales returns and allowances.

Now we have all the information we need to gross up Poncho's sales number. The analysis goes like this:

Net income	$ 450,000	Computed above
Overhead expense	1,000,000	Known
Subtotal gross margin	$1,450,000	Subtotal
Cost of goods sold	1,993,750	Computed (3)
Sales returns	181,250	Computed (2)
Targeted gross sales	$3,625,000	Computed (1)

1. *Targeted gross sales* was computed as follows: We know that gross margin runs about 45 percent. Therefore, cost of goods sold is the reciprocal of that, or 55 percent. To this add the sales returns allowance of 5 percent to arrive at 60 percent. The reciprocal of 60 percent is 40 percent—that's the number used to gross up the subtotal gross margin and turn it into targeted gross sales. The computation is

$$\frac{\$1,450,000}{0.40} = \$3,625,000$$

2. *Sales returns* are 5 percent of gross sales. The computation is

$$\$3,625,000 \times 5\% = \$181,250$$

3. *Cost of goods sold* is 55 percent of gross sales. The computation is

$$\$3,625,000 \times 55\% = \$1,993,750$$

Check gross margin to be sure you're correct:

$$\frac{\$3,625,000 - \$1,993,750}{\$3,625,000} = 45\%$$

That's how we work backwards from all company goals to convert them to hard sales targets. Depending on the type of goal we're talking about, the numbers change, but the technique remains the same.

Deriving the Sales Plan Schedules

We know the annual sales number the plan must hit. However, we must now establish a monthly schedule to track our progress toward that goal. Most companies have seasonal fluctuations in their sales levels. As we get farther into this chapter, we'll demonstrate how detailed the sales schedules sometimes get.

The emphasis is on *control*. We don't want detail just for the sake of detail. During implementation we want to identify which parts of the sales plan are working and which aren't. Sometimes this requires a breakdown by product and sometimes, for each product, by region, territory, and even salesperson.

Continuing to work backwards

The sales plan doesn't stop at just revenue. Indeed, many parts of the company can't use sales revenue projections. *Units sold* concern them more than the dollars generated. Production is one such department.

Therefore, the sales plan generates forecasts of unit volume from the revenue figures as well. Often companies prepare unit sales forecasts that target the specific volume of each individual product in each territory by each sales representative. Again, we don't want detail that's not necessary for controlling the plan. If it's needed, however, the sales plan must provide it.

USES OF THE SALES PLAN

We want to be sure that all those departments within the company that need the sales plan as a starting point have the necessary information. Further, we want it in a format that helps rather than hinders their planning effort. Let's take a look at other departments' uses for the sales plan to identify the best format.

Marketing

The marketing department supports the sales force. It creates the advertising and promotion programs necessary to get the sales staff into the customers' offices. The sales plan defines in quantitative terms the level of performance the marketing department must deliver.

Equally as important is the *timing* of each sales target. The marketing department, like everyone else using the sales plan, works backwards. To meet sales levels in June, we must have a marketing program in place and operational some time earlier. How much earlier depends on the length of the sales cycle. It may be only a few weeks in the case of some retail products. It may be several months if you're selling products to governmental and public entities that require drawn-out competitive bidding processes.

Some types of marketing efforts require extensively repeated messages to achieve maximum effectiveness. That's the case with most radio and television advertising campaigns. The company must purchase, produce, schedule, and repeatedly air spots designed to support a targeted sales level well in advance of required objectives.

Production

The production department also depends on the unit sales plan. As for the marketing group, timing is the key for Production. The sales plan schedules production. It identifies the timing for goods on hand in the finished goods warehouse ready for shipment. An accurate sales forecast makes such timing for the production department possible.

Finance

The sales *revenue* plan identifies the income of the company's entire business plan. Further—and more importantly for many firms—it's used to help create the cash flow forecast.

Cash and credit sales are two levels of detail the finance department must have from the sales revenue plan. Finance needs to forecast *when* it can expect to have the use of the money generated from sales.

Additionally, Finance includes the sales department costs for commission expense and promotions in its profit and loss projections.

Hiring to Meet Demand

Some companies delegate the hiring responsibility to one person. Others have a large enough requirement that they need a separate human resources department. Regardless of how you do it, the sales plan, along with requirements from the production, shipping, and warehouse departments, identifies the staffing level. The unit sales plan shows the company's general level of activity at any point in time. Those making hiring and firing decisions use the sales plan to adjust staffing levels.

STRUCTURING THE SALES PLAN

Sales plans don't have to be lengthy. Indeed, the shorter the better. Most people want only the numbers generated in the sales revenue and unit forecasts. However, *we* want a record of the supporting logic for these numbers, even though the rest of the company isn't interested in how the sales department arrived at the numbers for which it's responsible.

The act of creating a written record, no matter how brief, supporting the sales forecast gives it credibility. Further, it points out inconsistencies of logic that might otherwise have been overlooked. Figure 8-1 shows a sample outline of a sales plan.

Figure 8-1
Sales Plan Outline

Sales Plan Outline

Sales forecasts
    Revenue forecasts
    Unit sales forecasts
    Sales costs
        Commission expense
        Promotions
        Travel and entertainment
        Administrative support
Computations supporting overall company goals
Identification and bridging of capability gaps
Markets targeted
Customers targeted
Organization of the sales department
    Composition of the sales force
        Backgrounds
        Technical qualifications
    Sales force structure
    Assignment of quotas
    Sales territories
Pricing strategies
Use of sales resources

Notice that the forecasts are the first part of the sales plan. That's because they support the company's overall goals. We develop the plan logically. The forecast schedules identify where the sales department is going. The rest of the plan demonstrates how it gets there. Often, development of the logic identifies capability gaps that just can't be bridged during the current planning horizon. When that happens, the goals of the overall business plan may need changing.

FORECASTING SALES REVENUE

This is the number-crunching part of the sales plan. It usually begins with the dollar revenue requirements set forth in the company's overall business plan. We continue working backwards from there. The progression of work goes like that shown in Figure 8-2.

Figure 8-2
Flow of Sales Revenue Schedules

Notice how the flow of the sales schedules begins with a *lead schedule.* That's the seasonally adjusted sales revenue plan. Each succeeding schedule supports the one that went before. However, there's a word of caution when preparing any detailed schedule in the business plan:

Never prepare a plan schedule if you cannot get actual operating information against which to compare the plan.

> Without actual data to compare with the plan, we have no idea how we're performing and what changes to make. This renders the plan useless.

Using a Spreadsheet Program

Chapter 16, "Automating the Plan," demonstrates some of the techniques used to speed creation of the plan. Many people use a computer to assist in preparing *parts* of their plans. The sales revenue schedules are a good example. Use of a simple spreadsheet program not only accelerates the process and improves accuracy, it also helps in creativity.

For example, consider the assumptions used when preparing a revenue forecast. Often the sales plan calls for different price promotions for various products. Using a computer, we can change the *percentage* of the product mix that participates in the price promotion strategy. Further, we can alter the markups and markdowns. We can plot sensitivity analyses until we find just the right combination of price strategy and product mix participation that hits the sales targets. Such analyses would be laborious if done by hand.

Detailed product mix forecasts and pricing strategies make it easier to plan the marketing effort. We don't have to guess which products require aggressive advertising. Further, we can track actual performance against that planned to determine the effectiveness of our programs.

Figure 8-3 illustrates part of the sales forecast.

Figure 8-3
Unit Sales Forecast by Product Mix

DUDLEY PARTNERS, LTD.
UNITS SALES BY PRODUCT
Fiscal Year 199X

Product	Month 1	Month 2	Month 3	Total 199X
Copper flanges:				
Units sold	100	110	120	1,860
Average price	$10.00	$10.00	$10.00	$10.00
Total product	$1,000	$1,100	$1,200	$18,600
Beryllium faucets:				
Units sold	300	310	320	4,260
Average price	$15.00	$15.00	$15.00	$15.00
Total product	$4,500	$4,650	$4,800	$63,900
Shower door handles:				
Units sold	500	510	520	6,660
Average price	$12.50	$12.50	$12.50	$12.50
Total product	$6,250	$6,375	$6,500	$83,250
Total product lines:				
Units sold	900	930	960	12,780
Total revenue	$11,750	$12,125	$12,500	$165,750

If this were an actual schedule, it would include all twelve months. The next schedule after it might describe how the firm would achieve these sales. It could identify targets for specific regions, territories, and salespeople. If you prepared the schedules using a computer, the variable assumptions probably included such things as

- Percentage of total sales for each product • Prices • Discounts

FORECASTING SALES COSTS

Approach planning the sales costs the same way you developed the sales revenue and unit sales plan. Indeed, sales costs *support* projected unit sales and revenue. They help make it happen—just like the marketing plan coming up in Chapter 9. Further, the financial plan needs itemized sales costs for its forecast.

Sales Commissions

Commissions usually represent the largest single sales cost. Once you have the sales plan, computing commission expense becomes an easy task. However, some companies complicate it by offering special commission incentives for the sale of specific products. If you use such programs to motivate your sales force, be sure to schedule the various commission costs for each program. We don't want the business plan targeting one level of profit, only to find out that the costs were off because someone forgot about the special product sales commission program.

Price Rebates

Like discounts, rebates affect total *net* sales revenue. However, we usually include discounts in the pricing policies of the sales revenue plan. Treat rebates as a cost.

Not all customers take advantage of a company's rebate offer. The percentage expected to take advantage should figure into estimates of the costs. So should the timing. It may be that a percentage of your customers ask for their rebate within the first month after purchase. As time goes on, the percentage dwindles. Be sure to include this aspect in the cost plan. The controller needs it to forecast cash outflow.

Other Sales-related Costs

Every organization has its own unique set of costs associated with the sales effort. Many are peculiar to the industry or locale of the company. Here are a few of them to include in the schedule of sales costs:

- Sales meetings • Travel and entertainment • Auto expense
- Customer gifts • Promotional events sponsorship
- Sales staff gifts, prizes, and other incentives
- Brochures and sales materials • Sales training

COMPUTATIONS SUPPORTING THE SALES FORECAST

The way you arrived at the numbers usually doesn't interest those who read the sales plan. However, *you* should be interested. The sales plan needs a record of the logic behind each assumption. Where the sales revenue plan supports a target taken from the company's overall business plan, include the computations that support Sales's efforts in reaching that company goal. The analysis we did earlier in this chapter for return on owners' equity is a good example.

Additionally, the care people take in using assumptions they know they'll have to justify in writing will surprise you. Further, when it comes time to defend parts of the sales plan, a written record of just where you got these ideas comes in handy.

Using Work Papers

We want quick and easy access to the support for each assumption used in the sales plan schedules. The best way to accomplish this is by using work papers. Get a clean copy of the sales revenue, unit sales, and all the cost schedules. Using a colored pen, mark a reference number beside each assumption for which you have a supporting work paper. Match the work paper number with the reference number on the sales plan schedules. We want to refer sales numbers to the work papers and the work papers back to the sales numbers.

Using this system, it's easy to leaf through your *consecutively numbered* work papers to find the logic behind any assumption. However, make sure the work papers adequately (and accurately) describe how you arrived at the assumption. It's embarrassing to look through the documentation supporting a sales plan, only to find that your logic in arriving at the assumptions was wrong to begin with.

BRIDGING THE CAPABILITY GAP

The next part of the sales plan usually includes a section on bridging capability gaps. For example, the unit sales plan may identify a certain sales level in the Eastern region. The only problem is, we don't *have* an Eastern region. Or perhaps we're going after sales to a new market whose application of our product requires extensive technical explanation. However, our sales force doesn't have the background to make effective technical presentations.

This is the place in the sales plan to identify the capability gaps and describe the bridges you intend to build over them. Of course, you already included the costs for these bridges in sales costs (didn't you?). Further, the sales revenue and unit sales plans also assume that you successfully bridged these gaps.

Here is a list of the capability gaps you might discover in the sales plan:

- Number of salespeople • Their technical capability
- Sales training • Markets covered
- Sales staff orientation—retail when it should be wholesale
- Organization and structure of the sales department
- Pricing strategies out of line with competition
- Availability of inventory • Distribution channels

Whatever the capability gaps, they represent a risk to the sales plan if you can't bridge them in the time frame scheduled. The credibility of any plan increases when it is clear that the planners recognize their department's limitations and have taken steps to fix them. Questions like *have you thought of this?* should be answered positively and with a description of what you're planning to do about it.

MARKETS TARGETED

Chances are that everyone in the company already knows what markets the business has targeted. However, if the entire business plan may go to someone less familiar, such as a lender, include target markets. You might also need this section if you targeted entry into a new market. Additionally, sometimes it's good to take a fresh look at your existing target markets by defining them in the business plan. Try taking the tack of justifying inclusion of the target market as one of your major sales revenue generators. Ask yourself, Does it still make sense?

This section isn't as important as the sales revenue schedules. However, if you include it, here are some of the issues you might consider.

Segmenting the Markets

Market segmentation means that you specify parts of markets or their groups. The basis for market segmentation often includes the following criteria:

- Demographics • Geographic location
- Method of payment—cash, credit card
- Terms of purchase—trade credit versus C.O.D.
- Size of the targeted market segment
- Personal characteristics of buyers • Buying habits
- Type of intermediary used—jobber, wholesaler, factory direct, retailer
- Nature of targeted customer—federal, state, or local government; nonprofit; end user; consumer
- Intended application of the product

Targeting Your Best Markets

Sales professionals use six steps to evaluate and target markets for their products. If your business plan specifies new or changed target markets, use these steps in your analysis and include the analysis in the business plan.

Define the market

Clearly identify the market and industry targeted. Describe the products of yours that the target market buys.

Divide the market into targeted groups

Get as specific as possible in order to better focus the marketing strategy. Divide the market into its subgroups of discrete customers. Identify these customers using the bullet points for segmentation illustrated above.

Match the right market with the right product

The market segment must demonstrate the ability to absorb the company's products within the sales and marketing budget. We don't want to successfully penetrate a newly targeted market, but break the company in the process. The fit of designated products into the targeted market must be logical.

Customize strategy for the target market

Each target market is unique. By now we understand its specific requirements for the product we've targeted for it. Now, define a sales strategy that meets that specific demand. Southwest Airlines provides an example of one company that didn't follow this rule. Its no-frills, low-price strategy is a success among consumer passengers. However, when it targeted the business passenger, it forgot to customize its sales strategy and failed as a result. Business travelers wanted the pampering and food—they weren't paying for it.

Monitor performance of the market segment

Remember, newly targeted markets are experimental. We want to carefully track our performance. Don't stop at units sold or gross sales revenue. The bottom line is what interests us. We may successfully place our product in a new market. However, the cost of that effort may take away all the profit.

Integrate target markets into the plan

The last step is to make sure the newly targeted market matches the company's overall sales strategy. Does the segmented market move the company that much closer toward goals the sales plan must reach?

CUSTOMERS TARGETED

The best sales plans detail the customers they're going after. Often these aren't the same customers for each of the company's products. Good sales plans precisely target customers. Identify the customers' characteristics for each of your products. Determine what methods work best on which customers. Here's a list of the attributes many companies include in their sales plans when targeting customers and matching them with products and sales strategies:

1. *Lifestyle:* How does this customer prefer to buy? Match the distribution channel to that preference. When does the customer buy—during the week, on weekends, at trade shows, through the mail, over the phone?

2. *Customer expectations:* What does the targeted customer want in a sales presentation and in your product? Approach this attribute from the standpoint of

   - Product characteristics
   - Price
   - Availability
   - Post-sale service—800-number telephone hot lines are a plus
   - Service technicians
   - Quality of the sales presentation
   - Technical knowledge of the sales staff and their problem-solving skills
   - Logistics of the sales cycle—order taking, processing, shipping (just-in-time shipping is a plus), billing, payment terms

3. *Needs:* Identify the void your product fills for the customer. What problems does it solve? Does it save money, or can customers use it to proactively *make* money? Do they require products that are safer, cheaper, more durable, faster, or more adaptable to different applications?

4. *Customer niches:* Identify that group of customers that has a specific demand for your products. A good example is Bodine Corporation in Bridgeport, Connecticut. Bodine has built very specialized high-speed manufacturing machinery since 1933. Its equipment assembles Champion's spark plugs. It loads Sony's videocassettes. Each machine sells for around $1 million, and Bodine makes only thirty each year.

5. *Identify what works:* Past history with each target customer teaches us what works and what doesn't. Points that close the sale for some types of customers only make others yawn. An example is the importance of the vendor's service department for sellers of technologically complex equipment. Superior post-sale technical support is very highly rated among these customers. Yet for purchasers of services, it's not important at all. Instead, those customers want a salesperson skilled in solving their company's problems.

Evolution of the Sales Approach

Different customers buy for different reasons. The sales plan designs a different approach for each targeted customer segment. Sales techniques have evolved over the decades.

Personality

Before World War I, a salesperson's success depended on personality and charm. People bought because they liked the salesperson. The salesperson's force of personality persuaded them. Companies spent nothing on sales training. They believed good salespeople were born, not made.

The talking catalog

During the industrialization following World War I, sales pitches focused on product performance. A good salesperson was someone who knew the product. A typical sales presentation amounted to a mechanical recitation of the product's features. Just as much good would have come from the customer's simply reading the company's catalog.

Sales formulas

Between the 1930s and 1950s, sales techniques focused on use of a sales script. Many of them used a four-step sales approach:

- Attention • Interest • Desire to buy • Action

The salesperson learned to control the presentation. The goal was to elicit specific customer reactions to each of the sales points made in the presentation. The process walked the customer down a path that had only one logical conclusion: buy. The success of a presentation depended on communicating the product's benefits.

This approach often degenerated into a fencing match between salesperson and customer, each trying to outwit the other. For every objection voiced, there was a planned response—thrust and parry. The more objections blunted by the salesperson, the more likely he or she was to close the sale.

Solving customer's problems

In the 1950s, sales techniques began to evolve toward the professional presentations your sales plan should contain today. Sales tactics moved from manipulating customers to helping them solve their problems—possibly using the vendor company's products. Closing the sale became the last step in a series of solutions the salesperson helped the customer think through in their entirety. Professional sales staffs build long-term relationships with their customers.

Planning Appropriate Sales Approaches

Adjust your planned sales approaches for your different types of customers. Identify the customers and the most effective sales approaches for each. Put this in your sales plan. Then train your sales force to follow it. Here are a few of the different approaches you might include in the sales plan.

Selling the trade

Trade selling usually targets the retail industry. Its objectives focus on building sales volume. Train sales staff to assist customers with product promotion. The marketing plan plays an important role in trade selling. Not only does it promote the company's products, it promotes those of its customers as well. VISA credit cards routinely does this by targeting a particular retail establishment in an ad that promotes not only the card, but the establishment as well.

Selling for direct customers

This is an indirect but effective form of selling. It targets customers of the company's direct customers. For example, say we're a garment manufacturer that sells to wholesalers. Our wholesaler customers sell to retailers. Our sales plan targets these retailers—the customers of *our* customers. The chemical, airline, wholesaling, and pharmaceutical industries often use this strategy.

Technical consultative selling

Nothing sells like a technically competent person offering an effective solution to a customer's most pressing problem. Some of your target customers may have a common problem that your sales force can solve.

This occurred at some of the national CPA firms in the 1980s. Suddenly each of their bank clients had a common problem—interest rate risk that jeopardized earnings in the millions of dollars. The solution required mathematically rigorous computer simulation models and specific expertise in interest rate hedging. The job was a perfect match for the CPA-consultants. Yet, the entire sale of the project was of an extremely technical, problem-solving nature.

Selling cold

Most industries engage in cold calling on first-time customers. The sales force focuses its attention on customers who haven't asked for it. This is a difficult method of selling. However, many companies use it effectively. If your sales plan includes cold selling, define the type of customers targeted for these efforts. Determine how the sales force identifies likely prospects so that salespeople don't waste their time on unqualified customers. Identify the amount of resources devoted in the sales plan to cold selling. Then stick to it.

ORGANIZING THE SALES DEPARTMENT

Now that we've identified the targeted sales volume, strategies, and customers, it's time to determine the organization that makes it happen. Many sales plans include a section dedicated to structuring the department. Of course, if your company is of a size where only one person does sales, this is probably irrelevant.

However, if your firm does have a sales organization, it makes sense to identify its structure. Even if you don't intend to change it, how it looks on paper might spark some ideas.

Composition of the Sales Force

You've already identified the customers and the sales strategies most effective for them. Now determine if there's a difference between the type of sales presentations needed and the talents of your present sales staff.

Consider the backgrounds of your salespeople. Many sales situations require technical proficiency in the field. Does your team have the necessary degrees and work experience? Do their reputations in the industry give them ready access to customers' decision makers?

If the plan's requirements and current capabilities need enhancement, specify in the sales plan the necessary changes. Include a timetable for making the changes. Provide benchmark measurements so that you can track progress toward the needed goals. Also, be sure to enter the cost of upgrading current sales staff skills in the cost portion of the sales plan.

Sales Force Structure

People like to understand the chain of command. This is usually unnecessary in very small businesses. Everyone knows who's in charge. However, the larger the company grows, the more complicated reporting and responsibility relationships become. An organization chart of the sales department provides a quick illustration of reporting and responsibility relationships.

Include an organization chart in your sales plan if appropriate. Use it to make sure everyone knows his or her responsibilities. Figure 8-4 shows a sample sales department organization chart. Include all or just the relevant parts in your own.

Figure 8-4
Sales Department Organization Chart

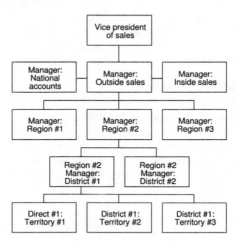

Of course, not every small business needs all this structure. Still, an organization chart along these lines that describes the sales group immediately communicates who works for whom.

Regionalizing the Sales Force

Regionalizing provides a niche specialization that the corporate level cannot implement. Many products suffer when managers are insensitive to regional differences in customer preferences and needs. McDonald's recognizes regional differences in its customers' preferences. It spends roughly 50 percent of its total marketing budget on regional advertising.

American Airlines is another company that recognizes regional niches. The Chicago region, for example, gets a completely different sales thrust in the winter than does the southwestern United States. After all, someone in Arizona isn't exactly aching to walk down Michigan Avenue in the snow and ice storms that blow off the Great Lakes. However, American could probably tempt those from the Windy City to take a sunshine break out West.

Here are some points to consider if you're planning to add regions to your marketing organization.

Regional distinctions in target markets

For regionalization to work effectively, there must be sharp differences between the various regions in which the company competes. These can be anything from uses of the product to customer demand and preferences. Make sure the sales programs that work for one region don't work for another—otherwise, what's the point in regionalizing?

Regional practices for trade outlets

Different regions have different trade customs. For example, in some states, grocery shopping is done at supermarkets. In others, warehouse stores predominate. The existence of visible differences in the way people buy often requires companies to regionalize.

Advertising media

Some regions simply don't support particular types of advertising media. In certain rural sections of the country, television and radio aren't as effective as newspapers and billboards. The sales approach that results from such different advertising support varies also. This further makes the case for regionalizing the sales force.

Legislative variations among regions

Some regions allow certain types of advertising but not others. Some don't allow certain products to be advertised over certain media. Florida at one time proposed a state tax on all advertising within its borders. All these regulatory requirements can form regional boundaries for your sales department.

Regional competitors

Here's the big question: Do your competitors employ regional sales strategies? Some companies believe they must respond to their competitors. Regionalizing the sales effort allows concentration on specific aspects of customers' preferences. Sellers who don't understand the peculiarities of the region often appear as outsiders.

Identify those products with the most to gain

Some products gain more from regional sales efforts than others. Generally, pick products for which advertising, use, and customer preferences differ sharply among regions. Additionally, make sure the national sales manager as well as the regional manager supports these efforts. One (the national sales manager) formulates *strategies* for the overall sales effort. The other (the regional manager) uses these strategies to create specific sales *tactics* unique to that region.

Structuring the Quota System

Every commercial organization needs just one thing from its sales force: sales revenue. For many companies, numbers are the only thing entered into the sales plan. However, some plans include other indicators of sales staff performance as well. These contribute to the bottom-line sales revenue numbers. Here are a few of these benchmark targets that you might consider putting in the sales plan:

- Number of sales per customer—encourages repeat business
- Number of sales calls
- Items purchased per order—tracks suggestive selling
- New accounts • Accounts lost

- Gross margin for each salesperson—controls excessive discounting
- Costs of sales support
- Number of technical educational courses completed
- Service calls per customer

Some companies even go so far as to include in the sales plan targets for behavior measurements such as loyalty, sincerity, and cooperation.

PRICING

Any company can give away its products. We want a sales plan that prices products at a level consistent with overall profit goals. Therefore, some companies include cost of goods sold targets in the sales plan to arrive at gross margin figures. This assists in planning both price and discount strategy.

Sales promotions offering price discounts for a limited time stimulate demand. Customers recognize that the offer won't last forever. They can either make their buying decision now and get the lower price or wait and pay the higher price. Often sales plans include price-off promotions to grab customers from the competition. They hope the customer stays once the discount offer stops.

Be sure to include the price promotion schedule in the revenue plan. These promotions often have material effects on the overall sales revenue and profit plan.

PLANNING SALES TOOLS

Sales tools provide support and incentives to the sales staff. They're also costly—a necessary cost, but a cash outlay nevertheless. Figure 8-5 shows a list of the management and motivational tools included in many sales plans.

**Figure 8-5
Sales Management Tools**

Administrative tools:
    Automated order entry
    Sales training courses, seminars, and meetings
    Sales staff participation in product design and development
    Customer seminars
    Clear credit authorization criteria
    Customer history reports

Motivational tools:
    Contests
    Rewards
    Achievement recognition prizes
    Bonuses for special promotions or products
    Participative commission structure
    Participative quota structure
    Timely commission payment schedule
    Territories fairly designed

Chapter 9

Creating the Marketing Plan

OVERVIEW

The marketing subplan provides the second step in getting your business plan up and running. It generates a detailed departmental blueprint that shows exactly *how* the company intends to execute its sales plan. If sales drives your business, then the marketing plan supports sales. The marketing plan identifies those things the company does during the planning period that help the sales staff generate the required demand for your company's products.

Chapter 9 identifies how the marketing plan integrates with the overall company plan. We'll define the specific targets and goals needed in all the areas of marketing.

Table of Contents

There are specific topic areas that should go into the marketing plan. Each deals with an aspect of the available marketing tools that can further sales goals. These also promote the goals of the overall company. Figure 9-1 (page 138) shows an outline of a sample marketing subplan.

INTEGRATING OVERALL COMPANY GOALS

Before drafting the marketing plan, first identify the ways it promotes the company's overall goals. Chances are that some of the most significant goals are financial. These generally have sales at their root. Since marketing drives sales, many of the marketing goals automatically integrate with overall company goals. Those are the easy ones to identify and integrate.

Targeting Issues Other than Sales

Often certain areas of the marketing plan foster goals other than merely sales. For example, say the company needs to float a public security issue. Parts of the marketing department's goals may focus on the company's public image. The firm may have an image, an industry, and a product line that haven't yet captured investors' interest. Often it's up to Marketing to change that image. If it doesn't, the offering may fail.

Focusing on the Big Picture

The marketing plan frequently deals with issues farther out on the planning horizon than some of the other departments. Marketing is an inexact science.

Figure 9-1
Marketing Subplan Outline

Marketing Subplan Contents

Current position
Capability gaps
Company image
Customer perceptions
    Identification of the customer
    Identification of the competition
    Purchase factors the marketing plan exploits
    Marketing to meet demand
Promotion campaigns
    Analysis of each program
Products
    Existing
    New
Packaging
Distribution
Advertising programs
    Product advertising
    Company advertising
Markets
    Existing
    New
Milestones, goals, and targets
Monitoring mechanism

Completion of specific goals often takes longer than a single planning cycle. That's frequently the case when the company recognizes a need to enter a new market or generate sales from a different customer base.

In such cases, the marketing plan produces a timetable that hits specific targets during this plan period. However, it doesn't accomplish its final goals until well into the next business planning cycle.

Marshaling the Marketing Resources

Marketing resources play a big part in achieving overall company objectives. The marketing department generates the message used by the firm's sales force. Additionally, it projects the company's image to the public, investors, lenders, and customers. The marketing plan aims these tools at the firm's overall targets:

- Advertising • Promotion • Market research • Imaging
- Product characteristics • Customer preferences and demand
- Competitor assessment • Pricing analysis

Some of the more technically oriented people in companies often view marketing as a "soft" discipline. They mean that the programs and results are often fuzzy. Some companies find it difficult to determine if their marketing efforts work. Figure 9-2 shows some of the objections you're likely to hear regarding integration of the marketing plan into the overall company plan.

Figure 9-2
Marketing Excuses

Reasons for Not Integrating the Marketing Plan

1. Our company is too small.
2. We can't predict the future.
3. There's no way to identify results with any certainty.
4. We don't have the resources to conduct research.
5. We can't afford to waste time and money on measures that may not work.
6. Take care of today and tomorrow will take care of itself.

Establishing Two-Way Communication

A good marketing department works like a sponge. It absorbs information from all over—both inside the company and outside. It processes this information. Then it *uses* the information to propel the company further toward its ultimate goals.

The only way to accomplish that synthesis of information is to generate a line of communication between the customer and the company. Here are some of the tools many companies use to maintain that communication:

- Regular sales meetings to find out what customers think from the people on the firing line
- Customer service teams whose job it is to fix problems
- Sales staff training programs • Field technicians

These are all tools used to integrate the marketing plan into the company's overall business plan.

TARGETING RESULTS

Like the other subplans, the marketing plan works backwards from a targeted end point. Therefore, we first identify the objectives of the marketing plan. These all integrate with the company's overall goals. Most marketing goals fall into these categories:

- Sales levels • Product support and image
- Company support and image

Sales Targets

The marketing plan provides ammunition for the sales force. Sales targets are a combination of both sales efforts and the tools Marketing provides. These include specific plans for advertising and promotional campaigns. They work in conjunction with the sales department's efforts. Be sure your plan ties each marketing campaign to specific and quantified sales results.

Small businesses cannot afford to throw money into marketing solutions that don't get the desired results. That's why we *compartmentalize* your marketing subplan by campaign. We want each campaign separated from the others. If we need to adjust or cancel one program, we don't want this to affect something else we're doing. This isn't always practical. Often one marketing program ties in with another. Nevertheless, where possible, we want each program discretely compartmentalized.

Target sales results for each tool employed in the marketing plan. Turn off those marketing programs that don't attain the desired results. Do this as soon as you make that determination.

A compartmentalized format may seem more structured than most marketing plans you've seen. That's deliberate. Marketing is expensive. Therefore, we specify and measure its objectives. Either the program hits its goals or it's terminated. The only way to monitor marketing performance is by using a structured approach.

Elements of each marketing compartment

Structure the elements in each compartment like this:

1. Identify each product marketing campaign. Describe the program and its mechanism.
2. Specify the marketing tools used. These include such things as
   - Advertising
   - Promotional programs
   - Pricing
3. Specify assignments, tasks, and responsibilities for each part of the campaign *by person.*
4. Be sure to put the campaign implementation on a monthly step-by-step timetable following the same course as the rest of the business plan.
5. Identify the costs associated with each part of the campaign.
6. Specify the projected sales resulting from this campaign. Match the sales projection by month with the costs for each part of the campaign.
7. Compute the profit and the return on the investment in marketing costs. Use these to track the marketing program throughout the business planning cycle.

This format allows us to watch the progress of each marketing program. By compartmentalizing (as much as possible), we can turn off the programs that don't work without affecting those that do.

Creating the Company's Marketing Portfolio

By compartmentalizing the plan, we've taken the company, its products, and the various marketing tools available to us and created an arsenal of weapons. In this arsenal we have a variety of items to market and methods to use. When we separate the marketing plan into its component parts, the task loses some of its intimidation. The plan also becomes more responsive to change.

Here are the items in the firm's arsenal that our marketing subplan should address:

- The company as a whole • Each product
- Each market for each product
- Customer segments for each product • Channels of distribution
- Competitive response to each marketing program

The baking industry provides an excellent example of the usefulness of the compartmentalization technique. Entenmann's is a high-volume commercial bakery. It distributes its breads and cakes in most major grocery store chains. Its business plan originally ignored no-fat products. However, when the market finally accepted low-cholesterol and no-fat ingredients, it changed the marketing plan in midstream.

It did this *within* the structure of the marketing plan. Entenmann's simply focused on one element of the portfolio of products—low-cholesterol and no-fat items. It took some of the marketing resources from other plan elements and plugged them into these products in what was soon an exploding market. The result was a sales increase of as much as 45 to 50 percent in some markets.

Without the structure of a compartmentalized portfolio of products and methods, the response would have been uncoordinated. It would have disrupted other marketing programs and products of the company. Instead, Entenmann's knew exactly what promotional and advertising resources it had to work with. By removing them from one part of the portfolio, it could predict the impact on sales. The decision process was organized, informed, and not destructive to the rest of the firm's goals and objectives.

Organizing Your Marketing Targets

Once you've established the marketing portfolio, you're in a position to organize the rest of the marketing plan. We want to identify

- Specific marketing targets for each product or portfolio segment
- Methods of marketing for each product or portfolio segment
- Total marketing costs scheduled out by month
- Total marketing results scheduled out by month

All of these should use the same time frames as the rest of the business plan.

That's the bottom-line orientation of the rest of the business plan. Our marketing plan conforms. Most likely the only thing catching other departments' interest will be the costs and results. The rest of the plan, such as competition's response to price changes, relates to the marketing planners' responsibilities. The rest of the firm probably doesn't care, so long as it doesn't affect what Marketing promised it could deliver.

CURRENT POSITION

We've identified where we want to go by targeting the marketing results. Now reality sets in. The marketing plan needs to identify the firm's current position. From here we determine the specific marketing tactics needed to get us there.

In some rare cases, the current market position already provides the company with the sales levels targeted in the plan. Perhaps the firm doesn't want an increase in sales. Maybe the product is too costly to service. It might be on the declining side of its life cycle with no resurrection in sight. Perhaps the company needs only maintenance marketing to retain its top market position. This happens.

Elements of the Current Position

Identify those elements of our current position that affect the marketing department's ability to deliver the support required to meet targeted sales levels. Chapter 3, "Where Is The Company Today?," identified each of the areas that might affect the marketing plan.

Products

Let's start with the current position of the products themselves. The sales plan identified the sales unit and revenue level for each product. Some plans specifically target not only the product, but for each product

- The customer type • Distribution channel • Sales territory

Analyzing the current positions of product sales this way takes more data and resources than many small businesses have available. However, it might help identify gaps in the firm's ability to generate sales in any of these portfolio segments.

Address issues related to benefits and uses of the current product. Compare them with the competition and customer demand. Identify how your products stack up against technological innovations that are just around the corner.

Market position

Identify the market position for each product in the portfolio. Address issues of

- Customer familiarity • Brand loyalty
- Perceived cost/benefit and quality
- Likely changes in market position
- Differentiation from competition • Price position
- Technological leadership

How does the current position of each product relate to these issues?

Customer requirements

Customers' needs change. They soon leave products that don't keep up with changing needs for those that do. This part of the marketing plan addresses how the company's products satisfy demand. Often the marketing plan identifies a product's current position as falling out of favor. That's how the plan predicts a capability gap. That's the first step in closing it.

Additionally, people in marketing and sales always look for ways to differentiate their products from those of the competition. The current position often identifies the true "differentiability" of the firm's products. The most usual ways to differentiate competing products include

- Technological capabilities • Style • Features • Installation
- Packaging • Delivery

Coors Brewing Company provides an example of attempted differentiation. Its advertising sought to distinguish Coors beer from the competition by marketing the fact that Coors uses *refrigerated* trucks to transport the product from the brewery in Golden, Colorado, to distributors around the country. No other company transports its beer in a constant-temperature environment, the ad campaign claimed.

This was a current position that remained constant. Coors hadn't changed its transportation policy in years. However, the company used this point to its best advantage.

Another viewpoint from which to look at your product's current position is that of the customer's needs, wants, and problems. The product must satisfy all three. The better a product does this, the more pronounced its *competitive edge*. There are three satisfiers for which customers buy your product:

- *Function*—what the product does to fulfill a need or solve a problem
- *Symbolism*—what the product means to customers or says about them
- *Service*—durability, repairs, delivery, installation, purchase terms such as trade credit availability

Customers

Many marketing plans revolve around customers' preferences. The current position section must assess these biases and the reasons the company's customers buy its products. Gaps open because companies fail to notice a change in their customers. Perhaps the targeted age group has changed. Ethnic or age groups may shift priorities and preferences over time.

Further, the competition educates your customers. The hair shampoo market provides a good example. In the 1950s Breck was the first to segment the market with three different types of shampoo—for dry, oily, and normal hair. Over the next twenty years, the industry bombarded consumers with pitches for all different types of hair care products. By the 1970s hair care offerings included products for basic cleaning, conditioning, moisturizing, fragrance, every day, children, teens, adults, elderly, and ethnic groups.

Understanding who buys your products helps you identify the segment's ability to buy in quantities sufficient to meet sales targets.

CAPABILITY GAPS

The marketing plan bridges those capability gaps that are most closely associated with customers' perception of the company and its products. So far we've identified the marketing targets that support our sales goals. We've also defined the firm's current position. By now the gaps between where we are now and where we need to go in terms of marketing are apparent.

This stage of the business plan specifies these gaps and quantifies them. Here we formulate the specific goals for each part of the marketing plan to bridge the gaps discovered between sales targets and the company's current position.

Product Differentiation

Many companies find themselves hopelessly mired in a field of look-alikes. Realizing planned sales targets requires breaking the company's products away from the pack. The problem is a task for Marketing, since there really is no difference.

Gaps in product differentiation between where the company is at present and where it needs to go can exist in several areas:

- Product function • Utility and durability • Service
- Distribution • Packaging • Price • Convenience

New uses for an undifferentiated product

Often the marketing plan identifies other uses for the product that differentiate its utility and service from the pack. Some such uses require only minor modifications. The story of 3M's yellow Post-it Notes is a case in point. The adhesive started as a superglue that didn't work. With some minor modification, 3M differentiated this product as something truly unique.

Bundling purchasing motivations

We can close some product differentiation gaps by combining two different products or buying motives and selling them as a bundled unit. Breakfast cereal is a good example. For years this was a no-growth industry. Then Kellogg combined the features of added nutrition *and* convenience in the marketing of Mueslix. Suddenly the targeted market segment, people aged 25 to 49, consumed 26 percent more cereal.

Differentiating by price

The business hotel market provides another marketing lesson. Many downtown hotels found that they were full during the week but empty on the weekends. They differentiated themselves by offering weekend price breaks. This bridged the capability gap by marketing to price-conscious consumers who wanted a mini-vacation.

Tie-ins

Some companies find it easy to differentiate their product using an unrelated partner. Citicorp's arrangement with American Airlines' frequent flier program works like this. For every dollar purchased on a Citicorp Visa card, the customer gets frequent flier mileage on the airline system.

Factory outlet sales

Factory outlet sales often bridge two capability gaps in the business plan. They get rid of surplus stock—sometimes items requiring rework or seconds—*and* generate sales revenue. Equally as important, these discount goods don't damage the company's market position. The company sells them through completely different distribution channels and usually to a different customer.

COMPANY IMAGE

Customers must believe the company capable of creating a product or service that fulfills their needs. Often the marketing plan calls for repositioning the company's image to one more consistent with its products and the market it's trying to penetrate.

Some companies want to promote a more socially responsible presence in the marketplace. The example of drug companies and their concern about product tampering illustrates this point. Through a crisis that staggered the nation, customers began to doubt the drug companies' ability to provide a safe product.

The marketing plans shifted to an emphasis not on any single product sold, but on the companies' image. Programs were made public to elevate the firms' social concern. Indeed, many companies had already implemented some of these measures. They widely broadcast research into safety caps and tamper-resistant seals. They pulled from production capsules that someone could spike. The industry accelerated research and introduced new caplet and gel-cap designs. This happened with all the publicity for image the marketing departments of socially concerned entities could gather.

Appealing to Specific Markets

Corporate imaging often targets particular market segments. It doesn't advertise the products. Instead, it promotes the company. Frequently, the marketing plan calls for perceptions of the corporation as

- Having high quality • Having high status
- Being scrappy price discounters • Being entrepreneurs

These companywide images translate into perceptions that spill over to all products the company sells. Additionally, they sometimes help the firm's image in the stock market.

Adding to Sales Force Credibility

It's a fact that salespeople from well-known, "important" companies often find it easier to see their clients' decision makers. Corporate imaging generates some of the customer's perception of company importance. Market shares and operating history provide the rest.

Sometimes a sales presentation focuses on issues of reliability. Such issues include

- Product availability and delivery schedules
- Post-sale technical support • Installation • Durability

These all go to the image of credibility the company's marketing plan created. Customers depends on the *company* to do something in each of these instances. It has nothing to do with the product they're buying. Computer software provides a good example.

Today, purchasers of software buy two things:

- A computer program that serves an immediate need
- An ongoing relationship with the software house

Computer users require future updates of their programs. They won't invest time and money in a system that grows technologically obsolete as companies develop new hardware and software. They want a company that is committed to an ongoing relationship. They demand stable vendors—those that will be around for the future.

If the company they're buying as well as its products concerns your customers, take careful note of imaging in the marketing plan. Your company must communicate and maintain the proper image as well as high-demand products.

Action Steps

Small companies don't spend a lot of money on corporate imaging and advertising for things other than specific products. However, here are some things that even small businesses can put into their marketing plan that promotes the company image they want to their target markets:

- Trade show booths
- Hospitality suites at industry conventions
- Company executives speaking before trade associations
- Technical articles in trade journals written by company executives
- Customer training seminars for the firm's equipment they've just bought
- Newsletters to customers
- Technical hotlines staffed by experts
- All staff that deals with customers being specially trained in presenting the company's proper image

None of these things is expensive or difficult to implement. The marketing plan can include such action items. Make the marketing department responsible for each program. Treat these performance indicators just as seriously as you do the more quantitative projects, such as production schedules.

CUSTOMER PERCEPTION

The marketing plan promotes those customer perceptions that best move its products. The company engages in advertising to sell more products. That's the only reason it advertises. We call this a demand-*pull* strategy—where advertising stimulates purchasing.

Specify Desired Customer Perceptions

This part of the marketing plan targets specific customer perceptions about the company's product that marketing campaigns must get across. Some of the issues it addresses are

- Familiarity • Customer loyalty to the brand and the company
- Product availability • Product characteristics
- Attributes of the competition
- Differentiation between your products and the competition's

The marketing plan identifies these perceptions. Then it determines the most cost-effective ways to get the point across.

Certainly it helps if you can identify the exact customers targeted for each product. The more you know about these people's buying motives and habits, the more accurately you can target the advertising campaigns.

The same goes for the competition. One drug company learned this lesson the hard way. Its sales force told it that doctors (its target market) associated its drug with an adverse side effect. However, it was clinically proven that the drug *did not* have this side effect. It never entered the sales presentations. None of the promotional material even mentioned the side effect.

However, the competition stressed that *its* product *didn't* have the side effect. It hammered this idea home in both its sales presentations and its advertisements.

Because the drug company never mentioned the side effect, doctors assumed the drug had it. That's why they avoided prescribing it.

Five Questions about Your Customers

Here are five questions that might help crystallize your marketing plan's goals for customer perceptions:

- Who are the customers in the markets in which we sell?
- Why do they buy our product over our competitors' and vice versa?
- Name the factors important to our customers.
- Do we meet them? More important, do the customers know we meet them?
- Can our marketing plan realistically support the sales projection? If not, how much additional time and money will it take?

PROMOTION CAMPAIGNS

All that has gone before in the marketing plan supports the design of the product promotion campaigns. This section of your marketing plan identifies the strategy that bridges the company's marketing capability gaps. The marketing plan designs specific bits of information about the product and the company. It targets communication channels aimed at particular customers.

Structure of the Promotion Plan

Design each promotion program in the marketing plan to deliver a message about the product and/or company to a specific customer. We'll judge the effectiveness of each promotion program on the basis of just one thing—the increase in sales it generates. Therefore, each program must have three characteristics:

- It must be achievable.
- To be successful, it must exactly do what we want.
- The results must be measurable.

A lack of any of these three characteristics eliminates almost any advertising or promotion campaign from the marketing plan of a small business. It simply can't afford taking chances on deploying scarce resources to a project it can't control.

Plan the promotion campaign for each product or product line. Often companies have spin-off campaigns to promote the same product to different market segments. If that's your case, then specify these as well. The point is to generate a precise promotional campaign for the company. Precision allows better control over plan implementation.

Designing the promotions

There are three targets for consumer advertising:

- Awareness • Attitudes • Behavior

Design your promotional campaigns around these purposes. Here are the steps in designing each promotional campaign and entering it into your marketing plan:

1. Identify existing and targeted markets for each product.
2. Assign responsibility for the execution and success of each campaign.
3. Specify the promotional mix needed to achieve the sales results for each product or revenue-generating segment.
4. Identify the costs for each promotional campaign and when they are paid.
5. Establish benchmark performance criteria and milestones to evaluate each campaign's results.

There's nothing mystifying about these five steps. If you're having trouble projecting results and creating the timetable, consult your media salespeople. They are the professionals. A reputable newspaper, magazine, or air-time salesperson can provide circulation statistics and advice on historical results.

Be sure you don't leave out the benchmark performance criteria. Promotional campaigns are so important that few small companies can afford those that don't do the job.

Media characteristics

Don't build promotional campaigns around a media channel, as the sellers of media would like you to do. Instead, design them around each revenue-generating segment you want to promote. There may be one or several media channels that produce the desired results. Figure 9-3 identifies the characteristics of various media solutions.

Figure 9-3
Media Characteristics

Television: Reaches the largest audience. Allows creative demonstration of the product. Precisely targets markets. But costs are high. Requires professional production of ads. Needs frequent repetition.

Radio: Lower cost than TV. More flexible production requirements. Can be used to target local customers. However, appeals to only one sense: audio. Can't display product. Requires frequent repetition.

Print: Newspapers and magazines have lower cost. Can include color or black-and-white layouts. Enjoys longer life than air media. Requires longer lead time than air media. Requires payment in advance to guarantee ad position.

Direct mail: Offers the most precise audience selection. Flexible and personal. However, has high throw-away rate. Mailing lists must be purchased and may be out of date.

Advertisement content

As much as possible, your promotional plan should identify the ad content. Plan readers want some idea of what you're going to say to the customer that's going to get the desired results. Here are some things that have proven effective in many types of ad campaigns:

- Factual messages dramatizing superior product performance
- Testimonials from satisfied buyers
- Endorsements from credible people and opinion leaders
- Facts about the product
- Demonstrations of the product
- Facts about the company behind the product
- Statements about product guarantees
- Warranties to ensure product performance

IDENTIFYING PRODUCTS

Include in your marketing plan each of the company's products. The existing ones should have some sales record on which to build a marketing program to reach the targeted sales goals. The plan must describe the new products in terms of how the marketing plan intends to deal with each of these issues:

- Benefits • Projected customer demand • Pricing • Quality
- Service • Durability • Competition and what they have to offer

- Technology • Sales terms

PACKAGING

Frequently packaging is both a marketing issue and an engineering issue. The package must communicate something about the product to the buyer. It also must protect the contents from a variety of things, including tampering. Bars of soap are a good example. The product engineers require a package sturdy enough to ensure that there is no damage to the product until the buyer uses it. Additionally, the package must keep potentially harmful contaminants in the product from leaking out.

Marketing, on the other hand, requires a package that gets people's attention and communicates the information its promotional campaigns have worked so hard to reinforce. Additionally, in the case of soap, consumers must be able to smell the product. Therefore, the package must be porous enough to allow it to pass this vital sniff test.

DISTRIBUTION

Include channels of distribution for each product (or product line) in the marketing plan. Frequently, changing channels or adding some for existing products increases sales, profits, or both. Existing products are often likely candidates for changes in distribution channels.

For new products, you need to experiment to see which channels net the most profit for the company. Identify the distribution channels for each new product. Include benchmark sales and profit figures for the various channels. Those that don't hit their targets may require some change. That's the purpose of the marketing plan—to identify problems in time to reduce damage to the overall plan.

Sometimes it helps to draw a picture of a distribution channel. Figure 9-4 shows a schematic of one company's paper distribution channel.

Figure 9-4
Harvey's Paper Company Distribution Channel

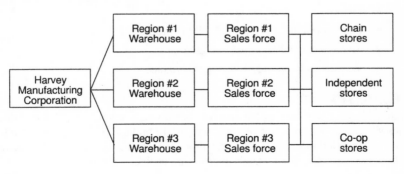

MARKETS

Small businesses don't change their markets all that much. Often they're selling just a few product lines to a few different markets. They have already established their market position. They count on it to generate a certain sales volume each year.

This business-as-usual scenario is exactly why the marketing plan identifies both existing and potential markets. The purpose of the business plan, and the marketing subplan, is to move the company from one point to another. It can't accomplish that without addressing *changes* in the way the company sells to existing and new markets.

Specify each market to which the company sells its products. Identify changes the marketing plan intends to make. Perhaps cross-selling the same product to different markets presents an opportunity. Maybe the plan calls for a completely new vehicle in a market never before specifically addressed.

Pizza Hut did exactly this when it teamed up with producers of the Teenage Mutant Ninja Turtles videocassettes. It offered dinner coupons inside each cassette. This *pack-up* idea allowed Pizza Hut exposure to 8 million households. The video producers suddenly had a value-added hook to offer along with the cassette. Both firms hugely benefited.

PERFORMANCE MONITORING AND MILESTONES

As with everything else associated with our approach to the business plan, we assign responsibility for results to particular people. The only way to achieve that is by establishing expected performance standards. This is especially crucial for the marketing plan.

Every cost and promotional effort identified in the marketing plan must have a projected return. Define this return in terms of dollars. Project them monthly over the marketing plan. The traditional marketing types may complain that they can't tell how much in sales a particular ad brings. They can't because no one asked them to before.

Many companies establish mechanisms that tally or estimate results from various promotional programs. The ethical drug companies are again a case in point. Most monitor all the shipments from the warehouse to hospitals and drugstores in each detail person's territory. This mechanism didn't exist before someone insisted on monitoring performance in this way. However, now they can track sales and marketing results right down to the Zip code for each customer if necessary.

The milestones for each marketing program provide signs along the way that the plan is on course. It's probably more difficult to create milestones for marketing results than for other parts of the business plan. However, they're just as important, if not more so because so much rides on hitting those sales targets.

Insist on identifying specific, quantifiable milestones for each major promotion and cost in the marketing department. Put these programs on a detailed schedule month by month. Make sure there's some way to report the results so we can track actuals against the plan.

If something isn't working, stop and fix it. If you can't fix it, then cancel the promotion and try something else. However, be sure the rest of the firm understands the shortfall and what it means to their particular part of the plan.

Chapter 10 creates the operations plan.

Chapter 10

Creating the Operations Plan

OVERVIEW

The operations plan is key for most companies, particularly those engaged in manufacturing and assembly. Chapter 10 incorporates uses of technology, production schedules, purchases of materials, inventory management, and labor costs into a comprehensive operations plan.

Different companies treat "operations" differently. For our purposes, the operations plan includes

- Manufacturing and production line operations • Quality assurance
- Inventory purchasing • Production costing
- Warehouse operations • Administrative overhead

The goals and targets set forth in this plan influence both the purchasing schedule and the cash disbursement timetable. The plan also creates the acquisitions schedule for the purchase of expensive machinery and equipment used throughout the company. Chapter 11, "Creating the Plan for Major Purchases," creates a detailed capital acquisition plan just for these items.

Operations plans in small businesses focus primarily on production and administration. At this point we've already prepared the sales and marketing department plans. Now we need to produce the goods for sale. To that end, the operations plan contains the topics shown in Figure 10-1 (page 154).

LINKING OTHER DEPARTMENTAL PLANS

The operations plan takes information from the sales and marketing plans. It processes the unit sales forecast into a production schedule. From the production schedule, the raw materials purchaser continues the process of working backwards to prepare a purchasing schedule. Figure 10-2 shows the linkages between the operations plan and the various other departmental plans.

Figure 10-1
Contents of Operations Plan

Operations Plan Outline

Production plan
    Use of technology
    Facilities plan
    Production schedules
Quality assurance program
    Production tolerances
    Test plan
    Acceptability levels
Inventory purchases plan
    Purchase schedules
    Economic order quantity calculations
    Computation of safety stocks
Materials availability and contingency plan
Analysis of production costs
Warehouse plans
    Materials handling
    Packing
    Shipping
    Receiving
Administrative cost schedules

Figure 10-2
Linkage of Operations Plan with Other Department Plans

Managing the Operations Plan

The production component of the operations plan considers issues such as

- Raw material and subassembly lead time
- Changes in warehouse space
- Production line retooling
- Manufacturing time
- Schedules for manufacturing the product mix
- Timing of staff changes

The operations plan coordinates the impact of the sales and marketing plans on each of these management issues.

Production Efficiency

The sales plan furnishes Operations with a blueprint for the production schedule. The production department knows what items it must produce and when. There are often options for organizing the production schedule to make the whole process more efficient. In many cases we can make setup and teardown of production runs less costly by knowing the production requirements and their timing as set forth in the sales plan.

Further, the production department schedules the most expedient and cost-effective production combination. Frequently the same subassemblies go into different products. It may make sense to produce *all* the subassemblies needed, even though only a portion of them go into the product now on the line, and store the others for use when the next product comes up for manufacture.

Tracking Sales Plan Performance

As we implement the business plan, the operations department tracks the sales plan against actual results. It gauges the risk of running short on supplies of raw materials and subassemblies. If unit sales run ahead of the plan schedule, Production may want to increase the safety stock of inventory for critical parts. Conversely, if the sales plan was overoptimistic, Operations slows its raw materials purchasing schedules.

Controlling Inventory

Operations uses the sales plan to identify how much inventory to order at a time. From these projections come closer approximations of optimum purchase quantities. This enhances use of the company's working capital by not having excessive inventory on hand, while maintaining a sufficient supply to avoid costly stock-outs.

Changing the Operations Department

Often one look at a projected sales plan reveals specific capability gaps in the production department. Inventory requirements targeted in the sales plan may require changes in equipment, personnel, machinery, and the production line itself. The production department includes all these items in its plan. However, it could not have the necessary information without its link to the sales plan.

Matching Operations with Cash Outflow

Just as the raw materials purchase schedule derives from the operations plan, so too does much of the company's cash outflow. The finance department uses the operations plan as a key link in forecasting timing of cash outflows resulting from

- Payments to raw materials vendors
- Payments to other suppliers of overhead goods and services
- Employee payroll
- Manufacturers to whom production items were subcontracted

Major Purchases

Many capital expenditures come as a result of requirements set forth in the operations plan. For small businesses, these often involve equipment used on the production line and in the production facilities. The operations plan identifies equipment requirements and their delivery times. It's the major purchases planner's job to get the equipment there when it's needed. The cash outflow schedule then passes to the financial plan.

CLOSING CAPABILITY GAPS

The most useful area of focus for small-business operations is the production facility. There, gaps in the company's capability to produce the necessary volume of goods at the stated costs surface. Sometimes the problem is the technology employed on the production line. Often it's the layout of the line itself. The production engineers also play a large role in the company's capacity to meet production schedule goals.

This section of the business plan specifically addresses shortfalls in the company's ability to meet the production schedule. Identify operational capability gaps, then demonstrate the bridge built in the operations plan.

Gaps in Production Volume Capacity

Operations—specifically Production—is charged with the responsibility of making enough of the right products to meet sales and advertising shipping targets. If that's the case at your company and if the operations plan must bridge a gap in production volume, consider addressing these questions in your operations plan:

1. Is the present manufacturing facility adequate for the production planned? If not, identify changes needed to make it adequate.
2. How does the current production line help or hinder the volume issue?
3. What changes in layout and equipment need to be made?
4. How much will it cost?
5. When will it be done?
6. How does the production volume gap affect inventory levels?
7. If raw materials, work in process, and finished goods inventories rise, how does the cost of carrying these items affect the profit plan?

8. Does availability of materials and labor affect the production gap? If so, identify how the plan overcomes those problems.

Part of your operational plan details answers to such questions. Where a gap in the firm's production capacity exists, demonstrate how this part of the plan fills the void.

Gaps in Products and Their Features

The operations department is heavily involved in developing new products and adding new features to existing ones. Much of the engineering and materials research for new products or enhancements falls to the operations department.

There may be gaps in the department's engineering and technical capability to fulfill the necessary development work. If this is the case, then the operations plan identifies the solution, costs, and timing. Often the solution is nothing more than hiring an outside engineering firm or a new product development manager.

If your operations plan has a gap in the products it's being asked to develop or change, consider addressing these stages of the development process in the plan:

- Scientific and engineering requirements, necessities, and limits
- Determination of feasibility in a controlled setting, such as the company's laboratory or R&D facility
- Creating an operational prototype
- Acceptance of the prototype by other departments
- Drafting engineering and production specifications
- Redesign of existing manufacturing facilities to accommodate the new product or enhancements
- Establishing revised quality tolerances
- Starting initial production runs
- Full-scale implementation of the production plan

These nine stages provide a logical progression for developing the new products or enhancements required. Be sure to include costs, personnel responsible, and timing for each stage.

Production Costs

Sometimes the company's overall profit objectives require squeezing the last bit of fluff out of the operations and production plans. For many small businesses, the best solution is to cut the manufacturing costs of the products.

This isn't easy. However, there are some bridges many firms have used in their businesses plans to successfully close the cost gap.

Subcontracting

Much as we might want to keep the entire manufacturing process under our complete control, that isn't always economically the best solution. Frequently a specialist subcontractor can take some or all of a production process and do an adequate job for less cost. The contracting firm becomes less of a manufacturer and more of an assembler of components it subcontracts out to others. There's nothing wrong with this. Indeed, often it produces better products for less cost.

Depending on the cost at issue, companies often send parts of production operations offshore. Most countries have a less expensive labor rate than that found in America. Further, if issues such as taxation and material costs are a problem, foreign production may be the answer.

One caution, however: Subcontracting components or entire assemblies raises the issue of quality control. Often QC procedures need adjustment to allow for the work ethic and customs of the subcontracting firms, especially if they're in less developed countries. The plan may include on-site QC inspectors in countries doing several subcontract manufacturing operations. Be sure to address this issue in the operations plan if you use subcontracting as a bridge to cover a capability gap.

Subcontractor and supplier dependency

Many small businesses are experts at hiring subcontractors for production of critical components—too much so. There comes a point where many firms find themselves at the mercy of their subcontractors or suppliers of critical material.

Such dependency places the company in the same vulnerable position as when it depends exclusively on just one large customer. Suddenly the subcontractor can dictate price, quality, and availability without risking its position.

Be sure the operations plan deals with situations that expose the company to overreliance on just a few subcontractors or suppliers. Implement a program of alternative sources. Include specifications the other sources have agreed to regarding price, availability, and quality.

Some companies plan for a maximum percentage of production parts or assemblies from any given supplier. Beyond that, they insist on alternative sources. This doesn't mean they stop using their primary sources. After all, often these suppliers are the best for the job and offer a great price. However, the plan does call for placing a portion of the firm's requirements with other suppliers.

The alternative sources may not be as competitive in price or quality as the primary source. However, it is often worth the added cost to establish and maintain a business relationship just in case the main supplier suffers a catastrophe.

Factory layout

Over the years production lines become like homes whose owners have simply added on as the need arose. Frequently they're no longer as efficient as they once were. Redesigning the plant layout often accelerates throughput of material and expedites the production process. This translates directly to manufacturing cost reduction.

Updating production machinery

Cost reduction and quality measures are usually the reason for replacing existing manufacturing equipment. Robotics and computer-aided manufacturing systems reduce errors, improve efficiency, lessen wastage, and generally reduce costs.

Reengineering work methods

If you haven't changed your production methods in recent memory, perhaps your operations plan should address hiring an industrial engineer to improve labor efficiency. Often labor costs, downtime, and mistakes raise production costs beyond what they should be. More efficient production techniques can be a good way of bridging a cost gap in the operations plan.

PRODUCTION TECHNOLOGY

Production represents a significant part of the operations plan for most small businesses. The use of technology on the production line often figures prominently in many operations plans. Small businesses can't afford to throw expensive labor at production problems. Thin profit margins dictate that they have the most efficient manufacturing facilities they can afford.

Technology is the answer for many. Modern machinery and equipment, materials, and work methods are usually less expensive in the long run than hiring more workers. Most businesses can finance or lease modern technology. We depreciate its expense over a useful life often spanning five years or more. Further, equipment won't turn around and sue for wrongful termination, discrimination, and all the other things real and imagined that plaintiffs' lawyers dream up.

Materials

Materials often play an important part in operation and production plans. The wrong material can drive up production costs. An example is Gilbey's gin. For years the company sold its product in neat frosted glass bottles. The problem, however, was that the frosting process was expensive. Even worse, some of the frosting came off the bottles during the packaging process. This introduced glass fragments into the delicate packing machinery. The packaging line was constantly going down for repair and cleaning. Idle labor costs were intolerably high.

The solution was to switch from a frosted bottle to a more conventional one. Contrary to what Gilbey's marketing seers feared, there was no substantial impact on sales volume. However, for this success, Gilbey's had to include the change and the advertising response both in the operations plan *and* in the marketing plan. The company adjusted advertising to handle the change in packaging that was once Gilbey's trademark.

Standardizing

High-volume production technology emphasizes standardization among components, assemblies, and packages. Where possible, we want to use the same part in several different products. It's all a matter of engineering such standardization into the production process.

The operations plan is the place to identify such fixes, cost them out, assign responsibilities, and create a timetable for completion. One example of this focused method comes from Unilever Export. It was producing detergent powders primarily for West African markets. The problem was that the packages it used were of a nonstandard size. That was what Unilever thought the market demanded. The packages didn't quite fit the production machinery. Consequently, they required filling *by hand.* Operations and Marketing teamed up and introduced a change to standard-sized packages. These fit the high-speed production line. Suddenly production costs fell and the company's profits rose.

Manufacturing Facilities and Machinery

Investment in facilities and production machinery is often a logical solution to small business's manufacturing cost and volume problems. If your firm requires new or modified facilities and equipment, consider putting these issues in the operations plan.

Plant location

Plant location involves a variety of important variables:

- Shipping and receiving facilities
- Geographic location
- Zoning
- Storage capacity

Further, all these things change over time. A brewery, for example, may be re-zoned by the city. No longer may it dump its treated waste into the river that flows outside the plant. Now the firm faces a planning dilemma: Move to another location or invest in costly secondary waste treatment equipment.

Some facilities simply become too small to accommodate planned production levels. This often necessitates either consolidating all operations under one large roof or adding still more facilities elsewhere.

Many companies require that the plant be close to major shipping points most often used by their customers. Perhaps the operations plan calls for moving the plant to a facility closer to an airport or rail terminal.

Conversely, receiving production materials from suppliers can sometimes be the driving force behind selection of plant location. Perhaps your major supply sources have moved their plants. Now availability of critical components is no longer as reliable as it once was. If that's the case, then the operations plan should include the solution to the problem along with costs and a detailed approach to what you intend to do about it.

Manufacturing equipment

For many companies, replacement of old production equipment with modern machinery is cost-justified. However, lowering production costs often requires new equipment. Some of the signs that this belongs in the operations plan include

- Higher production costs than competitors
- Unfavorable labor variances
- Excessive finished goods rework costs
- Poor quality control evaluation
- Excessive downtime on production equipment
- Poor safety record on dangerous machinery

Additionally, the equipment part of your operations plan should discuss the issues surrounding new equipment, such as

- Improved maintenance record • Labor efficiency savings
- Material usage efficiency savings
- Costs of preventive maintenance programs • Economic life
- Projected depreciation • Insurance
- Personal property taxes (if any in your state)

PRODUCTION SCHEDULES

Production schedules are the heart of most small-business operations plans. Here we take the sales plan and work backwards to arrive at the level of finished goods needed to fill the sales targets. From there, each component of the production process falls into place:

- From finished goods to work in process
- From work in process to raw materials
- From raw materials to vendor ordering schedules

Determining the Production Schedule

The technique used to back into the production schedule is similar to that employed in the marketing plan. However, creating a production schedule is easier, since it's more mathematically oriented. Figure 10-3 demonstrates how one company arrives at the number of units it needs to manufacture.

Figure 10-3
Determination of Units to Manufacture

LP ENTERPRISES
MANUFACTURING SCHEDULE
First Quarter 199X

	January	February	March	Total 1st Qtr
Planned sales	12,000	13,000	14,000	39,000
Plus required ending inventory	2,000	2,000	2,000	6,000
Less beginning inventory	-5,000	-2,000	-2,000	-5,000
Equals planned production	9,000	13,000	14,000	36,000

Computing required production with a safety stock

There's a simple variation on the equation in Figure 10-3 that is often used to compute the amount of production required. It assumes that we want a minimum ending inventory at the end of each production month *plus* our safety stock to avoid running out. Figure 10-4 shows how the formula works.

Figure 10-4
Computation of Required Production

PELE ENTERPRISES
PRODUCTION SCHEDULE
First Quarter 199X

	January	February	March
Planned sales	2,000	3,000	4,000
Plus desired safety stock	200	200	200
Plus ending inventory	500	300	300
Equals minimum required inventory	2,700	3,500	4,500
Less beginning inventory	300	500	300
Equals planned production	2,400	3,000	4,200

Notice how the production schedule comes from the equation. Additionally, the previous month's ending inventory becomes the current month's beginning inventory. We include safety stock by simply entering it as one of the inventory requirements.

Some companies base their production schedules on *equivalent units produced*. This assumes that work in process inventory is a certain percentage completed. They count that in the total of equivalent units manufactured during the planning period. Figure 10-5 shows how it works.

Planning for Contingencies

Contingency plans often accompany production schedules. After all, this is the most expensive part of a small-business operation. Most small businesses can't afford to overproduce products that just sit on the warehouse shelves. Eventually they sell these products at a discount that either eats into planned profit margins or creates an actual loss.

Contingency plans for the production area present benchmarks targeted by the sales department. For example, say the sales plan indicates second-quarter sales volume at 2,000 units, with the first 700 in April. The production department watches actual sales levels carefully. If sales aren't at 350 by the second week in April, the firm scales production back.

This has a domino effect through the rest of the operations plan. If finished goods are scaled back, then work in process declines accordingly. As this occurs, we cancel planned raw material purchases.

Figure 10-5
Computation of Production Schedule in Equivalent Units

PELE ENTERPRISES
PRODUCTION SCHEDULE IN EQUIVALENT UNITS
First Quarter 199X

	January	February	March	Total 1st Qtr
Planned sales	2,000	3,000	4,000	9,000
Plus ending finished goods inventory required	200	200	200	600
Equals total finished goods required	2,200	3,200	4,200	9,600
Less beginning finished goods inventory	-300	-300	-300	-900
Equals units to be completed for finished goods inventory	1,900	2,900	3,900	8,700
Plus equivalent units in ending WIP inventory (1)	300	500	300	1,100
Sub total	2,200	3,400	4,200	9,800
Less equivalent units in beginning WIP inventory (2)	-200	-300	-500	-1,000
Equals equivalent units to be manufactured	2,000	3,100	3,700	8,800

(1) Treat equivalent units in WIP as partially completed. In this case, in the month of January Pele estimated 600 units in WIP that were 50 percent completed.
(2) Beginning WIP inventory flows through the production plan. What was the ending equivalent WIP in the prior month becomes the beginning equivalent WIP in the current month.

Some operations plans include contingency production schedules assuming various errors in forecasting sales. However, most of these use a computer, so the actual computation of revised schedules is easy and fast.

Relating sales with inventory
Computation of the number of days of sales in inventory helps in monitoring the performance of the sales plan. The operations plan includes this index. From this we know how many days of sales in inventory we should have. Then throughout the planning period we recompute the index periodically to track sales and inventory levels. Departure of the actual from the planned index raises a flag that there's a problem with the inventory level.

Here's how to compute days of sales in inventory (DSI):

$$DSI = \frac{\text{inventory balance}}{\text{cost of goods sold}} \quad X \quad \text{\# of days in the period}$$

Assume we have $500,000 cost of goods sold for the month. We had an inventory balance of $175,000. The days of sales outstanding in this case is 128 days [($750,000 / $175,000) X 30 = 128]. That's over a four-month supply. The business plan may not support such an inventory buildup.

QUALITY ASSURANCE

The operations plan includes quality assurance (QA). Often companies adjust the relative measurements of quality in their products based on new engineering specifications and tolerances required by the marketplace. Meeting these often complex goals requires an organized plan of attack.

Planning the QA Program

The best QA plans establish definite goals, stated in the precise, quantitative language used by QA experts. For example, the format of a QA plan might include these specific topics:

- Numerical tolerances targeted for each finished product
- Statistical specifications designed to test a definite number of products to yield a predetermined confidence level that the answers represent the entire production run
- Identification of each QA inspection step, the kind of inspection, procedures, tests conducted, records of tests, and results
- Quality requirements (in mathematical terms) for vendors' raw materials and subassemblies
- Number of QA inspectors
- Test equipment used

Along with an outline of the plan comes a description of everyone's responsibilities. The operational plan describes the duties of the QA supervisor and all those involved in running the program. Some of the additional topics addressed in more comprehensive QA plans are

1. Organization of the QA program
2. Description of tie-in with production and marketing plans
3. Inclusion of the QA program and its written results in bid proposals
4. Description of standards not only in mathematical terms but in terms of product appearance as well
5. Inspection program for incoming raw materials and subassemblies
6. Training programs for QA personnel
7. Distribution of results to vendors, subcontractors, and customers
8. Support of management

INVENTORY PURCHASES

Obtaining raw materials and subassemblies requires an acquisition schedule. Most small businesses don't have the storage capacity to keep large amounts of materials waiting for use in Production. The objective is to get the items in stock as close to the time Production needs them as possible. This is the concept of just-in-time inventory management.

The plan for inventory purchases continues the process of working backwards from the finished goods production plan. This phase identifies what to order, when, and how much. These answers depend on

- Demand from the production line or warehouse in the case of retail businesses
- The time the firm takes in issuing a purchase order
- The lead time the vendors need in order to deliver the goods

Schedule out raw material and subassembly purchases with a bill of materials for each product manufactured during the planning period. A bill of materials is a complete list of all the things that go into each product. Create a purchasing schedule for each item on the bill of materials using the format shown in Figure 10-6.

Figure 10-6
Purchasing Schedule

MTH PARTNERS, LTD.
PURCHASING SCHEDULE—SUBASSEMBLY #12-89
First Quarter 199X

	January	February	March	Total 1st Qtr
Planned production usage	5,000	6,000	7,000	18,000
Plus planned ending inventory	1,000	1,200	1,400	1,400
Less planned beginning inventory	-700	-1,000	-1,200	-700
Equals planned purchasing schedule	5,300	6,200	7,200	18,700

Using this schedule, we know the quantity of each item to purchase. Next the process works backwards, considering the time it takes to issue a purchase order and vendor or subcontractor delivery lead times.

Disruption of Deliveries

Failure of key suppliers is every purchasing manager's nightmare. Sometimes it doesn't even have to be the fault of a key supplier. Often the weather prohibits delivering badly needed supplies. Companies in certain parts of Alaska suffer from early freezes. Suddenly that last shipment of goods for the winter sits on a dock in Seattle and won't move until spring.

Parts of many purchasing plans include actions the firm has lined up in case of a disruption in supplier delivery schedules. These often include remedies such as

- Alternative suppliers • Alternative materials
- Sharing agreements with overstocked manufacturers

Intercompany Sales

If your company has more than one division, these divisions may transfer inventory from one to another. Usually the issue of transfer pricing between corporate entities surfaces. The selling division may plan on making a profit on the sale of these goods to the sister company. From a profit planning standpoint, intercompany sales simply take money from one pocket and put it in another.

Define the terms of intercompany sales in the operations plan to keep peace in the corporate family. Regardless of the outcome, at least the players know the rules. Chapter 14 discusses intercompany pricing schemes

Establishing Purchase Quantities

An additional component of the purchasing plan is the computation of how much to order and how frequently. Apart from the amount needed by Production and lead times for delivery, there's a commonly used method for computing the optimum order size and number of orders a year. It's called the *economic order quantity*.

Economic order quantity

Often during the production planning process, manufacturing and purchasing managers determine the optimum quantities of inventory to purchase at one time. Orders different from the optimum only eat up precious working capital. Some companies purchase in whatever size yields the best price breaks without regard to the most economic order size. Nevertheless, the economic order quantity (EOQ) is the optimum order quantity considering both needs. EOQ represents the order size for an inventory item that provides the lowest possible overall cost to the company. Here's the EOQ equation:

$$EOQ = \sqrt{\frac{2ap}{sz}}$$

where a is the annual quantity of the item used in units
p is the purchase order cost
s is the annual direct and indirect carrying cost of a unit of inventory
z is the purchase price of the inventory item

Assume the following:

- Annual demand is 200,000 units.

- Cost to issue a purchase order, receive the goods, and stock the warehouse is $200.
- Annual cost of carrying inventory is 10 percent
- The cost of each item in quantities between 10,000 and 20,000 is $3.00.

$$EOQ = \sqrt{\frac{2 \ X \ (200,000 \ X \ \$200)}{10\% \ X \ \$3.00}}$$

EOQ = 16,330 units per order

If the company needs 200,000 units annually, it will issue about 12 orders (200,000 ÷ 16,330 = 12.25) during the year.

Safety stock

Many production managers insist on a cushion of inventory to avoid running out of raw materials and subassemblies. Stock-outs aren't just embarrassing, they cause costly disruptions to production runs. The sales staff also supports the idea of large safety stocks. Their livelihoods depend on there being sufficient finished goods inventory to fill orders.

However, there's a balance between safety stocks that meet production's requirements and those that are so large that they unnecessarily eat into valuable working capital. This method of safety stock computation marries the need for emergency stock with the controller's objective—to have as little inventory as possible and turn it quickly. Fortunately there's a way to compute the optimum safety stock. Here's the equation:

Probability of stock-out at a given level of safety stock X stock-out cost X number of orders per year (demand/EOQ) = expected stock-out cost + carrying cost of safety stock = total inventory carrying cost.

It's easiest if you set up the safety stock computation in tabular form. Compute the cost of various levels of safety stock. The lowest total cost is the best answer. Figure 10-7 provides an example.

In this example, the optimum level of safety stock is 80 units. When planning inventory purchases, make sure not to compute safety stock in a vacuum. For example, the manufacturing department might know of a risk to a steady supplier. That justifies increasing inventory well beyond any levels required by safety stock considerations. Anticipated cost increases also drive up inventories. The production department wants to maintain its cost plan, so it stockpiles low-cost inventory. In effect, the company is trading commodity futures. But instead of just buying an option to hedge against a possible price increase, it has taken delivery—a very risky enterprise.

PRODUCTION COSTS

Once we know the production schedule, the operations plan next identifies the associated costs. For most companies familiar with production operations, establishing standard costs for each production step isn't difficult.

Figure 10-7
Computation of Inventory Safety Stock

Units of Safety Stock	Prob. of Stock- out	Cost of Stock- out	# of Orders per Year	Stock- out Costs (1)	Carry Cost (2)	Total Cost (3)
60	60%	100	15	$900	$300	$1200
70	40%	100	15	600	350	950
80	35%	100	15	525	400	925
90	33%	100	15	495	450	945

(1) Compute stock-out cost as the probability of stock-out X cost of stock-out multiplied by # of orders per year (EOQ).
(2) Compute carrying cost as the cost of holding one unit per year (assumed to be $5.00) X safety stock. Carrying costs include things such as financing, space, handling, security, and insurance. The plan associates each with the cost to keep an item of inventory on the warehouse floor. Often carrying costs run as high as 25 percent to 35 percent of an item's acquisition cost.
(3) Compute total cost as stock-out cost + carrying cost.

The cost schedules use the same time frame as the production schedules. Indeed, the schedule matches production costs with items produced for each period. Here's a list of some of the things your production cost schedules should include:

- Raw materials • Direct labor • Indirect labor on the shop floor
- Allocation of supervisors' salaries • Maintenance labor and parts
- Manufacturing supplies allocation • Allocation of depreciation
- Allocation of insurance • Allocation of employee benefits costs
- Allocation of taxes • Telephone and other manufacturing utilities
- Fuel • Allocation of corporate overhead costs

Different companies allocate these overhead costs differently. Many use a percentage factor for each item related to all the items manufactured.

Planning Setup and Teardown of Production Runs

Another component of the operations plan is the scheduling of different production runs. This can be a complicated topic. We want the plan to reflect the most advantageous combination of production sequences. Often one item can use much of the production-line setup of the item manufactured previously.

The setup and teardown plan identifies these similarities and schedules the order of production runs accordingly.

WAREHOUSE

The warehouse section of the operations plan includes

- Materials handling • Scheduling physical inventory
- Packing • Shipping

Most of these are cost centers. They help the company fulfill the final part of the system that delivers goods to the company's customers.

Some company's forgo the inclusion of these four departments in the operations plan. However, frequently they become an issue. For example, take the warehouse itself. The production schedule may call for a significant increase or decrease in inventory items. Perhaps the warehouse isn't large enough to accommodate the additional finished goods inventory.

In that case, the warehouse plan calls for additional space. Maybe this is a permanent change and the existing warehouse needs expanding. Otherwise, the warehouse plan probably calls for lease of additional space.

Conversely, if the production plan clearly indicates a reduction in required warehouse space an opportunity may have opened. Perhaps the warehouse plan calls for subleasing excess space to another company.

Shipping

Organized shipping plans save companies huge amounts. Further, often a company's shipping system is the customer's first tangible contact with the company. We want to make a favorable impression. Shipping plans typically include such issues as

- Cost of shipping each type of commodity produced
- Insurance of parcels • Method of shipment
- Customer options offered, such as express delivery

Sometimes the methods a company uses to ship create a significant marketing distinction. Speed always seems to be an issue with customers. They procrastinate making the buy decision. However, when they finally make a decision, they want the product yesterday.

Shipping plans map out the solutions to accelerate product delivery. This may involve subcontracting with trucking firms. Perhaps it necessitates negotiating an air freight contract. Whatever the solution, the shipping plan often contributes greatly to the company's image and its profitability.

Receiving

The quality assurance plan ties strongly into the receiving department. Receiving's responsibilities often include inspection of raw materials and subassemblies from outside vendors entering the firm. The receiving plan should include specifics about these inspections, including

- Who does it • Their qualifications
- Inspection sampling policies • Acceptance criteria
- Rejection procedures

ADMINISTRATION PLAN

It's easy to overlook the plan for administrative costs. Yet, if a small business struggles with thin profit margins, poor control over administrative expenses often means the difference between profit and loss.

Administrative cost schedules identify each cost that is not related to a specific department. Usually these include costs that overlap departments. For example, the CEO's salary does not belong specifically to one department. The entire company benefits from the CEO's involvement.

Many companies establish Administration as a department like any other in the operations plan. Here the plan accumulates and summarizes all the costs and expenses, then feeds them into the financial plan.

More important, however, we have a plan not only for the costs but for specific actions for the upcoming planning period. The plan describes all administrative programs for the year. Perhaps it includes installation of a new computer system. In that case, the plan identifies the costs and assigns responsibilities to particular people. It establishes milestones to track implementation of the project.

Chapter 11 creates the major purchases plan and describes how to determine the value of large expenditures.

Chapter 11

Creating the Plan for Major Purchases

OVERVIEW

Small businesses have smaller margins for error than their larger counterparts. That's why small businesses pay at least as much attention, if not more, when planning their major purchases. They could be out a material amount of money if they misjudge the return on a capital asset. Even more important, that asset might not get them to the goal intended.

The gap in capability identified earlier defines the need for purchases of such durable goods. The major purchases plan identifies the assets, their costs, and the timing for their purchase. Since they represent significant increases in the company's capability—and possibly lower production costs and a significant cash outlay—we include a separate section in the business plan just for major purchases.

Chapter 11 shows how to schedule these purchases so that all the departments know their effect on them. We'll identify and structure a series of useful techniques to judge the performance of particular asset purchases. Often companies have several major asset programs competing against one another for scarce funds. Chapter 11 shows you how to compare one project with another by reducing them to a series of common denominators. Additionally, we'll look closely at the business evaluation of such expenditures. We won't get lost in the mathematical forest so that we lose sight of the asset's real purpose. Finally, after making the decision, we'll design a monitoring program to ensure that the project accomplishes its task.

BRIDGING THE CAPABILITY GAP

Major purchases build a bridge between the firm's present capabilities and the assets it must have to accomplish its business plan. Often physical assets enhance profit capabilities by lowering costs or increasing production capacity. Frequently companies need newer, larger, or just more of something to accomplish the tasks established in different areas of the business plan.

Many companies agonize over the decision to purchase an asset before putting it into the business plan. They go through all sorts of financial mathematics designed to give them insight into the asset's profit performance. In the end, however, the real decision comes down to these two questions:

1. Can we reach our planning targets better if we acquire this asset?
2. Does the increased profit that results from this purchase exceed its cost?

If both answers are yes, then buy the asset. If not, then pass.

Including Major Purchases in the Plan

Business planners usually call major purchases *capital expenditures* or *capital projects*. These terms refer to the purchase of durable goods—those that last more than one year. Indeed, most capital purchases of machinery or equipment give benefit for two years or more. A new production line qualifies as a capital purchase. So do the machines that go on the line. A company may need another warehouse to store its planned inventory increase. That's a capital expenditure. Perhaps the firm can get by with just expanding the existing storage facility. Include that in the major purchases plan as well.

Benefits from capital projects vary among companies. Some equipment reduces manufacturing costs. Modern computer-aided production machinery lowers labor costs and energy used for each item made. The production assets acquired from another company immediately increase production capacity.

Most major purchases use the company's capital or its purchasing power to create a flow of future profits for a period of several years. Once an asset is designated as a capital purchase for inclusion in the major purchases plan, two things happen:

- The asset must meet preset profit performance requirements.
- It must integrate with the company's overall business plan—not just for this year, but for the life of the asset.

The major purchases plan ensures that both these things happen.

Treating short-term assets

We don't include purchases whose benefits we derive for just one year in the more detailed analyses associated with the major purchases plan. The cash outlay or liabilities the firm undertakes to acquire short-term assets aren't usually as large as those for true capital assets. Instead, we include them as an operating expense in the beneficiary department's plan. We don't depreciate them because they don't last past the current operating period.

Assets providing no return

Some capital programs don't make the company a dime. The company does them just to stay in business. That's the case with the pollution control equipment required by a government agency. It produces no return on the investment. The company really has no choice in the capital expenditure decision. However, most firms still treat such expenditures as capital programs. We want to monitor their costs and make sure they accomplish their task.

Replacement Expenditures

Replacements are by far the most common major purchases. These are the routine acquisition of durable goods required to maintain the company's present level of operations. They don't inject an incremental profit increase into the company's business plan. With some exceptions, they don't usually require huge capital outlays. Purchase of a new delivery truck to replace one that's worn out is a good example.

Most companies don't do the extensive financial analysis for replacements that they do for other types of major purchases. Reasons cited are usually no more than, *because we need it.* Approval for the purchase comes from the executive whose department wants the expenditure.

For normal replacement acquisitions, that's usually sufficient. The problem comes when the same approval process (or lack thereof) creeps into the non-routine capital programs. Then the analysis we should have done falls by the wayside.

Nonroutine Expenditures

By nonroutine, we mean those major purchases that are new to the company. They may bring in some new sort of technology or capability. Perhaps they accelerate material throughput on the production line. If the company plans on going into a new line of business, the effort may well require one or more nonroutine purchases of capital equipment.

Some companies treat nonroutine capital projects without much analytical formality. Others have a whole series of hurdles each project must clear before the company consents to the acquisition. However, regardless of the approval process, most nonroutine capital purchases have these things in common:

- They upgrade or replace entire categories of equipment.
- They significantly reduce costs.
- Their benefits last more than one year.
- They consume large amounts of money.

Such major purchases are important to every small-business plan. The costs and benefits require analysis and planning. We want to ensure that the investment we're about to make is indeed the best use of the money. Further, we want to coordinate the acquisition with the rest of the company. The beneficiary department plans for the arrival of the purchase and the added capabilities it brings to the company. Perhaps delivery schedules of raw materials require adjustments because of the capital improvements to the production line.

The finance department also gets involved. It figures out the best way to pay for the purchase given the other parts of the business plan. This information makes its way onto the projected balance sheet, income statement, and statement of cash flows.

Approving nonroutine purchases

Often nonroutine expenditures are complicated. They usually involve amounts of money that are material to small businesses. If the company purchases sophisticated equipment, just study of the project often requires significant expenditure. For example, let's take something as seemingly simple as evaluation of an addition to the company's finished goods inventory storage facility. We require architect's renderings to provide drawings from which the engineering and construction consultants can determine the layout of the addition. Involving these professionals causes some initial cash outlay just to study the *possibility* of making this major purchase.

Continuing with this example, here's how the decision process leading up to approval might proceed:

1. The warehouse manager recognizes need for more space in which to store the additional finished goods required to meet the company's sales plan. The manager guesses that the addition will cost about $500,000.

2. The company president evaluates this seat-of-the-pants estimate. He appoints an evaluation team. On the team are people from Engineering, Marketing, Finance, Production, and Operations. They establish a budget for the initial evaluation to cover the outside experts needed.

3. The team generates a major purchase proposal for the addition at a cost of $530,000. This goes up to the president and board of directors for evaluation.

4. If this is a significant enough expenditure, the board may vote on the proposal itself. Otherwise, it delegates this decision-making authority to the company's management.

5. The construction project begins. The board reviews progress every month. The review compares actual costs with those presented during the project's analysis. Additionally, the review monitors various stages of construction to track progress against the time when the facility actually stores finished goods inventory. Any cost overruns or changes to the project require approval of whoever originally approved the expenditure in the first place.

PREPARING A MAJOR PURCHASES PLAN

Major purchases of capital equipment bridge gaps in the company's capacity to achieve some part of its business plan. We include major purchases in the business plan because

- They usually span a number of years. • They're expensive.
- Significant parts of the business plan rely on performance of the purchased items.

Several areas of the company rely on information from the major purchases plan. The finance group determines how best to pay for the project. Further, the cash flow plan relies on performance from the assets purchased. The department benefiting from the project identifies the impacts on its own business plan now and in the future.

Parts of the Major Purchases Plan

The parts of the major purchases plan that are most interesting to business plan participants include

- Description of all projects
- Financial schedules associated with each project
- Demonstration of how each project integrates into the company
- Impacts on the company

Identifying projects
Include a brief description of each major purchase. Highlight cash outlays and inflows. Tell why the company accepted each project. Include sufficient detail to assess progress each month. The plan should let you know immediately if the programs deviate from their planned course.

Scheduling purchases
The financial schedules associated with each project interest people the most. List all major purchases on a monthly schedule. Include on this schedule

- Projected cash inflows, revenues, and any other income item listed individually by project
- Projected cash outflows, costs, and expenses listed individually by project

Additionally, include milestones scheduled for completion at particular points in time—again for each project. This is the basis for our tracking mechanism to ensure that the acquisition does what we said it would.

Integrating with the overall business plan
This part of the plan identifies changes for each department as a result of the major purchases. For example, if the company builds a new production line, either current production stops during construction or the old line moves elsewhere. The business plan must communicate these impacts to all affected departments.

Detailing each purchase
The last part of the major purchases section provides the detail for each program. Most companies just include the analysis they did when deciding on the purchase. This information provides a detailed reference base for each project.

EVALUATING RISK
There's always risk involved with large expenditures that require a number of years to generate return on their investment. Major capital purchases carry risk mostly in three areas:

- Risk of financing costs
- Risk that the expected return may not be reached
- Risk that costs exceed those originally planned

Of these, the last, cost overruns, is most typical. Consider the nature of a major purchase. Frequently the item is new to the company. Many times it is custom-made. The proposal estimates installation costs on the front end. Often industrial equipment requires special power and air-conditioning systems. Sometimes it sits on concrete pads. If not considered in the original proposal, all these cause the overall cost to rise above the plan.

However, that's one of the benefits of creating a major purchases plan. We monitor and control the costs during construction and through the payback period. The plan lets us know if something happens that causes our return on investment to fall below the estimates when the project was first approved. Chances are there's something we can do to bring the project back in line.

Managing Risk

Adding major purchases to your business plan helps you manage the associated risk. The plan creates a conduit that

- Defines the investment requirements for major purchases
- Establishes a formal approval procedure • Monitors performance

One of the best ways to control risk is by requiring major purchases to return their original investment in a short period. The shorter the payback time, the less the risk. This also reduces risk from long-term market fluctuations, since capital projects usually go on for several years.

Insulating the plan from error

Astute planners often analyze major purchases using three different sets of assumptions: best case, worst case, and most likely case. One way to further refine these scenarios is to identify the probability of each one occurring. From there, we arrive at the *expected value* of the project's return. Figure 11-1 illustrates one such computation.

Figure 11-1
Expected Value of Return on a Major Purchase

MTH ENTERPRISES, LTD.
CAPITAL PROJECT ANALYSIS—BONE MILLING LINE
Expected value of project return

	Return	Probability	Expected return
Best case	$500,000	25%	$125,000
Most likely case	450,000	60%	270,000
Worst case	300,000	15%	45,000
Total		100%	$ 440,000

The computation in Figure 11-1 is nothing more than the weighted average of MTH's expected return using three cases. By using the different scenarios, we arrive at the dollar return we actually expect the investment in a new bone milling line to make. Of course, the accuracy of this analytical technique depends on the correctness of the probabilities attached to each case. For MTH, the expected value of the project's return is $440,000. That's the number MTH's planners use to evaluate the original investment, along with profit. They'll also use parts of this analysis to evaluate the project's risk.

Using the best, most likely, and worst cases creates what planners call a *range of tolerable error.* This is the change in a project's outcome that the company can accept and still call the project successful. We define the range of tolerable error as the boundaries created by outcomes from the best and worst cases. Within those borders, the project is a go. Graphically, the concept looks like Figure 11-2.

Figure 11-2
Range of Tolerable Error

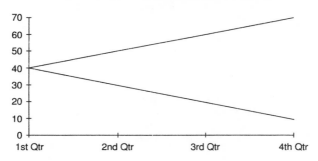

Note the area between the best-case and worst-case lines. This is the range of tolerable error. As long as the mill's actual performance falls somewhere between these two lines, the project makes sense. Management's decision becomes whether it thinks the project can perform within those boundaries.

Some companies look just to the worst-case scenario. They assume from the start that the return never rises above that projected in the *worst* of circumstances. If the project still passes, chances are that the company's capital is safe. The firm views any results better than that as a windfall.

However, this view throws out many valuable capital projects because management was overcautious. Companies make the most profit when they're willing to take a calculated risk.

Sensitivity Analysis

Projecting the financial results for a capital project uses many assumptions. Often they're beyond the control of management. Interest rates on the financing used to acquire the project is one such variable. Projecting these variables is particularly difficult if the project requires several years before earning back the initial investment.

Because of this unpredictability, we frequently take apart the assumptions used in analyzing the merits of a major purchase. We're searching for those assumptions that *drive* the project's profitability. Such driver assumptions control the outcome of the project more than other assumptions. A relatively small change in one such driver assumption can cause the project's overall profitability to change drastically.

Once we have discovered them, we compute a range of tolerable error for the driver assumptions. We ask, Will this assumption remain within the range that keeps the project profitable over its lifetime?

We call the technique used to determine the range of tolerable error *sensitivity analysis.* It involves testing the outcome of the project under different ranges for each major assumption.

If you're using a computer model, it's easy to develop a quick sensitivity analysis for capital projects. Most of the popular spreadsheet programs have specific sensitivity analysis features that make this process fast and easy. Figure 11-3 shows a simple sensitivity matrix.

Figure 11-3
Sensitivity Matrix

DOOBIE PARTNERS, LTD.
CAPITAL PROJECT ANALYSIS—AUTOMATED PARACHUTE FOLDER
Net Income
Sensitivity Analysis—Sales Volume vs. Interest Rates

	Sales Volume		
Interest Rates	200,000 Units	250,000 Units	300,000 Units
10%	$75,000	$85,000	$100,000
9%	85,000	95,000	110,000
8%	95,000	105,000	120,000
7%	100,000	110,000	125,000

Notice how Doobie's net income fluctuates depending on these two driver variables: sales volume and interest rates. Using the sensitivity table, we can quickly estimate projected net income over the likely ranges of our assumptions. Our range of tolerable error is, say, net income between $95,000 and $120,000. Anything below that is unacceptable. Anything above is nice, but not expected. Therefore, the range of tolerable error for our assumptions is

- Interest rates no higher than 8%

- Sales volume no lower than 200,000 units

Within these boundaries, the purchase makes sense according to Doobie's criteria. Doobie can analyze any other critical assumptions the same way. This technique zeros in on the risk associated with various assumptions that the firm accepts with a capital project.

Obtaining Adequate Reward for the Risk Taken

People who plan major purchases for a living see a certain level of reward for every level of risk they take. The more risk taken, the more compensation they demand. For purposes of planning major expenditures, we treat risk as a function of

- Sensitivity to changes in specific key assumptions
- The amount of money spent or liability undertaken
- The time the project runs before it returns us "adequate" compensation

Ideally, our projects should all be low risk and high reward—the upper left quadrant of Figure 11-4. Unfortunately, many firms find themselves in the lower right quadrant—high risk, low reward. Those are the ones that fail to adequately control their plans for major purchases.

Figure 11-4
Risk-Reward Matrix

There's nothing wrong with taking investment risk—as long as

- You're appropriately compensated for the risk undertaken.
- You've identified all the variables that influence the project's outcome.
- You monitor the project's performance.

The worst (and most embarrassing) thing is being surprised by something you should have considered in the first place. Often, these things are simple. Had we thought about them, we might have arrived at a different conclusion about the project in the beginning.

PREPARING PROPOSALS FOR MAJOR PURCHASES

Most companies try to analyze each capital purchase independently of all other proposals. This isn't always easy. For example, many times a series of major purchases, one linked to the others, comes up. However, if we plan each independently of the other, they're easier to track.

Contents of Major Purchases Proposals

Small businesses don't need to draft elaborate proposals to justify the purchase of an expensive piece of equipment or capital project. The proposal has just one purpose: Clearly describe the project considering all the issues important to the decision makers. Contents of the proposals for major purchases include just three topics:

- The reasoning behind the recommendation
- The assumptions used and their likelihood of fulfillment
- Estimated profits and the level of risk undertaken

The capital purchases part of your business plan shouldn't get all caught up in the presentation. We're looking for *realistic* proposals, not fancy justification for a marginal purchase. A pretty package won't make a project that's a dog to begin with anything more than a pretty dog.

Highlight all the options available for the project. Indicate why you chose the course you did. You just may need to go back to that reasoning later if there's a problem.

Identify all unknowns or soft numbers used in the analysis. Communicate them in the proposal. Often we know that certain numbers are nothing more than guesses. However, they don't affect the final outcome that much—they're not driver assumptions—and nailing them down any more would be prohibitively costly. Never mislead the reader into thinking the analysis is more reliable than it really is. This damages your credibility for presentation of future projects.

Here's a list of the sections that are usually helpful in presenting major capital project proposals:

- Executive summary and highlights • Background of the project
- Statement of the need • Benefits of the project
- Analysis of alternatives • Economic justification
- Assumptions used • Risk and opportunities
- Implementation plan • Plan for periodic monitoring

Helpful Hints for Capital Project Proposals

Don't design proposals to persuade the reader. They are factual accounts. Period. The facts, numbers, and computations do the persuading. The text explains and amplifies on the numbers. It doesn't influence.

Help the audience

Identify the proposal's audience. Write the proposal specifically for that audience. Determine the things *they* require to make a decision on the project, then deal with them point by point. Don't prepare analyses the audience won't use. Don't waste everybody's time with long explanations. Be brief.

Defend the proposal

Don't do it. Analysts who win the battle may end up ultimately losing the war. Major purchase proposals should present an objective description of all aspects of the project. Avoid turning into an advocate for the project. Be sure to keep the project in perspective. The company probably won't go broke if it doesn't do the project. Your readers can't make an unbiased evaluation of a proposal that attempts to convince them of its validity.

Often a project that results from a successfully defended proposal fails because it was weak to begin with. The person who successfully defended it suffers loss of credibility. Everyone looks at that person's next project proposal more carefully. It may be a good one, but those already burned hesitate before taking another chance.

Provide comparisons

Often capital projects are new to the company. No one on the decision team has a frame of reference for the project. Compare the assessments and analyses with things that are more familiar. Show how it relates to past projects.

Maintain context

Good capital projects communicate the context in which they work. They describe how the program fits into the company's overall plan. If the equipment or assets acquired bridge capability gaps, the plan demonstrates how. If the purchases replace worn-out items, it shows how they've worn out and why replacements are needed to keep the company's overall targets on track.

Sometimes a major purchase plan is just the first step in a huge, ambitious project. In this context, decision makers want to know what happens to their investment if they get halfway through the project, then decide to abort. How much does the firm lose? What happens to the equipment purchased so far? Can other parts of the firm use it?

Be specific

Avoid generalizations. Employ summary tables that describe the points quantitatively. We definitely want the plan for all major purchases to schedule cash inflow and outflow by month for the period covered by the business plan. Without these schedules, we can't track planned performance against the actual. Suddenly, there's no accountability for getting results. Without accountability, no one is responsible for making these expensive assets perform as promised.

Graphs demonstrate trends and concepts faster and more accurately than most text. Explain how the assets purchased integrate into the overall business plan if it's not obvious. Do not litter your text with adjectives. Increases that seem huge to one person may not be to someone else. Instead, talk in terms of absolutes—an increase of $45,000, for example. Such specifics avoid possible misinterpretations of value judgments.

CALCULATING HURDLE RATES

Plans for major purchases must demonstrate how the assets recoup the firm's original investment. That's not enough, though. The proposals must explain additional compensation for things such as profit and risk of the company's capital.

Analysts call the rate of return that accomplishes all these goals the *hurdle rate*. If the cost of capital is, say, 8 percent, then the hurdle rate rises to some point above that. Many companies require that capital projects return 20 percent, 25 percent, or more before they clear the hurdle rate and the company approves the project. The difference between the cost of capital and the hurdle rate compensates the firm for its risk and its time, and maintains its profit margin.

Building the Hurdle Rate

Some companies arbitrarily establish a minimum rate of return for major purchases. This is easy but not very analytical. It often quashes projects that might otherwise provide a good return for their lower level of risk.

A better solution is to derive hurdle rates from the items that create the return necessary for purchase of a major asset to make economic sense. Comprehensive hurdle rates usually consider the following factors:

- Cost of capital
- Compensation for risk
- Profit margin
- Compensation for time and effort

Cost of capital

Cost of capital isn't difficult to figure. Purchases financed using loans specifically for those purchases have a cost of capital equal to the interest rates on the loans. Other purchases require no outside financing. Instead, the company pays for them using internally generated funds. In these cases, the planners use a *blended* or aggregate cost of capital that includes all the company's funding sources.

In these cases, using an aggregate cost of funds makes sense. We don't know where the money used to pay for the capital asset came from in the first place and what it cost. How could we? It came from all the company's various funding sources. We aggregate these funds into one pool.

Find the aggregate cost of funds by computing the weighted average of all your company's borrowing. It's not complicated. Figure 11-5 shows how one company did it.

Figure 11-5
Computation of Aggregate Cost of Funds

PEACHES CORPORATION
COMPUTATION OF AGGREGATE COST OF FUNDS

Funding Source	Amount	% of Total	Interest Rate	Interest Rate Factor
Bonds—8.75% due 6-1-2001	$1,500,000	46%	8.75%	4.0%
Loan—Community redevelopment	750,000	23%	5.00%	1.2%
Revolving loan—Citibank	500,000	16%	11.25%	1.8%
Loan—Guardian Bancorp	475,000	15%	9.875%	1.5%
	$3,225,000	100%		8.5%

Peaches' aggregate cost of funds is 8.5 percent. The company uses this number in computing the hurdle rate for major purchases funded by internal resources.

Paying for risk

There's a rate for every risk. However, everyone has his or her own concept of the appropriate compensation for a given level of risk. A good way to begin the process of identifying risk is to compare the purchase with other investments that have a known return. Begin with a Treasury bond, for example. It has a known return at any point in time. It also has a known risk—none. T-bonds form the bottom of our risk scale.

Next, identify the top of the scale. Let's use second mortgages. They appear somewhere near the top of most investors' risk scales. Seconds also have a known return—considerably above that of T-bonds to compensate for the additional risk. Since secondary markets actively trade both, their returns to investors are fairly accurate. Now, fill in the risk scale with other types of investments that have a known return and an active market to prove that return.

Liquidity

Liquidity has a great deal to do with the perceived risk of an investment. The less liquid an investment, the greater the risk factor. When identifying similar investments for comparing risk, be sure to select investments that have a similar liquidity factor. This isn't always easy. For example, there probably isn't a ready market for the resale of an industrial mixer at a commercial bakery. However, we did say that risk was the most fuzzy of the hurdle rate components. Do the best you can to identify various investments against which to gauge risk and compensation to investors for undertaking that risk.

Eventually you'll see the capital project presently under consideration falling between two investments with similar risks. Use the return from the most similar investment to gauge compensation for the risk of the major purchase you're planning.

Compensating for profit margin

Few companies make a major purchase without assurance of making at the very least their normal profit margin. Otherwise, they continue with their normal line of business and don't risk trying something new.

Companies with several divisions probably have a different profit margin for each entity. Therefore, the profit margin component of the investment hurdle rate differs depending on the entity requesting the purchase. Some companies want to build strategically important areas of the company. They do this by *lowering* the profit margin component of the hurdle rate. They're willing to forgo some profit today in return for a larger return in the future.

Compensating for management's time

The last component of the hurdle rate is a factor to compensate the company for management's time and effort in overseeing the capital purchase. This is similar to the overhead burden allocated to a division profit plan. Much time and effort go into planning a major purchase program. The firm buys the assets and puts them on line. They begin to produce income. Someone supervises their performance and makes corrections to ensure that they achieve planned targets.

All this draws management attention away from the other things they could be doing to earn the company a profit. Essentially, supervision of a major purchase plan creates a potential *opportunity cost*. The hurdle rate should include some form of compensation for that forgone opportunity.

Joining hurdle rate components

We've just identified the four components of a hurdle rate. Now let's put them together. Figure 11-6 shows how one company built its hurdle rate.

Figure 11-6
Components of a Hurdle Rate

PEACHES CORPORATION
CAPITAL PROJECT PROPOSAL—INDUSTRIAL MIXER
Hurdle Rate Computation

Hurdle Rate Variable	Rate
1. Cost of capital: 1-ton mixer is purchased using an installment loan from Wells Fargo	7.75%
2. Profit margin for Industrial Bakery Division last year	6.50%
3. Risk: Similar to that of a bond rated AA	4.50%
4. Compensation for management efforts	2.25%
Computed hurdle rate	21.0%

The one-ton industrial mixer must return at least 21 percent to justify its purchase. Anything less than that fails to adequately compensate the firm for risk, profit margin, cost of capital, and management time.

Use Hurdle Rates with Caution

Many companies pride themselves on the precision with which they derive their hurdle rates. Major purchases must at least meet this minimum standard of return. Yet as precise as the methods described above are, they have several problems.

First, hurdle rates ignore cash flow. Yet cash flow is the life blood of most small businesses. Investments that take longer to return their initial cash outlay are more risky than those that return money from the beginning. However, arbitrary hurdle rates don't consider periodic cash flows.

Analyses of major purchases done fairly incorporate the reduced risk associated with regular cash inflows into hurdle-rate computations. Projects that immediately throw off cash toward repayment of the purchase outlay have a lower hurdle rate than those that don't.

Second, many hurdle rates are too ambitious. They tend to creep upward as interest rates increase and the company's required profit margins rise. Soon they're appreciably above the going rate of return for most investments at the risk level the company can live with. Without consciously doing so, companies place themselves at even greater risk by demanding higher and higher return on their capital projects. Remember, there's a rate for every risk. The higher the return, the greater the risk.

JUDGING RETURN ON INVESTMENT

Business planners use several financial analyses to evaluate the return on major purchases. These aren't difficult to compute. As with hurdle rates, don't use these mathematical benchmarks as a substitute for common sense. Frequently the return on the investment in a particular purchase doesn't meet the hurdle rate of return. Yet, the purchase's other merits justify the expenditure. One such circumstance might be the strategic advantage a project gives the company.

There are four main computations we use to judge the return on a major purchase:

- Net present value
- Internal rate of return
- Accounting rate of return
- Payback period

Discounted Cash Flow Rate of Return

This method considers the project's cash inflows and outflows. Since we're dealing with durable goods, these take place over a number of years. Discounted cash flow accounts for the time value of money flowing in and out of the firm over the duration of the project. Essentially the technique translates cash flows into their *present value*. That's the common denominator for comparing two purchase proposals with different cash flows.

The other discounting technique is *internal rate of return*. This method computes the rate that repays the project's initial investment out of discounted future cash flows.

Net present value

Net present value (NPV) analysis converts the future value of a project's cash inflows into today's dollars. Between two different projects, the one with the greater NPV is the winner—in this particular measurement. However, keep in mind that NPV isn't the only evaluation method we use. Don't jump to the conclusion that one major purchase is better than another without completing the evaluation. NPV is just one part of the total pie. Here's how to do it.

Assume we're deciding between two projects for MTH, Ltd.:

- An automated product bagging line
- A secondary recovery system for water used by the manufacturing facility

MTH's cost of borrowing money is 12 percent. Let's assume the following about the two projects:

- Automated bagger: Cost is $500,000 and cash inflows for the next ten years are $75,000 per year.
- Secondary recovery system: Cost is $400,000 with cash inflows of only $65,000, but for the next 15 years.

Use the NPV tables in any finance book or any good financial calculator. The NPV of the two projects is

- Bagger: $423,767 • Recovery system: $442,706

Therefore, from this standpoint, the secondary recovery system seems the better investment. Now, let's compute the return on investment for each project:

$$\text{ROI} = \frac{\text{NPV / Initial cash outlay}}{\text{\# of years}}$$

Bagger: ($423,767 / $500,000) / 10 = 8%
Secondary recovery: ($442,706 / $400,000) / 15 = 7%

Therefore, the bagger, even though it's more expensive, has a smaller NPV, and lasts only ten years, has a better return on investment. Did you notice that these calculations considered the 12 percent cost of funds by discounting the future cash inflows back to present value?

Internal Rate of Return

Internal rate of return (IRR) discounts the future cash inflows back to present value so that they exactly equal the initial cash outlay. IRR computes an interest rate, whereas net present value computes a dollar amount. Computation of internal rate of return requires two steps:

Step 1: Determine annuity factor of future cash inflows

Find the table factor for the present value of an ordinary annuity of $1. Use this in step 2. Compute the table factor using this formula:

$$\text{Annuity table factor} = \frac{\text{net cash outlay}}{\text{average annual net cash inflow}}$$

The factors used for MTH's two projects are

- Bagger: $500,000 / $75,000 = 6.67
- Recovery system: $400,000 / $65,000 = 6.15

Step 2: Use the annuity table for IRR

Look up the two factors using the table for present value of an ordinary annuity of $1. Use the row corresponding to the correct number of years for the project. Then look *up* the column to find the IRR that discounts us back to the initial cash outlay. Here are the results:

- Bagger: For ten years, the factor was 6.67. This gives an approximate IRR of 8 percent.
- Recovery system: For fifteen years, the factor was 6.15. This provides an approximate IRR of 14 percent.

From an IRR perspective, the secondary recovery system is a better project. That's primarily because it has a longer period over which we can count on cash inflows. Common sense also tells us that.

Accounting Rate of Return

The accounting rate of return focuses on *net* cash inflow or net profits and the average investment to measure a project's productivity. If the computation uses net profit rather than cash flow, it's called *return on net assets (RONA)*. The equation for the accounting rate of return is

$$\text{Cash return} = \frac{\text{average annual net cash inflow}}{\text{cash outflow}}$$

$$\text{RONA} = \frac{\text{net income} + \text{after-tax interest expense}}{\text{total assets} - \text{current liabilities}}$$

For MTH's project, the accountant's cash return is

- Bagger: $75,000 / $500,000 = 15%

- Recovery system: $65,000 / $400,000 = 16%

Payback Period

We use this method in part to help us gauge risk. Longer payback periods mean greater exposure to market fluctuations and more risk. Payback is also a measure of a project's *liquidity* rather than its actual return. This computation determines the number of years (or payment periods) it takes to return the initial investment. Compute payback as

$$\text{Payback period} = \frac{\text{cash outlay}}{\text{constant cash inflow}}$$

The payback periods for MTH's two projects are

- Bagger: $500,000 / $75,000 = 7 years
- Recovery system: $400,000 / $65,000 = 6 years

In this case, the recovery system repays the lower initial investment a year earlier even though its annual cash inflows are $10,000 less per year.

There are problems with payback as well. Primarily, it ignores the time value of money. In our example with MTH, suppose the bagger project had a $95,000 annual cash inflow instead of $75,000. Now its payback time would be only a little over five years ($500,000 / $95,000 = 5.3 years). This gives us a faster payback than for the recovery system. However, the bagger stops paying after ten years. The recovery system continues generating a cash return for another five years. Payback computations ignore that significant part of the equation.

Rules of Thumb

Use these three general rules when working with discounted cash flow computations:

1. If NPV (in dollars) equals cash outlay (also in dollars), the project is at break-even. It hasn't returned us anything over the discount rate used in the present value computations.

   The same holds true when the IRR (in percentage) equals the cost of capital (also in percentage). The firm has not received compensation for its risk, its profit margin, or its time.

2. If NPV is negative, reject the major purchase proposal. The same holds true if IRR is less than the cost of capital—don't do the project.

3. If NPV is positive and IRR exceeds the cost of capital, the project may be a good deal.

COMPARING PROJECTS

To compare different project proposals, we must reduce them to a common denominator. Our analysis won't work if we find ourselves comparing apples to oranges. Usually two projects have different cash flows, and their initial payments are different as well. Most likely, the financing requirements aren't similar either. Use the criteria in Figure 11-7 to compare two different projects.

Figure 11-7
Major Purchases Comparison

Project description
Project benefits: cost reduction, better manufacturing throughput, improved quality—describe what the project does for the company
Schedule of cash outflows (often there's more than one)
Schedule of cash inflows and all assumptions used to arrive at the schedule
Required hurdle rate and its computation
NPV
IRR
Payback
Residual value

MONITORING THE PROJECTS

We prepare major purchase plans to document required performance. Then we use the plan to track actual results. The plan focuses on the accountability of the people who proposed a project in the first place. We don't make decisions to buy expensive equipment based on excessively ambitious projections. Instead, the plan holds those who prepared the proposal responsible for the accuracy of their estimates. Such accountability creates a deterrent to making a proposal unjustifiably attractive just to get it pushed through.

The major purchases plan does four things to assist monitoring performance:

1. It points out differences between projections in the proposal (on which we based the authorization to proceed) and actual results.
2. It provides a base on which to make corrections if necessary.
3. It holds project management responsible for the accuracy of the proposal estimates.
4. It involves senior management in the investment process.

Chapter 12 moves on to forecasting wages and salaries.

Chapter 12

Forecasting Labor Expenses

OVERVIEW

Chapter 12 demonstrates how to prepare the cost side of a people plan—the labor expense schedules. There's a lot more to forecasting labor expense than just entering everyone's salary on a monthly schedule, though that's the finished product of our labor expense plan.

Chapter 12 identifies the steps required to get there. We begin by establishing the plan for salary reviews. This section shows how to conduct salary surveys. From this, the labor expense forecast provides a salary range for each job classification. Additionally, Chapter 12 demonstrates the points included in a salary review. The end product is a schedule of wages, salaries, raises, and bonuses.

Along with normal wages and salaries, the labor expense forecast includes the costs for overtime premiums, temporary help, and consulting fees. Chapter 12 shows how to connect this section of the business plan with other departments in the company. Finally, Chapter 12 identifies the indirect costs associated with a complete schedule of labor expenses. This includes all the employee benefits such as pension and profit-sharing contributions, insurance, parking, cafeteria subsidies—the list goes on.

PLANNING SALARY INCREASES

Most companies adjust their employees' salaries at least annually. Rather than make this adjustment in a casual manner, as many companies do, our business plan *schedules* the increases according to levels set by our profit targets. This organizes the effort and establishes a planned labor expense level *after* raises.

The first step in preparing for salary reviews is to identify the amount labor expense can rise and still meet profit goals. This isn't a difficult computation. Just compute the financial forecast using different assumptions for total labor expense increases.

The process requires two steps:

- Identify the total labor expense increase in dollars.
- Subtract out the likely increase in uncontrollable indirect costs.

The amount left goes to wage and salary raises. We'll plan distribution of the raise pool with care. The wage and salary plan recognizes such issues as

- Competitive labor rates at other companies
- The need to retain key employees
- The firm's need to build its skill levels

Computing the Amount Available for Raises

Companies control the amount of raises they give their labor force. However, they can't always control the increases in indirect costs. We allocate these first. Indirect labor expense includes such things as insurance premiums, parking expense, and subsidy of the company cafeteria. Such perks cost money. Often the only way to control their increase is to either scale them back or stop them entirely. Some companies now require a larger contribution from the employees for the group health plan.

Here's how we determine the amount available for wage and salary increases:

1. List all uncontrollable indirect costs included in total labor expense.

2. Identify the amount for each over the planning period.

3. Adjust levels of service or benefits to match the business plan. Perhaps the company needs a dental plan to remain competitive in the labor market. Maybe it needs to remove its employee parking subsidy. Whatever the adjustments, make them now.

4. Subtract indirect costs from total planned labor expense. The amount left over goes to salaries and wages.

5. Subtract last year's wage and salary expense from the result. This amount represents raises for the planning period.

Figure 12-1 provides a schematic for this computation.

Now we know just how much our business plan allows for wage and salary raises. Next we allocate raises where they will do the most good—in specific areas of the work force.

Conducting Salary Surveys

Allocating raises requires identifying those positions where you're likely to see turnover because current rates are low. An easy way to identify these positions is through salary surveys.

Effective salary surveys require comparison of like-kind jobs. Often titles are misleading, so have a good idea of the duties and responsibilities of the jobs you're surveying. We want to compare apples with apples.

Professional associations sponsor salary surveys each year. The National Association of Printers is one such organization. Personnel recruiting organizations sometimes sponsor surveys for the industry in which they specialize.

If you are not able to use someone else's salary survey, it's not difficult to conduct your own. The first step might be to contact a personnel recruiting firm and ask the going rate for the positions that interest you. Another source of wage rates is the want ads in newspapers. However, rates usually appear only for

Figure 12-1
Computation of Allowable Wage and Salary Increases

Computation of Labor Raises	Month 1	Month 12
Total planned labor expense	————	————
Uncontrollable indirect costs:	————	————
Health insurance	————	————
Dental insurance	————	————
401(k) contribution	————	————
Stock purchase and profit sharing	————	————
Van pool	————	————
Sick time	————	————
Vacation time	————	————
Family leave time	————	————
Federal taxes paid by employer	————	————
Compliance with worker's laws	————	————
Parking subsidies	————	————
Child care subsidy	————	————
Cafeteria subsidy	————	————
Subtotal indirect costs	————	————
Amount available for wages and salaries		
Less last year's wages and salaries	————	————
Amount available for raises	════	════

lower-level jobs. Call competing firms to find out their pay rates for particular jobs. Be sure to write down the survey results. This provides a good record for future reference.

Allocating raises to positions with less than competitive rates

Some positions in companies just don't keep pace with the going market. Labor, especially in low-level jobs, goes to the highest-paying employer. If your survey uncovers one or more job categories that don't pay competitive rates, chances are you'll see turnover or attract unqualified people.

If such turnover or the quality of people is a problem for the firm, then the plan must bring these job categories up to competitive levels. Therefore, these are the first jobs that get allocated a portion of the pool available for wage and salary raises. These aren't merit raises. The labor market requires them to keep pace.

Most employers don't automatically give raises just because someone's compensation is below the going rate. However, plan on raising these rates during the planning year through either

- Hiring more costly labor to replace turnover

- Bidding up rates for valued employees to meet offers from the competition

Establishing Wage and Salary Ranges

Wage and salary ranges give the company a chance to employ some strategy. Most firms opt for salary ranges where the competitive rates hit the middle of the range. However, if your company has some particular benefit that sets it apart from the competition, target the midpoint of a salary range slightly below the competition's.

Some companies fine-tune this strategy for specific job classifications. Interns at teaching hospitals provide a good example. The most prestigious hospitals pay their interns less than the competition in return for the superior training their institution provides along with its name.

Conversely, some companies demand a superior work force. Some job categories are so vital to a company that it must have the best people possible. These firms peg the midpoint of their salary range *above* the competition's average rate.

The size of a salary range depends on the job and how long the firm wants employees to stay. For example, jobs where employees should stay five years before moving up should have around a 30 percent difference between the top and bottom of the salary range. This allows for rate increases of around 5 percent each year. Other jobs require wider ranges because of larger increases or longer tenure. Some jobs have narrow ranges based on the short time it takes to train a replacement and the low cost of turnover.

Regardless of the job range, always remember that there's a top rate for every job. Beyond that, it doesn't make sense for the company to retain an employee. He or she should move up to a more responsible job or just receive cost of living increases.

Using Job Descriptions

Though not part of the wage and salary plan, job descriptions certainly assist in establishing ranges for pay rates. Job descriptions provide the most information to larger companies with more complex tasks where everyone doesn't already know exactly what everyone else does.

Job descriptions also establish a method of comparing jobs, both within the company and with other firms. Small businesses usually don't have such a formal system of job descriptions. Here are some of the things normally included:

Duties

List the tasks of the job. Describe the level of complexity, difficulty, frequency of each task, and importance to the firm. For example, the tasks associated with an accounting clerk might include

- Total daily cash receipts
- Post cash receipts in accounts receivable subledger
- Transfer receivables subledger entry to general ledger

- Account for $100,000 of monthly income

Supervision

Describe the supervision required of the job and that given others by the job. This brackets the relative level of authority and responsibility. Be sure to identify the other job titles related to supervision given and received. *Numbers* of people supervised under this job description are important.

Authority levels

Describe the level of authority the job has. For example, a purchasing agent may have the authority to sign contracts up to $25,000. Purchases beyond that require review and approval from a higher authority. Authority levels also identify where the job description fits in the company's hierarchy of responsibility.

Special requirements

Include all special skills, knowledge, and extraordinary demands of the job. Perhaps the job requires knowledge of toxic chemicals. Maybe the person *works* around them. Often jobs require odd hours or long hours during peak season. Be sure to include these as well.

PLANNING FOR TEMPORARY HELP

Temporary help fills a breach for many firms whose business is seasonal. Some companies discover a core of very specialized temporary workers whose skills and experience border on those of consultants. Nurses fall into that category. Hospitals and other health care providers often call on individuals or nursing registries that provide qualified temporary help as needed.

Most positions for which companies use temporaries, however, require skills that can be learned very quickly. Generally, temps cost more than the pay rate for a regular employee. However, there's no insurance and little of the liability associated with an employee.

The labor expense plan must recognize and schedule the need for temporary help. Most companies with an operating history know when they need temporary help. They project approximately the number of full-time equivalents (FTEs) by which the work force should increase. With this background, scheduling temporary help is no mystery.

Computing Temporary Expense

Look at the increase in labor capacity the firm requires during its peak season from a mathematical standpoint. Say the company normally staffs to meet 50 percent of the peak demand. Overtime and temporaries fill the remaining 50 percent gap. The salary budget provides for a specified labor expense during this time. We already know that half of that labor expense goes to regular employees.

Therefore, the issue is how much of the remaining 50 percent goes to temps and how much goes to overtime. Figure 12-2 shows one way to figure this out.

Figure 12-2
Computation of Temporary Help Required

Assume:

Production capacity for regular employees is 10 units per 8-hour day
(10 ÷ 8 = 1.25 units per hour).
The production shift has 20 people.
Normal capacity is 200 units per day.
Peak demand is 400 units per day.
Maximum hours regulars can work is 12 hours per day.
Only 15 regulars volunteer for overtime during peak season.
Temporaries produce 8 units in a normal 8-hour day
(8 ÷ 8 = 1 unit per hour).

Computation:

1. Units produced by 5 regulars not working OT [(5 X 8) X 1.25 = 50 units]	50
2. Units produced by 15 regulars working 12-hour shifts [(15 X 12) X 1.25) = 225	<u>225</u>
Subtotal units produced by regulars	275

3. Temps required:
Units required is 125 (400 - 275 = 125)
Temps produce 1 unit per hour and work
12 hours. Therefore, number of temps is
125 ÷ 12 = 10 temporary employees

Once we know the number of temporary employees, it's easy to compute their expense. Most temps charge by the hour. Simply extend the number of temps required by their hourly rate. Enter that number in the labor expense schedule by month.

Use the same computational method when forecasting overtime and temporary expense for nonproduction jobs. Instead of units produced, many firms base their computation on some aspect of the work.

For example, bill collecting firms have their peak period during the second quarter of every year—after their clients have given up on delinquent receivables from the Christmas buying rush. They figure the need for temporary collectors based on the number of accounts a single collector handles.

PLANNING FOR CONSULTING EXPENSES

We don't structure the forecast for consulting expenses as rigidly as that for temporary labor. When planning the consulting part of labor expense, you'll probably have to check with the individual departments that need the consultants. Consulting engagements vary in cost. The department head can tell you the nature of the engagement and the approximate expense the firm should incur.

The consulting part of the labor expense forecast should identify each engagement by name and department. Everyone should be aware of the money planned for outside expertise. If using certain consulting expertise becomes a regular routine, maybe you should consider hiring someone with that kind of background. Alternatively, the firm can always train existing employees to do what the consultant does.

Policy Regarding Consultants

The best consulting engagements are those that do not require an intimate knowledge of the company. Consultants with particular expertise come in, apply their knowledge to the issue, draw conclusions, report them to the company, and leave. These engagements become expensive when the consultant must spend time gaining familiarity with the particulars of the company.

The labor expense plan should identify the firm's posture regarding employment of consultants. Many companies include in this policy specifics regarding

- Conditions for hiring a consultant
- Structure of the consulting contract
- Range of fees quoted
- Authority for approval of the expense
- Scope of the consultant's involvement
- Consultant's approach to the engagement
- Anticipated work product
- Definite start and end dates
- Policy in dealing with cost overruns

This list structures consulting engagements that might otherwise begin without the necessary thought.

Training Consultants

Small businesses often hire consultants to train their staff. This is an excellent engagement for a consultant. We can immediately see both their expertise and their ability to impart knowledge to our people. Experienced training consultants identify a set time for their work and usually have a predetermined fee. Additionally, companies need fewer high-priced consultants with people trained in that area of expertise.

SCHEDULING WAGES AND SALARIES

This schedule incorporates all the work done so far on the forecast of labor expense. It tells every department the detailed labor expense associated with its operation month by month throughout the business plan. The plan forecasts each person's wage and salary expense along with increases scheduled at the appropriate times.

The labor expense schedule includes all

- Wages • Salaries • Bonuses • Overtime
- Temporary expenses • Consulting fees • Indirect costs

If you're using an automated spreadsheet program to build the labor expense schedule for each department, consider this technique: Build each department's labor expense schedule based on the major headings listed above. Often planners include the different departments on separate parts of one large spreadsheet. Alternatively, each department might have its own spreadsheet, with all departments using an identical format. Then we consolidate them into the lead labor expense schedule for the whole company. Use the file, combine, and add commands.

Figure 12-3 (page 198) shows a sample labor expense schedule for a five-person department.

Using this technique, we have a permanent record of the method used to arrive at the grinding department's labor expense. Further, this schedule provides a blueprint for implementing planned rate increases and bonuses.

Scheduling Indirect Costs

Indirect costs often add up to a substantial percentage of actual wages and salaries. Even though the company doesn't pay indirect costs—or benefits—in cash to employees, they're a real business cost nonetheless. You must have a place for them somewhere in the business plan. Usually the labor expense schedules are a good place, since they already address employee costs.

Identifying Indirect Costs

Indirect costs include all labor-related expenses not paid directly to employees. Don't confuse this use of the term *indirect costs* with its meaning in cost accounting. There, indirect costs are production expenses not related to any particular work in process.

Instead, here we're talking about the perks and benefits other than cash payments that companies provide employees as part of their total compensation package. Figure 12-4 shows a partial list of indirect costs.

Figure 12-4
Indirect Costs

- Health insurance
- 401(K) and pension plan contributions
- Profit-sharing contributions
- Stock purchase plan
- Company-owned child care facilities or subsidies paid for child care
- Company-paid employee parking
- Company-paid or subsidized van pool
- Paid sick time
- Paid vacations
- Substance abuse rehabilitation programs
- Company payments to state employment development departments
- Federal taxes paid by employer
- Company-paid changes at the demand of OSHA
- Maintenance of employee manuals

Figure 12-3
Grinding Department Labor Expense Schedule

	Month 1	Month 12	Total
Assumptions—Grinding			
Stanley (supervisor):			
Monthly salary	2,500	3,200	
Bonus		1,000	1,000
Day:			
Hourly base pay rate	$11.00	$12.00	
Standard hours	140	140	
Bonus		400	400
Pogue:			
Hourly base pay rate	$10.00	$11.75	
Standard hours	140	180	
Bonus		350	350
Gunner:			
Hourly base pay rate	$10.00	$12.00	
Standard hours	140	160	
Bonus		500	500
Jones:			
Hourly base pay rate	$10.00	$12.50	
Standard hours	140	180	
Bonus		500	500
Salaries and wages:			
Stanley (supervisor)	$1,400	$2,250	$25,487
Day	1,540	1,680	19,500
Pogue	1,400	2,115	22,300
Gunner	1,400	1,920	22,450
Jones	2,500	3,200	20,000
Total salaries and wages	$8,240	$11,165	$109,737
Bonuses:			
Stanley (supervisor)	0	500	1,000
Day	0	400	400
Pogue	0	350	350
Gunner	0	500	500
Jones	0	1,000	500
Total bonuses	$0	$2,750	$2,750
Total salaries, wages, and bonuses—Grinding	$8,240	$13,915	$112,487

Allocating Indirect Labor Costs

Indirect labor costs get allocated to each department. The method of allocation always seems to be an issue with department managers—especially when bonuses depend on bottom-line performance. Regardless of the care with which we allocate such overhead expenses, people complain. For labor overhead items, the argument usually focuses on the "unique" composition of a department and the fact that its employees don't use or incur indirect expenses in the amount allocated.

Methods of allocating indirect labor costs vary. Most companies don't take the time to devise an allocation percentage based on the actual usage of individual indirect expenses by each department's employees.

Fixed allocation per employee method

One way of allocating indirect labor and other overhead expenses is simply to take all the indirect labor costs and divide them by the total number of employees. Then each department gets allocated this fixed amount multiplied by the number of employees in the department.

This method is misleading if a department's staff truly does not use (or overuses) a particular benefit. The counterargument goes, *but they could use these benefits.* Either way, fixed allocation is the most common method.

Apportionment of indirect labor expenses

This is more complicated and still doesn't make everyone happy. Apportionment attempts to identify particular groups of employees with specific indirect costs. For example, say the company pays a subsidy of $50 per month to each employee for every child they have requiring day care up to a maximum of $150.

Under apportionment, that indirect cost gets allocated to those departments whose employees take advantage of the program. It makes sense when viewed like this. However, what about indirect costs such as health insurance? Certainly some employees with a costly medical history drive up the insurance premium for the company. Is the firm's accountant going to dig into the premium bill, itemize it by employee, then apportion *that* cost to the department in which each individual works? Probably not. Yet that's what apportionment requires when done correctly.

Figure 12-5 displays a sample schedule for indirect costs. This schedule follows the one in Figure 12-3 for wages, salaries, and bonuses.

Figure 12-5
Allocation of Indirect Costs

Indirect Labor Expenses— Grinding Department	% of Total	Total Amount	Amount Allocated
Allocation percentages of total			
Group health plan	10%	$25,000	$2,500
Employer's contribution to 401(k) plan	5%	$197,000	9,850
Employer's contribution to pension and profit-sharing plan	5%	$100,000	5,000
Child care subsidies	20%	$50,000	10,000
Parking subsidies	15%	$10,000	1,500
Van pool subsidies	15%	$5,000	750
Allocation of paid sick time	10%	$100,000	10,000
Federal and state employment taxes paid by employer:			
Stanley (supervisor)	Actual	13%	3,315
Day	Actual	13%	2,535
Pogue	Actual	13%	2,899
Gunner	Actual	13%	2,919
Jones	Actual	13%	2,600
Total federal and state taxes			$14,268
Other overhead allocations	5%	$50,000	2,500

From this point, the labor expense schedules distribute the indirect cost allocation month by month over the planning horizon for the grinding department. Most companies distribute an equal amount to each month for all indirect costs except federal and state employer-paid taxes. For these, they base the allocation on the actual employee payroll for each month.

CONDUCTING SALARY REVIEWS

Once the company has determined the planned wage and salary schedules, it needs to implement them. Do that using salary reviews between the workers and their supervisors. The salary forecast identifies the month in which each person in the company receives a salary review. Within reason, we already know the amount of each person's pay rate change from the labor expense schedules.

Well-run companies schedule both performance and salary reviews in advance of the anniversary date. This gives the discussion the level of importance that it should have. The wage and salary plan already includes the pay rate adjustment date for each employee. It makes sense that this part of the business plan should also schedule both performance and salary reviews.

Often companies separate performance and salary reviews. They aren't the same thing. Performance reviews may occur annually on the employee's anniversary. Salary reviews sometimes occur at the same time for all employees. Other companies stagger them by division or department. Some conduct performance reviews before completion of the business plan. Then salary reviews come afterwards, during implementation of the business plan.

Regardless of timing, performance and salary reviews are *linked*. The performance review provides a basis for adjusting employee salaries and pay rates. We document the reasoning behind any salary adjustment and include it in each employee's personnel file. In the event future questions arise concerning the reasons for particular pay rate adjustments, the performance and salary reviews provide the necessary documentation.

Contents of Salary Reviews

Plan salary reviews carefully. This is a two-way street between supervisor and subordinate. Include these things in a salary review:

1. *Derivation of the company's overall pay rate increases.* The wage and salary plan arrived at an overall increase for the firm's pay rates. Communicate this so that there's no mistaking where the company is going and how that direction affects everyone's pay rate.

2. *Identify the pool allocated for pay rate increases.* Every department gets allocated a part of the overall rate increase pool. Identify its derivation.

3. *Identify the employee's pay rate adjustment.* Explain how the adjustment ties to the employee's performance review.

4. *Explain where the employee falls in the salary range for that position.* People wants to know where they stand in relation to their growth potential. The salary range for each position provides a scale on which to grade an individual's progress.

Figure 12-6 shows some of the things to include in your plan for salary reviews.

Figure 12-6
Salary Review Checklist

- Scheduled date for each employee's salary review
- Mechanism to ensure that salary reviews are conducted on time and in accordance with company policies
- Deadline for drafting any salary review forms
- Supervisor training on giving salary reviews
- Criteria for merit increases
- Identification of the planned increase in overall compensation for the firm
- Bonus plan and criteria for administration
- Identification of the bonus pool

Chapter 13 demonstrates how to create the financial plan.

Chapter 13

Creating the Financial Plan

OVERVIEW

Chapter 13 formulates the financial plan. Its purpose is to provide a quantitative measure of the financial results for each department's goals and targets. In this chapter we'll pull together all the departments' plans and integrate them into one financial projection. That way we create a tracking mechanism for implementation of the business plan.

Many managers of small businesses want the financial plan to answer only one question: How much money do we need and when do we need it? Cash flow planning is certainly important—in Chapter 14 we'll create a cash flow plan. However, the financial plan deals with all other aspects of the business plan's goals. For instance, it identifies the level of accounts receivable resulting from the sales plan. This has a direct impact on the amount of working capital required by the company. Further, it tells us something about the speed with which the firm can afford to pay its vendors through accounts payable.

Smart business planners *derive* their cash flow plans from the overall financial plan, not vice versa. Doing otherwise allows borrowing requirements to dictate how you run your business. It should be the other way around—we manage our business and require funds to help us meet our goals.

The prospective financial statements resulting from the financial plan quantify each department's subplan in a standard format. This way we quantify the firm's objectives, tactics, and policies for the entire plan in dollars and cents. Further, we reduce all targets and goals to a standardized format that everyone understands—prospective financial statements.

Segments of the Financial Plan

Financial plans have three segments:

1. The projected income statement presents the company's operating plan. This section includes forecast results from the sales, production, distribution, advertising, and administrative subplans.

2. The forecasted balance sheet presents the company's financial position over the course of the planning horizon. It includes the assets, liabilities, and owners' equity of the firm. Here results of operations and the major purchases plan get projected.

3. The cash flow plan tells how much to borrow and when.

Financial plans have a reputation for being too complex. This comes from the dependence of one department's performance on another. This linkage only makes a financial plan seem complicated. Indeed, components of financial plans are like dominos—as one moves, the others farther down the line move as well.

Our financial plan won't require the services of a CPA. We get around that in two ways:

1. We'll isolate the key variables that drive the financial plan—sales volume estimates, for instance. Understanding all the areas in the financial plan changed by each variable makes the mystery disappear.

2. We'll develop a simple spreadsheet computer model to create the financial plan. The results of that analysis appear at the end of this chapter. Financial planning doesn't require the use of a computer; however, its use speeds the process along. It also allows for more creativity, since we can test ideas quickly without much effort. Further, a computer relieves us of the arithmetic when cranking through changes to the financial plan. Even if you don't use a computer for your financial planning, you'll find the ideas helpful.

Each department's operating goals plug into the financial plan. From there we see how they further the company's overall objectives. Presentation of the financial plan in financial statement format gives everyone a common point of reference.

DEVELOPING THE FINANCIAL PLAN

Our financial plan derives from three components:

- Assumptions • Financial schedules • Work papers

Assumptions

Accurate assumptions create a credible financial plan. Often the first question people ask when they see a number they don't understand is, How did you get that? Financial plans take most of their assumptions from the subplans of other departments. We'll use these to create the revenue and expense numbers feeding into our financial plan.

Some of the assumptions remain specific to the financial plan. These include projected interest rates and borrowing capacity. The finance department usually consults outside experts for many of these assumptions. Most of us aren't in the business of projecting such things as interest rates. Attempting to do so only impugns the credibility of the financial plan.

We'll begin our financial plan by assembling all of the assumptions we use. We want to remember where these numbers came from and why we used them. Our financial plan has a separate section devoted to explaining the assumptions used and their derivation. This section is extensive, especially the work papers that derive the major assumptions. The most useful assumption sections explain

- The derivation of each assumption

- The impact changes in the key assumptions have on the overall financial results

This section provides a written record that's used throughout the implementation of the business plan. Don't get the idea that the assumption section is an academic exercise simply for purposes of being thorough. You *will* refer to it often.

However, temper documentation of your assumptions with actual need. Most smaller businesses have less need for extensive documentation because everyone is close to the numbers. Further, people who are not familiar with the company probably won't see the financial plan. Nevertheless, as time goes on, people forget what they were thinking when they created the assumptions. The assumption section becomes increasingly valuable the more complex the financial plan and the more time that passes.

Time horizon
The time horizon used in our financial plan should match that used in the rest of the business plan. For our purposes, this is just one year. However, many companies produce multiyear financial plans.

If your financial plan goes out more than a year, look carefully at the level of detail projected. The accuracy of financial projections falls off dramatically the farther into the future you go. This is especially true when you are using volatile assumptions over which the company has little control. Interest rates are a good example. How much credibility does a five-year financial plan have when one of its major assumptions turns out to be a forecast of interest rates? Any of our guesses is probably as good as the next.

What happens when the time horizon diminishes the credibility of your assumptions? Reduce the level of detail contained in the financial plan. For example, many companies abbreviate the income statement to show only major revenue and expense items. These don't forecast net income. However, they are often sufficient for tracking the financial performance and current position of the business plan. Equally as important, their credibility as a management tool doesn't decline. The precision of the forecast matches the precision of the underlying assumptions. That's the important thing.

For purposes of tracking plan implementation, the interim milestones of each department's subplan should exactly coincide with the time horizon of the financial plan. For example, if your sales forecast goes out one year by month with quarterly subtotals, so should the financial plan.

Driver assumptions
Your financial plan has two types of assumptions:

- Driver assumptions   • Secondary assumptions

Driver assumptions move the plan. For example, sales is a driver assumption. Such things as cash inflow from collections depend on sales. State your driver assumptions in terms of dollars. They represent the hard targets established in the business plan.

The fewer driver assumptions, the better. That way, using an automated financial model, a change in one key variable automatically flows through the entire financial plan without much additional work.

Secondary assumptions

Most financial plan assumptions depend on the few driver assumptions. For example, state advertising expenses as a *percentage* of the sales they generate. The same goes for accounts receivable. They become a percentage of sales and key on the aging and collection process.

Make sure your secondary assumptions automatically change when the driver assumptions on which they depend change. The best way is to make the secondary assumptions a percentage of the drivers. That makes the financial plan a useful *what if* tool. If one set of targets for a department doesn't fulfill the firm's financial objectives, it's easy to determine which ones do.

Input from other departments

Departmental subplans feed into the financial plan. Include such items as

- Projected sales revenue from the marketing subplan
- Cost of goods sold from the manufacturing subplan
- Shipping costs as a percentage of sales from the warehouse department

Plug each department's operating goals into the financial plan. See how they further the company's overall objectives. An automated spreadsheet program computes the impacts of changes quickly and accurately. From here we can identify the errors department assumptions contain before they risk keeping us from achieving the targets of the overall business plan.

Departmental assumptions that appear excessively ambitious and could damage the business plan pop out of such analyses. This illustrates the utility of the financial planning mechanism as a creative planning tool.

Results of financial plans often become the performance benchmark of the business plan. That's what we want. Using the financial plan as a tracking mechanism, it's easy to compare actual results with those planned on a monthly basis. Without a clear understanding of where the planned financial targets came from, it's impossible to track implementation of the plan.

Change is another reason for carefully documenting the assumptions used in the financial plan. Often departments come up with various *scenarios* that they plug into the financial plan. Unless you identify the assumptions used, determining exactly which scenario each department employed to formulate its contribution to the financial plan becomes confusing.

For these reasons, document the assumptions. Make sure your notes trace each assumption back to its source. Additionally, if those responsible for assumptions can't explain them or if the explanations don't sound logical, something is wrong. Those preparing the financial plan are responsible for its assumptions. Excessively ambitious or ill-conceived assumptions do no one any good. They diminish the credibility of the entire business plan.

DATA REQUIRED BY THE FINANCIAL PLAN

The financial plan needs information from every department that creates a sub-plan to further the overall goals of the business plan. Most small businesses orient their financial plans toward sales and marketing. That's usually because the firm is sales-driven. It bases all other activities on sales levels.

Sales and Marketing

Don't recreate the sales plan in the financial plan. Make sure the assumptions specify dollar level or a percentage of another variable and their timing. Here are the key pieces of sales and marketing information required by the financial plan:

Sales

Make sales one of your financial plan's primary driver assumptions. Chances are that many parts of the overall plan assumed particular sales levels. This makes it easier to change the entire financial plan by changing only sales.

If your company carries several products or product lines, identify sales levels for each one in the financial plan. This makes it easier to identify where sales revenue comes from. It also makes changing the sales expectations of specific products faster.

If your financial plan doesn't show sales revenue detail, make sure you have it readily available in your work papers. Everyone reviewing the financial plan asks questions regarding sales revenue.

Customer mix

Customer mix has an impact on the accounts receivable and collections segment of the financial plan. This drives the cash plan. New customers have un-known payment habits. The financial plan adjusts for this anticipated change in the collection and bad debt projections.

Additionally, the sales plan may target a new geographic location of customers. This also affects the speed of collections and the effort expended (such as possible use of a lock box system).

Credit criteria

Policies surrounding the firm's granting of trade credit influence the quality of customers entering the Receivables system. Often the rules for granting trade credit change for specific marketing campaigns. This is important to the financial plan in forecasting future receivables balances, cash flow, and bad debt expenses.

Sales commissions

Make commissions a percentage of sales, net of returns and allowances. That way the expense changes automatically as sales change. Sales commissions should appear as a separate line item in the financial plan.

Warranty service expense

Marketing campaigns often utilize warranty programs. They can be part of either the marketing or the production plan. If warranty expense is material in re-lation to gross sales, include it as a separate line item in the financial plan. The warranty assumptions should include timing and amount from past experience. If engineering or warranty contract terms changed as part of the business plan, include the anticipated financial effect as well.

The sales plan is a logical driver assumption for warranty service expense. Make it a percentage of total sales. Then lag it behind sales revenue according to the time it usually takes for customers to require service.

Developing new products

New product development expenses and costs associated with changes to existing products should hit the financial plan. If your company has many such expenses, detail them in your work papers. Then get a total for each month in the planning horizon and include only the total number in the financial plan.

If your firm incurs new product development expenses, be sure the *benefits* of these efforts make it into the sales forecast. Additionally, questions regarding new product development or enhancement of existing products often revolve around cost overruns and overly ambitious projections of results. It's often a good idea to include projections of these costs and their benefits.

Manufacturing Cost of Goods Sold

This is the bottom-line number that comes from the manufacturing department. If it has done its job, all of the costs associated with producing the firm's products appear in the manufacturing plan. This includes allocation of overhead as well as indirect and fixed expenses shared by all the items produced. Two examples are rent for space occupied by the production line and the salary of the production manager. All products benefit from these expenses and should bear their fair share.

It's a good idea to present cost of goods sold in the financial plan as a secondary assumption. Make it a percentage of the gross sales revenue before returns and allowances. Compute a cost of goods sold percentage of gross sales for each product produced. That way, as the sales levels for each product fluctuate, the financial plan maintains an accurate cost of goods sold expense without having to recompute this complex number.

Note also that the difference between the sales price and the cost of goods sold (stated as a percentage of the sales price) is the gross margin. Most people understand gross margin and use it as a reference point. Indeed, many financial plans compute this number and display it right on the projected income statement.

Alternatively, many companies don't schedule gross sales and cost of goods sold for each product. Instead, they compute an overall CGS number and use that. Though this makes creating the financial plan easier, tracking implementation of the financial plan is more difficult. Identify variances, then research their causes. Often negative variances result from any number of problems, such as

- Unit sales for any given product
- Prices at which any given product sells
- Production costs for any given product

Show the sales revenue and production cost of each product separately on the face of the income statement. This technique makes tracking performance of the sales and manufacturing departments that much easier. Further, problems with specific products show up more readily.

Other manufacturing costs

Cost accounting is a complex subject that is beyond the scope (or necessity) of our job here. Chapter 11 of *Accounting for the New Business* in the Adams series shows how to establish a cost accounting system. However, the financial plan must forecast all manufacturing expenses somewhere. Most get allocated when you compute cost of goods sold. Be sure that any production costs not allocated to individual products get put into an account called *unallocated production costs*. Make this a percentage of total production expenses. Such costs might include

- Shipping and packing • Warehousing
- Repair and maintenance of material handling equipment
- Quality control • Production engineering

When companies—especially smaller ones—first begin financial planning, they often make it unnecessarily complex. They spend hours analyzing costs and trying to allocate every single expense, no matter how tiny.

Don't make this mistake. A plan that's less than 100 percent accurate is still better than no plan at all. As time goes on, the firm's ability to create and execute its financial plan grows. With that growth may come added sophistication and complexity of the financial plan—but only if it adds to the final product.

Transfer pricing

Many companies with more than one division sell products between themselves. These appear in the financial plan. Assign price policies to these "sales." Most firms choose one of these three methods when pricing product transfers between divisions:

1. *Market value* of the goods sold from one division to another. Many companies favor this method because it places the purchase decision in real-world terms.

2. *Cost plus a mark-up.* If the financial plan uses this technique, it's liable to pass along operating inefficiencies of the selling division—the higher the manufacturing cost, the greater the profit dollars to the "seller." This is misleading in the selling division's financial plan because the "profits" merely transfer money from one pocket to another.

3. *Actual cost.* This method shows no profit. It isn't fair to the selling division, which could have sold the same goods to a third party at a profit.

Consider these factors when selecting a transfer pricing policy:

- Organizational goals

- Performance evaluation and fairness to the "buyer" and "seller"
- Autonomy of divisions
- Legal and regulatory requirements

The last item, legal conformity, is important. The IRS takes a dim view of firms managing their profit (and therefore their tax liability) using transfer pricing schemes.

People costs

Cost for wages and salaries usually runs a close second behind cost of goods sold for the largest expense. Take the salary and wage projections directly from the people plan and its salary subplan. Work papers of the financial plan should include wage and salary schedules along with projected raises and bonuses from the people plan. There's no need to duplicate these in the financial plan.

Along with schedules of salaries, wages, and raises, include the following in this section of the financial plan:

- *Overtime expense.* The only way to control over-time expense through the financial plan is to include it as a separate line item in the financial plan. Every month compare actual and planned OT expense.
- *Bonuses.* Show them separately in the periods when earned. This helps improve the accuracy of the cash forecast. Include the bonus policy (percentage of net income, for example) and those eligible in the financial plan work papers. Schedule each individual separately in the work papers, then flow the total up to the projected income statement.
- *Recruiting expenses.* Include schedules from the people plan identifying the positions for which you are recruiting, the timing of payment, and the amount in the financial plan work papers. Total the schedule and flow it up to the income statement.
- *Legal fees.* If legal and settlement fees for pending lawsuits are part of the people plan, be sure to include them in the work papers of the financial plan. Since work papers are confidential, the risk of disclosure is slight. Total them in the work papers and flow them up to the forecasted income statement.
- *Outside services.* Include here such things as temporary workers and consultants. If you want complete control and accountability for these expenses, include them as separate line items in the financial plan.

FINANCIAL ASSUMPTIONS

The financial plan requires some assumptions that don't come from other departments. These include

- Interest rates   • Collections forecast   • Payables forecast
- Minimum level of cash required   • Borrowing capacity
- Capital expenditures forecast

- General and administrative and overhead costs • Management fees
- Opening balance sheet • Ratios and statistics

Interest Rates

Interest income and expense may be a material item to the financial plan depending on the nature of the business and its investments or need for borrowed funds. The amount of invested or borrowed funds and interest rates dictate the level of interest income and expense.

However, where can you get a reliable interest rate forecast? Economists have a poor track record in projecting the value of future interest rates. However, they're good at projecting *a range* in which the rates will probably hit.

Astute planners use a range of interest rates in their financial plan. There are many economic forecasting firms that supply interest rate forecasts (Chase Econometrics and Data Resources, Inc. are two).

We want two things from interest rate assumptions:

- The appropriate interest rate for our purposes—maybe it's Treasury bills, maybe it's prime, or maybe it's the Fed's Eleventh District cost of funds. Some plans use several rates in various parts of the plan.

- Three interest rate scenarios: best case, worst case, and most likely—we'll use all three in creating a range of tolerable error. This is especially important if the interest income or expense item has a significant influence on the financial plan results.

Collections Forecast

The financial plan uses the collections forecast to help produce the ending cash number that appears on the balance sheet each month throughout the planning period. Some of the assumptions used to create the collections forecast are

- The percentages of cash sales and credit sales. Use these as secondary assumptions, driven by sales.

- The percentage of receivables that customers historically pay within 30, 60, 90, and 120 days.

- The percentage of receivables that roll through the collections system to write-off as bad debt.

- The timing and amounts received by factoring or selling accounts receivable.

- The collection rate for receivables based on the sales forecast.

Payables Forecast

Include these assumptions regarding accounts payable in the financial plan:

- Trade credit allowed by vendors. This helps you project the balance in payables over the planning horizon.

- Payment due date for major payables, such as inventory purchases and taxes.
- Trade discounts.

Minimum Level of Required Cash

Cash is a safety net. Many financial plans establish floors below which the company doesn't want cash balances to fall. Further, some bank loans require maintenance of compensating balances in non-interest-bearing accounts. If so, include these in the minimum level of cash required.

Borrowing Capacity

The narrative portion of the financial plan describes the funding available and the timing necessary to obtain it. Borrowing capacity consists of

- Lines of credit • Secured loans • Capital infusion
- Debt or equity offerings

The financial plan identifies the need for funds and the amount as well as the type of borrowing. Once this is known, the financial plan charts a course to make sure the appropriate funds arrive when needed.

General, Administrative, and Overhead Costs

Include most of the company's expenses in the departmental subplans that flow into the financial plan. Therefore, G&A and overhead costs shouldn't be very large. However, be sure not to overlook those you have not already counted. We don't want any surprises as the plan unfolds.

Some G&A items you might look for are

- Executive and supervisory salaries, including bonuses, that don't belong to any single department
- Office staff salaries and wages • Repairs and maintenance
- Utilities expenses • Telephone • Postage and messenger service
- Office supplies • Travel and entertainment
- Depreciation and amortization of office equipment • Insurance
- Taxes—federal, state, local, and property
- Auto expenses not already allocated to the consuming department
- Professional fees, such as legal and accounting

Management Fees

Companies with several divisions sometimes allocate their corporate office expenses to these divisions in the form of management fees. The corporate division takes these fees as income, and the divisions count them as expense. The financial plan must eliminate the income entirely and just count the expense. Here's how:

Corporate office financial plan:

Revenue from management fees charged	$50,000
Overhead expenses	(50,000)
Net income	$ -0-

Division A's financial plan:

Management fee expense charged by corporate office	$35,000

Division B's financial plan:

Management fee expense charged by corporate office	15,000
Total management fees paid by divisions	$50,000

Add management fees back at the division level, thus eliminating them as expense items on the division's financial plans. At the corporate level, remove the management fee revenue as an income item. All this adding and subtracting leaves the overhead expenses originally charged at the corporate level intact so they don't fall through the cracks.

For purposes of producing the projected income statement, the divisions that benefit from these costs absorb them. However, for cash flow purposes, eliminate corporate management fee income. This leaves the firm with just one corporate office expense, paid to outsiders, not within the company.

Opening Balance Sheet

The financial plan must begin with an opening balance sheet. This comes from the balance sheet accounts at the end of the prior operating period. It provides the beginning numbers used in the financial plan. Even if your firm is brand new, it still has an opening balance sheet, although it may have just two accounts:

- Cash
- Capital contributed by owners

Ratios and Statistics

Many experienced financial planners take some of their opening financial benchmarks from the beginning balance sheet. Then they convert the financial goals and targets to financial ratios. This creates convenient benchmarks against which to track changes in the financial plan throughout the planning period.

WORK PAPERS

The sources of information that went into the financial plan become more valuable as time passes. That's why astute planners prepare, maintain and update the sources of financial planning information. Very few of the people who receive a copy of the plan ever see the work papers. They generally remain in the financial director's possession. However, managers consult them frequently.

Work Paper Contents

Keep these things in your work paper files:

- A marked copy of the financial plan, showing work paper references for each assumption and number appearing in the financial plan
- Derivation of assumptions and explanations or references to the department's subplan from which they came
- Subschedules that compute specific figures flowing up to the projected financial statements.

An example of the subschedules contained in the work papers is the collection plan for accounts receivable. From this schedule you should be able to trace the complete derivation of cash inflows from collections. It should begin with the sales projections that create receivables. From there it should crank through using assumptions such as

- Customer payment habits
- Percentage of receivables that roll through the various aging buckets in the receivables system
- Bad debt

The result is a comprehensive plan for the collection system to produce both the cash inflows and the receivables balances presented on the face of the projected financial statements. Cash outflow from payment of accounts payable and funds inflow from borrowing are two more examples of detailed work paper subschedules supporting the financial plan.

Work papers should explain every assumption used in preparation of the financial plan. If the origin of an assumption isn't obvious from looking at the face of the financial plan, then create a work paper schedule or narrative explanation to clarify it.

Two-Way References

Number all work papers at the lower right using a colored pencil. This facilitates quickly flipping through them to find the right one. Referencing goes from the lead financial schedules in the financial plan to the work paper that explains each number.

However, referencing goes the other way too: from the work papers back up to the lead schedule. To do that, we mark references to the financial plan on the work papers. In some cases we'll refer these back to the appropriate line on the financial statement.

FINANCIAL SCHEDULES

Everyone sees the financial schedules presented in the financial plan. The level of detail presented varies depending on readers' familiarity with the operation. Larger firms in which people are unfamiliar with the financial operations of the company usually need more detail.

The purpose of the financial plan is to give a clear picture of exactly how the company plans to meet its financial goals. Don't include a lot of fluff that goes beyond that. Adding unnecessary data, superfluous schedules, and charts runs the risk of confusing people.

Supporting Information

Make sure the financial plan uses accounts that tie exactly to the general ledger. We need this congruity for purposes of tracking performance. This also helps avoid confusion among those looking for particular benchmarks.

Our financial plan begins with three financial statements:

- Balance sheet
- Income statement
- Statement of changes in financial condition

Balance Sheet

The company's projected balance sheet begins with the opening balances described earlier. From there, it evolves as the rest of the company's business plan unfolds.

Don't use the balance sheet to demonstrate computations of particular numbers. Put those in the work papers. The balance in accounts receivable is a case in point. A/R begins with the prior period ending balance. Sales increase it, and payments reduce it. After we write off uncollectable accounts, the balances rise again with more sales. All this is necessary information that belongs in the work papers.

Figure 13-1 shows the sources of some of the balance sheet information that flows from the assumptions and from the other financial statements and sub schedules.

Figure 13-1
Sources of Projected Balance Sheet Information

Balance Sheet Item	Source of Information
Cash	Statement of changes and/or statement of cash flows
Accounts receivable	Schedule of accounts receivable
Inventory	Production schedule/raw material purchase schedule
Prepaid expenses	Financial assumptions
Investments	Investment maturity schedule
Property, plant, and equipment	Schedule of fixed assets, capital expenditure schedule, and depreciation schedule
Furniture and fixtures	Schedule of fixed assets, capital expenditure schedule, and depreciation schedule
Other assets	Financial assumptions
Trade accounts payable	Schedule of trade accounts payable
Inventory accounts payable	Schedule of inventory accounts payable

Balance Sheet Item	Source of Information
Short-term debt	Debt repayment schedule
Deposits and advance payments	Schedule from sales department
Accrued income taxes payable	Computed from rate assumption and income statement
Accrued property taxes payable	Financial assumptions
Other liabilities	Financial assumptions
Partners' capital	Financial assumptions
Capital stock	Financial assumptions
Retained earnings (if a corporation)	Prior period balance sheet plus net income for this period

Income Statement

This is probably the most interesting report in the financial plan. Indeed, many of the financial targets appear on the income statement—profit, for instance. The income statement provides a convenient gauge for tracking actual performance against the plan.

Major sections of the income statement include the following.

Revenue

The largest component of projected revenue comes from the company's main business. However, be sure not to forget income from the lesser product lines, sale of assets such as equipment, and interest income. Additionally, many firms carry some sales over from one year to another because of accounting cutoff requirements.

If your company falls into this category, be sure you apply these carryover and cutoff rules consistently. We don't want to compare apples with oranges when tracking the actuals versus plan or when comparing one year to the next.

Cost of goods sold

Computation of cost of goods sold is sometimes complicated. That's why many financial plans compute it on a separate detailed subschedule in the work papers and report only the one number on the projected income statement. It's often good to test the CGS computations when preparing projected financial statements. Here's how:

Beginning inventory + purchases – ending inventory = cost of goods sold

Most of this information comes from the manufacturing plan. The ending inventory figure usually combines the safety stock with the amount left over after the planning period.

Other costs and expenses

All other costs associated with running the firm go in this section. These include such things as legal and accounting, interest expense, rent, and utilities.

Make sure that *other costs* include every expense not previously accounted for in the manufacturing operation.

Statement of Changes in Financial Position

The statement of changes combines the *results* from both the balance sheet and the income statement. It doesn't use assumptions from the rest of the business plan. Instead, it is purely a mathematical product of the interaction between these two financial statements.

The most valuable presentation of a statement of changes for a small business emphasizes cash. Here is the format to follow.

Sources of working capital converts net income (not a cash number) from the income statement into a source of working capital. The working capital items added to net income to recognize all cash sources include

- Depreciation and amortization
- Cash inflows from sale of capital stock, partnership contributions, and financing
- Paydowns of accounts receivable
- Reduction of inventory

Include in this section of the statement of changes anything from the income statement or balance sheet that is considered a source of working capital or cash.

Uses of working capital are such things as

- Purchase of capital equipment • Paydown of loans
- Repayment of balance due in accounts payable • Tax payments
- Payment of deposits • Expense prepayment

An easy way to make sure all the sources and uses of working capital hit the statement of changes is to compare each line of the balance sheet. Make sure that the changes from last period to this period appear on the statement of changes.

Many analysts prefer the statement of changes to compute the ending cash balance. Do this at the bottom as follows:

Beginning cash + cash sources - cash uses = ending cash

That's where the cash balance on the balance sheet comes from. If the balance sheet balances, it's a pretty good assumption that all three financial statements tie with each other. Figure 13-2 (pages 218-224) shows a sample financial plan.

Chapter 14 takes the next step and creates the cash flow plan.

[this page intentionally left blank]

Figure 13-2: Sample Financial Plan

COMPANY NAME
FINANCIAL PLAN ASSUMPTIONS
TIME PERIOD

	BEG BALANCE	MONTH 1	MONTH 2	MONTH 3	MONTH 4	MONTH 5	MONTH 6	MONTH 7	MONTH 8	MONTH 9	MONTH 10	MONTH 11	MONTH 12
ASSUMPTIONS													
BALANCE SHEET ASSUMPTIONS:													
CASH	100,000												
ACCTS RECEIVABLE ASSUMPTIONS:													
ACCOUNTS RECEIVABLE (% OF SALES)	350,000	50%	50%	50%	50%	50%	50%	50%	50%	50%	50%	50%	50%
BEGINNING BALANCE	350,000												
PERCENTAGE OF SALES ON CREDIT		100%	100%	100%	100%	100%	100%	100%	100%	100%	100%	100%	100%
COLLECTION RATES:													
% COLLECTED CURRENT		65%	65%	65%	65%	65%	65%	65%	65%	65%	65%	65%	65%
% COLLECTED W/IN 30 DAYS		50%	50%	50%	50%	50%	50%	50%	50%	50%	50%	50%	50%
% COLLECTED W/IN 60 DAYS		98%	98%	98%	98%	98%	98%	98%	98%	98%	98%	98%	98%
% COLLECTED W/IN 90 DAYS		85%	85%	85%	85%	85%	85%	85%	85%	85%	85%	85%	85%
BAD DEBT %		2%	2%	2%	2%	2%	2%	2%	2%	2%	2%	2%	2%
INVENTORY (% OF SALES)	200,000	35%	35%	35%	35%	35%	35%	35%	35%	35%	35%	35%	35%
CORPORATE OFFICES	2,500,000	2,500,000	2,500,000	2,500,000	2,000,000	2,000,000	2,000,000	2,000,000	2,000,000	2,000,000	2,000,000	2,000,000	2,000,000
MACHINERY & EQUIPMENT	1,500,000	1,500,000	1,500,000	1,500,000	1,000,000	1,000,000	1,000,000	1,000,000	1,000,000	1,000,000	1,000,000	1,000,000	1,000,000
FURNITURE & FIXTURES	1,000,000	1,000,000	1,000,000	1,000,000	1,200,000	1,200,000	1,200,000	1,200,000	1,200,000	1,200,000	1,200,000	1,200,000	1,200,000
LEASEHOLD IMPROVEMENTS	750,000	750,000	750,000	750,000	800,000	800,000	800,000	800,000	800,000	800,000	800,000	800,000	800,000
ACCTS PAYABLE ASSUMPTIONS:													
ACCOUNTS PAYABLE (BEG. BAL. ONLY)	325,000												
ACCOUNTS PAYABLE (% OF INVENTORY)		75%	75%	75%	60%	60%	60%	60%	60%	60%	60%	60%	60%
BEGINNING BALANCE	325,000												
% OF INVENTORY PURCHASES ON CREDIT		75%	75%	75%	65%	65%	65%	65%	65%	65%	65%	65%	65%
PAYMENT RATES:													
% PAID CURRENT		75%	75%	75%	75%	75%	75%	75%	75%	75%	75%	75%	75%
% PAID W/IN 30 DAYS		40%	40%	40%	40%	40%	40%	40%	40%	40%	40%	40%	40%
% PAID W/IN 60 DAYS		85%	85%	85%	85%	85%	85%	85%	85%	85%	85%	85%	85%
% PAID W/IN 90 DAYS		100%	100%	100%	100%	100%	100%	100%	100%	100%	100%	100%	100%
ACCRUED INCOME TAXES PAYABLE	0												
BANK NOTE	500,000	500,000	500,000	500,000	500,000	500,000	500,000	500,000	500,000	500,000	500,000	500,000	500,000
REVOLVING LINE OF CREDIT	250,000	250,000	250,000	250,000	250,000	250,000	250,000	250,000	250,000	250,000	250,000	250,000	250,000

ACCTS RECEIVABLE ASSUMPTIONS:
NOTE: The A/R schedule assumes collections from prior periods not shown in the planning horizon.
Additionally, A/R is assumed to be a fixed percentage of sales. This percentage can be altered in the assumptions.

ACCTS PAYABLE ASSUMPTIONS:
NOTE: The A/P schedule assumes that only inventory is included in the A/P balance. In practice this is not usually the case.

218

	C1	C2	C3	C4	C5	C6	C7	C8	C9	C10	C11	C12	C13
RETAINED EARNINGS	100,000												
COMMON STOCK	3,800,000	3,800,000	3,800,000	4,000,000	4,000,000	4,000,000	4,000,000	4,000,000	4,000,000	4,000,000	4,000,000	4,000,000	4,000,000
PREFERRED STOCK	625,000	625,000	625,000	800,000	800,000	800,000	800,000	800,000	800,000	800,000	800,000	800,000	800,000
DIVIDENDS PD ON COMMON STOCK	N/A	0	0	0	0	0	0	0	0	0	0	0	0
DIVIDENDS PD ON PREFERRED STOCK	N/A	0	0	0	0	0	0	0	0	0	0	0	0
INCOME STATEMENT ASSUMPTIONS:													
SALES	550,000	575,000	650,000	700,000	675,000	650,000	625,000	600,000	575,000	550,000	525,000	500,000	
COST OF GOODS SOLD (% OF SALES)	30%	30%	25%	25%	25%	25%	25%	25%	25%	25%	25%	25%	

NOTE: CGS as a % of sales keys off of the assumption in month #1. The purpose was to use this in the sensitivity analysis.

	C1	C2	C3	C4	C5	C6	C7	C8	C9	C10	C11	C12	C13
ADVERTISING (% OF SALES)	5%	5%	2%	2%	2%	2%	2%	2%	2%	2%	2%	2%	
BAD DEBT EXPENSE (% OF A/R)	2%	2%	5%	5%	5%	5%	5%	5%	5%	5%	5%	5%	
COMMISSION EXPENSE (% OF SALES)	10%	10%	10%	10%	10%	10%	10%	10%	10%	10%	10%	10%	

NOTE: Commissions as a % of sales keys off of the assumption in month #1 and computes that assumption for every other month. The purpose was to use this in the sensitivity analysis.

	C1	C2	C3	C4	C5	C6	C7	C8	C9	C10	C11	C12	C13
DEPRECIATION:													
CORPORATE OFFICES	500,000	2,500	2,500	2,500	2,500	2,500	2,500	2,500	2,500	2,500	2,500	2,500	
MACHINERY & EQUIPMENT	100,000	1,800	1,800	1,800	1,800	1,800	1,800	1,800	1,800	1,800	1,800	1,800	
FURNITURE & FIXTURES	75,000	1,500	1,500	1,500	1,500	1,500	1,500	1,500	1,500	1,500	1,500	1,500	
LEASEHOLD IMPROVEMENTS	125,000	1,750	1,750	1,750	1,750	1,750	1,750	1,750	1,750	1,750	1,750	1,750	
INSURANCE													
SALARIES & WAGES (% OF SALES)	5,750 / 14%	5,750 / 14%	5,750 / 14%	5,750 / 14%	5,750 / 14%	5,750 / 14%	5,750 / 14%	5,750 / 14%	5,750 / 14%	5,750 / 14%	5,750 / 14%	5,750 / 14%	

NOTE: Salaries as a % of sales keys off of the assumption in month #1 and computes that assumption for every other month. The purpose was to use this in the sensitivity analysis.

	C1	C2	C3	C4	C5	C6	C7	C8	C9	C10	C11	C12	C13
PAYROLL TAXES (% OF SALARIES)	12%	12%	12%	12%	12%	12%	12%	12%	12%	12%	12%	12%	
UTILITIES (% OF SALES)	8%	8%	8%	8%	8%	8%	8%	8%	8%	8%	8%	8%	
TRAVEL & ENTERTAINMENT (% OF SALES)	5%	5%	5%	5%	5%	5%	5%	5%	5%	5%	5%	5%	
TAX ACCRUAL %	38%	38%	38%	38%	38%	38%	38%	38%	38%	38%	38%	38%	

COMPANY NAME
PROSPECTIVE BALANCE SHEET
TIME PERIOD

	BEG BALANCE	MONTH 1	MONTH 2	MONTH 3	MONTH 4	MONTH 5	MONTH 6	MONTH 7	MONTH 8	MONTH 9	MONTH 10	MONTH 11	MONTH 12
CURRENT ASSETS:													
CASH	100,000	167,579	170,397	249,567	1,502,698	1,643,474	1,791,641	1,928,904	2,057,474	2,177,445	2,288,911	2,391,966	2,486,704
ACCOUNTS RECEIVABLE	350,000	376,250	395,625	466,000	535,000	587,000	625,625	667,250	707,000	744,875	780,875	815,000	847,250
INVENTORY	200,000	192,500	201,250	227,500	245,000	236,250	227,500	218,750	210,000	201,250	192,500	183,750	175,000
TOTAL CURRENT ASSETS	$650,000	$736,329	$767,272	$943,067	$2,282,698	$2,466,724	$2,644,766	$2,814,904	$2,974,474	$3,123,570	$3,262,286	$3,390,716	$3,508,954
FIXED ASSETS:													
CORPORATE OFFICES	2,500,000	2,500,000	2,500,000	2,500,000	2,000,000	2,000,000	2,000,000	2,000,000	2,000,000	2,000,000	2,000,000	2,000,000	2,000,000
MACHINERY & EQUIPMENT	1,500,000	1,500,000	1,500,000	1,500,000	1,000,000	1,000,000	1,000,000	1,000,000	1,000,000	1,000,000	1,000,000	1,000,000	1,000,000
FURNITURE & FIXTURES	1,000,000	1,000,000	1,000,000	1,000,000	1,200,000	1,200,000	1,200,000	1,200,000	1,200,000	1,200,000	1,200,000	1,200,000	1,200,000
LEASEHOLD IMPROVEMENTS	750,000	750,000	750,000	750,000	800,000	800,000	800,000	800,000	800,000	800,000	800,000	800,000	800,000
SUBTOTAL FIXED ASSETS	$5,750,000	$5,750,000	$5,750,000	$5,750,000	$5,000,000	$5,000,000	$5,000,000	$5,000,000	$5,000,000	$5,000,000	$5,000,000	$5,000,000	$5,000,000
ACCUMULATED DEPRECIATION	800,000	807,550	815,100	822,650	830,200	837,750	845,300	852,850	860,400	867,950	875,500	883,050	890,600
FIXED ASSETS	$4,950,000	$4,942,450	$4,934,900	$4,927,350	$4,169,800	$4,162,250	$4,154,700	$4,147,150	$4,139,600	$4,132,050	$4,124,500	$4,116,950	$4,109,400
TOTAL ASSETS	$5,600,000	$5,678,779	$5,702,172	$5,870,417	$6,452,498	$6,628,974	$6,799,466	$6,962,054	$7,114,074	$7,255,620	$7,386,786	$7,507,666	$7,618,354
CURRENT LIABILITIES:													
ACCOUNTS PAYABLE	325,000	279,844	173,109	154,875	161,766	149,231	141,225	135,975	130,725	125,475	120,225	114,975	109,725
ACCRUED INCOME TAXES PAYABLE	0	47,095	96,544	167,406	243,478	315,302	383,132	446,910	506,673	562,455	614,293	662,223	706,279
REVOLVING LINE OF CREDIT	250,000	250,000	250,000	250,000	250,000	250,000	250,000	250,000	250,000	250,000	250,000	250,000	250,000
CURRENT LIABILITIES	$575,000	$576,939	$519,653	$572,281	$655,244	$714,533	$774,357	$832,885	$887,398	$937,930	$984,518	$1,027,198	$1,066,004
BANK NOTE	500,000	500,000	500,000	500,000	500,000	500,000	500,000	500,000	500,000	500,000	500,000	500,000	500,000
STOCKHOLDERS' EQUITY:													
COMMON STOCK	3,800,000	3,800,000	3,800,000	3,800,000	4,000,000	4,000,000	4,000,000	4,000,000	4,000,000	4,000,000	4,000,000	4,000,000	4,000,000
PREFERRED STOCK	625,000	625,000	625,000	625,000	800,000	800,000	800,000	800,000	800,000	800,000	800,000	800,000	800,000
RETAINED EARNINGS	100,000	176,840	257,519	373,136	497,254	614,440	725,110	829,169	926,676	1,017,690	1,102,268	1,180,469	1,252,350
TOTAL STOCKHOLDERS' EQUITY	$4,525,000	$4,601,840	$4,682,519	$4,798,136	$5,297,254	$5,414,440	$5,525,110	$5,629,169	$5,726,676	$5,817,690	$5,902,268	$5,980,469	$6,052,350
TTL LIAB. & STOCKHOLDERS' EQUITY	$5,600,000	$5,678,779	$5,702,172	$5,870,417	$6,452,498	$6,628,974	$6,799,466	$6,962,054	$7,114,074	$7,255,620	$7,386,786	$7,507,666	$7,618,354

COMPANY NAME
PROSPECTIVE INCOME STATEMENT 199X

	MONTH 1	MONTH 2	MONTH 3	MONTH 4	MONTH 5	MONTH 6	MONTH 7	MONTH 8	MONTH 9	MONTH 10	MONTH 11	MONTH 12	TOTAL YEAR
SALES	$550,000	$575,000	$650,000	$700,000	$675,000	$650,000	$625,000	$600,000	$575,000	$550,000	$525,000	$500,000	$7,175,000
COST OF GOODS SOLD	165,000	172,500	162,500	175,000	168,750	162,500	156,250	150,000	143,750	137,500	131,250	125,000	1,850,000
GROSS MARGIN ($)	$385,000	$402,500	$487,500	$525,000	$506,250	$487,500	$468,750	$450,000	$431,250	$412,500	$393,750	$375,000	$5,325,000
GROSS MARGIN (%)	70%	70%	75%	75%	75%	75%	75%	75%	75%	75%	75%	75%	74%
ADVERTISING	27,500	28,750	13,000	14,000	13,500	13,000	12,500	12,000	11,500	11,000	10,500	10,000	177,250
BAD DEBT EXPENSE	7,525	7,912	23,300	26,750	29,350	31,281	33,363	35,350	37,244	39,044	40,750	42,363	354,231
COMMISSION EXPENSE	55,000	57,500	65,000	70,000	67,500	65,000	62,500	60,000	57,500	55,000	52,500	50,000	717,500
DEPRECIATION:													
CORPORATE OFFICES	2,500	2,500	2,500	2,500	2,500	2,500	2,500	2,500	2,500	2,500	2,500	2,500	30,000
MACHINERY & EQUIPMENT	1,800	1,800	1,800	1,800	1,800	1,800	1,800	1,800	1,800	1,800	1,800	1,800	21,600
FURNITURE & FIXTURES	1,500	1,500	1,500	1,500	1,500	1,500	1,500	1,500	1,500	1,500	1,500	1,500	18,000
LEASEHOLD IMPROVEMENTS	1,750	1,750	1,750	1,750	1,750	1,750	1,750	1,750	1,750	1,750	1,750	1,750	21,000
INSURANCE	5,750	5,750	5,750	5,750	5,750	5,750	5,750	5,750	5,750	5,750	5,750	5,750	69,000
SALARIES & WAGES	77,000	80,500	91,000	98,000	94,500	91,000	87,500	84,000	80,500	77,000	73,500	70,000	1,004,500
PAYROLL TAXES	9,240	9,660	10,920	11,760	11,340	10,920	10,500	10,080	9,660	9,240	8,820	8,400	120,540
UTILITIES	44,000	46,000	52,000	56,000	54,000	52,000	50,000	48,000	46,000	44,000	42,000	40,000	574,000
TRAVEL & ENTERTAINMENT	27,500	28,750	32,500	35,000	33,750	32,500	31,250	30,000	28,750	27,500	26,250	25,000	358,750
TOTAL COSTS AND EXPENSES	$261,065	$272,373	$301,020	$324,810	$317,240	$309,001	$300,913	$292,730	$284,454	$276,084	$267,620	$259,062	$3,466,371
NET INCOME BEFORE TAX	$123,935	$130,128	$186,480	$200,190	$189,010	$178,499	$167,837	$157,270	$146,796	$136,416	$126,130	$115,937	$1,858,629
TAX ACCRUAL	47,095	49,448	70,862	76,072	71,824	67,830	63,778	59,763	55,783	51,838	47,929	44,056	706,279
NET INCOME	76,840	80,679	115,618	124,118	117,186	110,669	104,059	97,507	91,014	84,578	78,201	71,881	1,152,350

COMPANY NAME
PROSPECTIVE STATEMENT OF CHANGES IN FINANCIAL
199X

	MONTH 1	MONTH 2	MONTH 3	MONTH 4	MONTH 5	MONTH 6	MONTH 7	MONTH 8	MONTH 9	MONTH 10	MONTH 11	MONTH 12
FINANCIAL RESOURCES PROVIDED:												
CASH FROM OPERATIONS	$76,840	$80,679	$115,618	$124,118	$117,186	$110,669	$104,059	$97,507	$91,014	$84,578	$78,201	$71,881
ADD NON-WORKING CAPITAL EXPENDITURES:												
DEPRECIATION	7,550	7,550	7,550	7,550	7,550	7,550	7,550	7,550	7,550	7,550	7,550	7,550
TAX ACCRUAL	47,095	49,448	70,862	76,072	71,824	67,830	63,778	59,763	55,783	51,838	47,929	44,056
TTL WORKING CAPITAL FROM OPERATIONS	$131,485	$137,677	$194,030	$207,740	$196,560	$186,049	$175,387	$164,820	$154,346	$143,966	$133,680	$123,487
EFFECTS OF CHANGES IN COMPONENTS OF WORKING CAPITAL ON CASH:												
INCREASE IN ACCOUNTS RECEIVABLE	(26,250)	(19,375)	(70,375)	(69,000)	(52,000)	(38,625)	(41,625)	(39,750)	(37,875)	(36,000)	(34,125)	(32,250)
INCREASE IN INVENTORY	7,500	(8,750)	(26,250)	(17,500)	8,750	8,750	8,750	8,750	8,750	8,750	8,750	8,750
DECREASE IN ACCOUNTS PAYABLE	(45,156)	(106,734)	(18,234)	6,691	(12,534)	(8,006)	(5,250)	(5,250)	(5,250)	(5,250)	(5,250)	(5,250)
CASH FROM OPERATIONS	$67,579	$2,818	$79,171	$128,131	$140,776	$148,167	$137,263	$128,570	$119,971	$111,466	$103,055	$94,738
DRAWDOWN ON LINE OF CREDIT	0	0	0	0	0	0	0	0	0	0	0	0
PROCEEDS FROM BANK NOTE	0	0	0	200,000	0	0	0	0	0	0	0	0
ISSUANCE OF COMMON STOCK	0	0	0	175,000	0	0	0	0	0	0	0	0
ISSUANCE OF PREFERRED STOCK	0	0	0		0	0	0	0	0	0	0	0
TOTAL FINANCIAL RESOURCES PROVIDED	$67,579	$2,818	$79,171	$503,131	$140,776	$148,167	$137,263	$128,570	$119,971	$111,466	$103,055	$94,738
FINANCIAL RESOURCES APPLIED:												
PURCHASE OF CAPITAL ASSETS	0	0	0	(750,000)	0	0	0	0	0	0	0	0
DIVIDENDS PAID TO PREF'D STOCK	0	0	0	0	0	0	0	0	0	0	0	0
DIVIDENDS PAID TO COMMON STOCK	0	0	0	0	0	0	0	0	0	0	0	0
TTL FINANCIAL RESOURCES APPLIED	$0	$0	$0	($750,000)	$0	$0	$0	$0	$0	$0	$0	$0
INCREASE (DECREASE) IN CASH	$67,579	$2,818	$79,171	$1,253,131	$140,776	$148,167	$137,263	$128,570	$119,971	$111,466	$103,055	$94,738
BEGINING CASH BALANCE	100,000	167,579	170,397	249,567	1,502,698	1,643,474	1,791,641	1,928,904	2,057,474	2,177,445	2,288,911	2,391,966
ENDING CASH BALANCE	$167,579	$170,397	$249,567	$1,502,698	$1,643,474	$1,791,641	$1,928,904	$2,057,474	$2,177,445	$2,288,911	$2,391,966	$2,486,704

COMPANY NAME
SCHEDULE OF ACCOUNTS RECEIVABLE
PLANNING PERIOD 199X

	MONTH 1	MONTH 2	MONTH 3	MONTH 4	MONTH 5	MONTH 6	MONTH 7	MONTH 8	MONTH 9	MONTH 10	MONTH 11	MONTH 12
BEGINNING BALANCE	350,000	376,250	395,625	466,000	535,000	587,000	825,625	667,250	707,000	744,875	780,875	815,000
PLUS CREDIT SALES	275,000	287,500	325,000	350,000	337,500	325,000	312,500	300,000	287,500	275,000	282,500	250,000
LESS COLLECTIONS:												
FROM 90 DAYS AGO	(45,500)	(45,500)	(45,500)	(35,750)	(37,375)	(42,250)	(45,500)	(43,875)	(42,250)	(40,625)	(39,000)	(37,375)
FROM 60 DAYS AGO	168,000	168,000	132,000	138,000	156,000	168,000	162,000	156,000	150,000	144,000	138,000	132,000
FROM 30 DAYS AGO	(52,500)	(41,250)	(43,125)	(48,750)	(52,500)	(50,625)	(48,750)	(46,875)	(45,000)	(43,125)	(41,250)	(39,375)
FROM CURRENT SALES	178,750	186,875	211,250	227,500	219,375	211,250	203,125	195,000	186,875	178,750	170,625	162,500
ENDING ACCOUNTS RECEIVABLE	$376,250	$395,625	$466,000	$535,000	$587,000	$825,625	$667,250	$707,000	$744,875	$780,875	$815,000	$847,250

COMPANY NAME
SCHEDULE OF ACCOUNTS PAYABLE
PLANNING PERIOD 199X

	MONTH 1	MONTH 2	MONTH 3	MONTH 4	MONTH 5	MONTH 6	MONTH 7	MONTH 8	MONTH 9	MONTH 10	MONTH 11	MONTH 12
BEGINNING BALANCE	$325,000	$279,844	$173,109	$154,875	$161,766	$149,231	$141,225	$135,975	$130,725	$125,475	$120,225	$114,975
PLUS CREDIT PURCHASES (INTY ONLY)	144,375	150,938	170,625	147,000	141,750	136,500	131,250	126,000	120,750	115,500	110,250	105,000
LESS PAYMENTS:												
FOR CURRENT PURCHASES	106,281	113,203	127,969	110,250	106,312	102,375	98,438	94,500	90,563	86,625	82,688	78,750
FOR PURCHASES 30 DAYS AGO	(113,750)	(50,531)	(52,828)	(59,719)	(51,450)	(49,612)	(47,775)	(45,938)	(44,100)	(42,263)	(40,425)	(38,588)
FOR PURCHASES 60 DAYS AGO	146,250	146,250	64,969	67,922	76,781	66,150	63,787	61,425	59,062	56,700	54,337	51,975
FOR PURCHASES 90 DAYS AGO	48,750	48,750	48,750	21,656	22,641	25,594	22,050	21,263	20,475	19,688	18,900	18,113
ENDING ACCOUNTS PAYABLE	$279,844	$173,109	$154,875	$161,766	$149,231	$141,225	$135,975	$130,725	$125,475	$120,225	$114,975	$109,725

SENSITIVITY ANALYSIS
COST OF GOODS SOLD % VS. YEAR-END NET INCOME
PLAN YEAR 199X

CGS %	NET INCOME
50%	$1,012,850
45%	1,082,600
40%	1,082,600
35%	1,117,475
30%	1,152,350
25%	1,187,225
20%	1,222,100
15%	1,256,975

COMPANY NAME
SENSITIVITY ANALYSIS
SALES COMMISSION % & SALARY % VS.
YEAR-END NET INCOME
PLAN YEAR 199X

	SALES COMMISSION %				
SALARY %	14%	12%	10%	8%	6%
19%	$751,985	$759,623	$767,262	$774,900	$782,538
17%	840,955	848,593	856,232	863,870	871,508
15%	929,925	937,563	945,202	952,840	960,478
13%	1,018,895	1,026,533	1,034,172	1,041,810	1,049,448
11%	1,107,865	1,115,503	1,123,142	1,130,780	1,138,418

Chapter 14

Creating the Cash Flow Plan

OVERVIEW

Creating a cash flow plan isn't difficult once the financial plan is in place. Chapter 14 shows how the cash flow plan evolves from the financial plan. For small businesses that are strapped for cash, this part of the planning effort answers two all-important questions:

- How much do we need? • When do we need it?

The biggest problem in creating the cash flow plan is to distinguish between *financial* transactions appearing in the company's projected financial statements and *cash* transactions. They aren't the same. Companies that attempt to view projected net income as disposable cash soon find themselves without funds to pay their bills.

This stems from the difference between the accrual basis of accounting and the cash basis. Most companies use the accrual basis. This automatically creates a timing difference between recognition of income and expense items and the arrival of spendable cash.

The cash flow plan is really a mathematical derivation from components of the business plan already created. It doesn't really create any new ideas. Rather, it uses those generated by others. It tells us the firm's cash balance at the end of every month throughout the planning horizon.

Places in the business plan other than the cash flow plan correct inadequate cash balances. An example is the cash shortfall that frequently hits companies toward the end of their slack season. By then all receivables from the busy season have been collected. The firm has already stretched its payables to their maximum, and now the creditors are demanding payment.

The cash flow plan identifies the timing and amount of additional cash required. The controller or treasurer then takes steps to adjust the business plan to accommodate the company's cash needs. This may involve doing something in the financial arena, such as borrowing. Alternatively, there might be something in the major purchases plan or the wages and salaries plan that needs changing. Once the problem is identified, the cash flow plan continues cranking out results again until it finds a solution.

STRUCTURING THE CASH FLOW PLAN

The cash flow plan has a specific purpose: Identify the cash balance throughout the planning horizon. Its structure is simple:

Beginning cash balance + cash inflows – cash outflows = ending cash balance

The ending cash balance in one period becomes the next period's beginning cash balance. The projected balance sheet uses this bottom-line number in the cash account balance, which usually appears at the top of the statement.

The complicating factors in creating the cash flow plan involve the timing of cash inflows and outflows. We want enough *spendable* cash available to meet the firm's obligations without incurring unnecessary interest expense from borrowing.

Time Horizons

The cash flow plan uses two different time horizons. The first is month by month, just as in the financial plan. This matches the timing used in the rest of the business plan. It provides a good mechanism for tracking the company's planned cash position.

The second time horizon focuses on the actual money available to pay the company's obligations. It is much more detailed in terms of time periods and shows

- The first week by day
- The first month by week
- The first quarter by month

Many companies update this schedule throughout the year as the business plan unfolds. It provides not only a detailed estimate of cash position but also a monitoring mechanism to remind everyone of anticipated cash inflows and outflows. If these aren't forthcoming, then someone knows when and where to look for them.

IDENTIFYING CASH INFLOWS

Most companies have a variety of cash inflows coming in throughout the year. The cash flow plan identifies each one in terms of

- Timing
- Amount
- Source
- Relation to the forecasted balance sheet and income statement

Figure 14-1 lists some of the cash inflows you might put into your cash flow plan.

Figure 14-1
Sources of Cash Inflow

- Cash sales
- Collection of accounts receivable
- Additional contributed capital
- Sale of stock

- Sale of bonds
- Borrowing
- Insurance settlements
- Lawsuit settlements
- Maturing investments
- Sale of assets
- Payment received from installment sales
- Payment received on loans made by the company

Collection of Accounts Receivable

Unless most of your firm's sales are to the retail public for cash, collection of accounts receivable is probably your largest source of cash inflow. The cash flow plan builds the collection segment of the financial plan, shown in the schedules at the back of Chapter 13.

Measuring cash inflow from receivables involves understanding the proportion of sales that hit the receivables system. It also requires knowledge of your customers.

Assumptions of the cash collection plan

Like any part of the business plan, the projected cash flow requires several assumptions. Each is subject to change. Indeed, as the plan unfolds, you'll probably update the collections plan to better reflect actual experience. This makes the cash flow plan that much more accurate as the year goes by.

The assumptions required in the collections plan include

- Accounts receivable balances for the months prior to the start of the cash flow plan
- Percentage of all sales made on credit that hit the A/R system
- Percentage of new credit sales paid within thirty days
- Percentage of new credit sales paid within sixty days
- Percentage of new credit sales paid within ninety days
- Percentage of new credit sales uncollectable

Using these assumptions, it's just a matter of cranking the arithmetic through. New credit sales roll into the receivables system, and payments reduce the balance in accordance with our assumptions. What's left is the ending receivables balance. This flows to the next month. Figure 14-2 shows a simple collections model that computes cash inflow from credit sales.

Notice how the collections from thirty, sixty, and ninety days ago reach back into the prior year. Our cash flow plan recognizes transactions that took place prior to the start of the current planning horizon. This happens for both cash receipts and disbursements.

Figure 14-2
Cash Inflow from Credit Sales

	January	February	March
Sales	$350	$400	$600
% of credit sales	75%	75%	75%
Collections rates:			
% current	50%	50%	50%
% in 30 days	65%	65%	65%
% in 60 days	85%	85%	85%
% in 90 days	98%	98%	98%
% uncollectable	2%	2%	2%
Beginning A/R	$400	$436	$521
Add new credit sales	262	300	450
Less collections:			
From 90 days ago	25	15	25
From 60 days ago	30	20	52
From 30 days ago	40	30	45
From current sales	131	150	225
Ending A/R	$436	$521	$624
Cash collected	226	215	347

Additionally, note the flexibility of the assumptions. This allows us to change the cash flow plan as we gain experience about our customers' payment habits. Finally, note that the change in the accounts receivable balance differs from the actual cash received from collections.

Additional Sources of Cash Inflow

Most companies have other sources of cash inflow besides collection of accounts receivable. Insurance settlements frequently fall into this category. So do settlements of lawsuits. Both insurance companies and losing litigants are notorious for dragging their feet when making settlement payments.

People tend to forget nonroutine payments during the crush of their normal responsibilities. Including them in the cash flow plan creates a reminder.

Investment maturity schedules

Other cash inflows sometimes come from companies' investments of excess cash. Many firms have extensive holdings with a variety of maturity dates. There's no place better than the cash flow plan to keep these dates straight.

If we see that a particular investment at a certain bank or brokerage firm is due to mature on a certain date, we look for the money to hit our account. If it doesn't, then we contact the institution immediately and find out what happened.

If your firm has investments, be sure to create a maturity schedule and enter it in the cash flow plan. Include these items in the schedule:

- Security description • CUSIP number if applicable
- Maturity date • Gross amount • Interest income expected
- Net amount • Institution holding the investment
- Company's account that should be receiving the money

Knowing what to expect, when, and where go a long way in making sure the company receives the funds as promised.

Notes receivable

Few small businesses normally loan money. However, many find themselves in exactly that position at one time or another. Often a loan or note arises from the sale of an asset.

Notes and loans usually run for several years. As people change jobs and turn over, the details of who owes what and when sometimes get lost. Including such nonroutine payment receipts on the cash inflow plan (as well as the projected balance sheet and income statement) prevents them from being forgotten.

Contributed capital

Sometimes small businesses have scheduled payments from partners for their capital contributions. Make sure these get posted to the cash flow plan. Most partners won't forget. However, unless the plan recognizes all sources of cash inflow, it can't accurately forecast ending cash balances and the amount of additional needed (or excess available) funds.

IDENTIFYING CASH OUTFLOWS

The key to controlling cash outflows is knowing the disbursement schedule and managing it. The cash outflow plan facilitates this. One thing we don't want is to omit a category of cash disbursement, then finalize the business plan, only to discover an unplanned cash shortfall.

Accounts Payable

Routine accounts payable are the largest cash outflow of most small businesses. This includes payments for inventory purchased and all the other operating expenses of the company. Companies whose payment policies vary often separate their trade payables from their inventory payables.

Many firms discover that the terms of payment for most of their accounts fit into just a few categories. For example, say you studied your accounts payable portfolio and determined the following normal pay dates:

- 20 percent have terms of 2/10, net/30
- 10 percent have terms of 1/20, net/30
- 50 percent are due in thirty days with no discount terms
- 5 percent have no payment due date stated on their invoices

- 15 percent have special terms exceeding thirty days negotiated by the purchasing department

Further, say that your payment policy is to

- Take all trade discounts.
- Age all other payables forty-five days regardless of thirty-day payment terms.

Now you have a good idea of *when* the expenses identified in the forecast income statement actually require cash disbursement.

Compilation of a payables forecast requires these two additional assumptions as well:

- Accounts payable balances for the two months prior to the start of the cash flow plan
- Percentage of all expenses using trade credit that hit the A/P system

Using the same technique as for the collections forecast, we're in a position to identify the cash outflow resulting from accounts payable. Figure 14-3 illustrates the assumptions used and their results.

Figure 14-3
Disbursements Plan

	January	February	March
Purchases	$500	$450	$600
% of credit purchases	85%	85%	85%
Payment rates:			
% paid in 10 days	10%	10%	10%
% paid in 20 days	20%	20%	20%
% paid in 30 days	50%	50%	50%
% paid in 45 days	15%	15%	15%
% paid in more than 45 days	5%	5%	5%
Beginning A/P	$400	$334	$364
Add new purchases	425	383	510
Less disbursements:			
From 10 days ago	43	38	51
From 20 days ago	86	76	102
From 30 days ago	212	218	255
From 45 days ago	150	21	19
From more than 45 days ago			
Ending A/P	$334	$364	$447
Cash disbursed	491	353	427

Notice that January shows a $150 payment from the prior month (forty-five days ago). This is exactly the type of payment our cash outflow plan should capture. That payment could have been anything: a tax payment, for example, or a deposit for a major purchase already scheduled elsewhere in the business plan. The point is that once it's been identified and scheduled for disbursement, the cash flow plan can deal with it.

Also note that the change in the accounts payable balance differs from the actual cash disbursed. The difference is the beginning balance and the payables that came into A/P during the month.

Other Disbursements

Along with accounts payable, our cash outflow plan includes the nonroutine payments that so often catch unwary planners by surprise. These include.

- Deposits • Income tax payments • Property tax payments
- Payroll tax payments • Principal and interest on debt
- Major purchases • Dividends paid to shareholders
- Rent payments—especially when they change

When creating the cash outflow schedules, be sure to note items appearing on the projected income statement that are *accrued* for a particular period but not necessarily paid in that period. Employee and executive bonuses often fall into this category. Sometimes a company declares a bonus earned on, say, December 31, but actually pays it on January 3.

That way the company counts it as a current business expense, but the employee doesn't pay tax on it (except for withholding) for fifteen months (January 3 to April 15 of the next year). Some companies get around that by legally counting this as payment to someone who gets a Form 1099 and isn't subject to withholding. However, there too, the employee must pay estimated taxes.

Shareholder dividends always fall into this "deferred payment" category. The board of directors declares a cash dividend on a particular date for shareholders of record as of a certain date. However, the *payment* date usually isn't for at least thirty days thereafter.

Debt payments

Be sure to include both principal and interest payments for outstanding debt and their due dates on the cash flow plan. Since many companies have several debt payments, to avoid confusion, list each separately on the disbursement schedule. Additionally, many companies show principal and interest amounts separately. This answers the question, "Did you include the principal pay down?" before it's asked. Further, it provides two different numbers that tie to two different forecasted financial statements:

- Interest expense ties to the interest expense line on the forecast income statement.

- Principal paydown ties to the difference between two months' debt balances on the balance sheet.

If these numbers don't all tie, then one of the statements omitted something.

Watch for debts with balloon payments or lines of credit with annual cleanup requirements. Additionally, keep track of term loan expiration dates. If one or more such loans expire during the planning period, assess the likelihood of rolling them over. If the probability isn't high, then the cash flow plan should provide for this funds requirement. Loan repayments use large amounts of cash. It never hurts to identify these disbursements well ahead of time so you can plan their funding.

If your firm issued bonds, you'll probably disburse interest payments twice a year. The cash flow plan must provide for available ("good") funds in the disbursing agent's account on the bond interest payment date.

Tax payments

Tax payments come at various times throughout the year. Income tax is due either on April 15 or after your firm's fiscal year-end if it doesn't use a calendar year. However, your firm may have filed for an extension. In that case, the actual payment probably isn't due for another six months.

Some companies have operations in several states. If you pay income tax or property tax in other states as well as in your corporate state, include that on the disbursement plan as well.

Changes in wages and salaries

Sometimes we can forecast significant changes in wages and salaries at the beginning of the planning period. This doesn't just include the standard rate increases and bonuses already projected in the salary plan. If you run a unionized company, for instance, your labor contract may come up for renewal during the planning period. Inclusion of what you think might be the final settlement makes the cash flow plan that much more accurate.

Changes in suppliers' terms

If your firm has an operating history, perhaps it also has working relationships with its suppliers and vendors. Use these to help formulate a more accurate cash flow plan. For example, ask your purchasers or major suppliers questions regarding

- Price changes • Changes in purchase terms
- Changes in product features that may alter your firm's usage of raw materials or subassemblies

Material changes in these items affect the cash flow plan.

TYING WITH OTHER PLAN COMPONENTS

The cash flow plan takes information from other parts of the business plan. Most of this appears on the forecast income statement and balance sheet. However, make sure the cash flow plan picks it up as well. The statement that we use to forecast cash balances is the statement of changes in financial condition—cash basis. This statement utilizes the changes in both the income statement and balance sheet that affect monthly cash balances throughout the planning horizon. Figure 14-4 shows how the cash flow plan ties with the financial plan.

Figure 14-4
Matching the Cash Flow Plan with the Financial Plan

Cash Flow Plan	Financial Plan
Cash from operations	Income statement—net income
Depreciation	Income statement—expenses
Amortization	Income statement—expenses
Accrued taxes	Income statement—tax provision
Collections from accounts receivable	Balance sheet—change in A/R balance and collections subschedule
Collections from notes receivable	Balance sheet—change in account balance and notes receivable subschedule
Proceeds from borrowing—includes loans and bond issue	Balance sheet—change in liability accounts
Proceeds from stock issue, additional capital from partners and investors	Balance sheet—changes in owners' equity sections
Payment of accounts payable	Balance sheet—change in A/P balance and A/P payment subschedule
Payment for purchase of capital assets	Balance sheet—asset account changes and major asset purchases plan
Payment of nonroutine expenses	Balance sheet changes such as accrued taxes payable, loan payments due, cleanup of credit lines

Converting Net Income to Cash

Many companies begin their cash flow plan using forecast net income. Then they convert that number to actual spendable cash. This provides the number many call *cash flow from operations*. The conversion process merely identifies noncash items in the net income figure and eliminates them. What's left is pure spendable cash, appropriately timed.

Depreciation and amortization

Most people identify depreciation and amortization of fixed assets as the first noncash expense to eliminate when converting net income to cash. These two expense items don't cost the company a penny of spendable cash. Remove depreciation and amortization expenses by *adding* them back to net income. Since these are expense items, adding them back negates their effect.

Tax provisions

The second most common conversion number used to eliminate noncash expense is the tax accrual. Net income includes the anticipated provision for federal and state income taxes. As with depreciation and amortization, add this provision back to net income to eliminate its effect.

Changes in Balance Sheet Items

The next step is to identify cash impact of changes in the balance sheet. These items provide both cash inflows and outflows. Earlier we identified changes from the accounts receivable and payable forecast. Put these cash sources and uses in this section of the cash flow plan.

Every change on the balance sheet means a potential source or use of cash. First identify the asset or liability change on the cash flow plan. Next insert the correct timing. Most often the timing is that shown on the forecast balance sheet. However, sometimes—such as with the purchase of major assets—there's a timing difference between the asset hitting the books and the actual cash disbursement.

Funds flowing in from outside sources

From the beginning, many cash flow planners know that they'll need to access debt sources. Often the major purchases plan specifies such debt sources from the start. Include these as funding sources from the balance sheet.

Along with the normal sources of debt, such as bank installment loans, term loans, and lines of credit, this section of the cash flow plan includes funding from

- Owners • Partners • Shareholders • Bondholders
- Other investors

Once again, all these sources of cash should appear on the balance sheet as well. If they don't, there's a problem.

Funds flowing out

Funds flow out of the cash plan from departments all over the company. Inventory and capital assets purchased are two good examples. As the major asset purchases plan unfolds, the assets appear on the balance sheet. These require cash outlays in accordance with the timing in the purchase contracts. The raw materials and subassembly purchasing plan takes its lead from the manufacturing plan. Make sure you include the timing for these items in the cash plan.

Additional cash outflow items sometimes get omitted from the forecasted balance sheet and income statement because they're nonroutine. Be sure the cash flow plan includes

- Dividends to common and preferred stockholders
- Interest payments to bondholders

The balance sheet should reduce shareholders' equity to reflect payment of a cash dividend. The income statement should record interest paid to bondholders as an interest expense.

Totaling the Cash Flow Plan

Once all the cash inflows and outflows appear on the cash plan, we can determine the cash balance for each planning period. The easiest way is to total all cash inflows and outflows separately. Then add and subtract them from the opening cash balance. What's left is the ending cash balance. This becomes the opening cash balance for the next operating period. Figure 13-2 illustrated a completed cash flow plan in the form of a Prospective Statement of Changes in Financial Condition.

Additionally, it's often useful to graph the cash flow plan. This quickly communicates where the cash excesses and shortfalls appear during the planning period.

Chapter 15 establishes the benchmarks used to track implementation of the business plan.

Chapter 15

Establishing Benchmarks

OVERVIEW

This section shows how to establish meaningful benchmarks in each critical area of the plan. These establish a link between the blueprint for plan implementation and the company's everyday operations. Well-chosen benchmarks provide the yardsticks by which we measure progress toward achieving the business plan's goals.

The benchmarks we create here have the same characteristics as the rest of our business plan:

- Their computation is simple and straightforward.
- They track plan goals.
- Often they detail the steps toward hitting intermediate targets.
- Their timing mirrors that of the rest of the business plan.
- They point us toward specific problems and solutions.

MATCHING BENCHMARKS TO PLAN GOALS

In Chapters 4 and 5, when we set the company's overall goals and those for each department, we mentioned the need to track our progress toward the goals. Now we're ready to expand that. The benchmarks serve to identify specific milestones needed for implementation of the plan. They combine with the overall company and department goals to tell us how we're progressing.

Trying to implement a business plan without benchmarks is like flying an airplane without a compass. You can't tell if you're on course just by watching the ground whiz by. The same goes for our business plan. Benchmarks provide a reference point to help us stay on course.

Establishing a Blueprint for Plan Targets

Benchmarks provide a blueprint for meeting plan targets. Often the company's overall plan sets broad targets and goals. For example, return on shareholders' equity is an often-used target. However, many things go into reaching that target. Each provides a quantitative benchmark by which we track progress. Further, we must accomplish each benchmark by a particular time. Failure to meet the planned timing affects the steps that follow.

Anticipating the Effects of Some Benchmarks

Careless choices for benchmarks sometimes have unanticipated results. For example, let's say your company targets earnings per share (EPS = net income / number of shares outstanding) as its primary end point. The firm judges the success of the business plan by this one number.

How does this affect the firm's ability to pay shareholder dividends? The answer is that reduced dividends allow more money for reinvestment in the firm. Any return on this invested capital falls right to the bottom line and helps achieve the benchmark EPS. Therefore, a danger in using this particular benchmark is a cut in shareholder dividends. Did management have in mind reduced shareholder dividends? Maybe not.

Some companies use return on equity (ROE = net income / owners' equity). This encourages the most profitable investment of equity capital. But wait. There's a problem here, too. Let's say the company plans on earning $200,000 on equity of $1,000,000. The ROE plan target was, therefore, 20 percent ($200,000 / $1,000,000 = 20%). That's the incentive benchmark.

However, the business plan calls for investing $300,000 in new production line equipment. The expected return is 15 percent. Where do we get the $300,000? Selling more stock increases the numerator in the ROE equation by $45,000 ($300,000 X 15% = $45,000). However, the denominator (shareholder's equity) would also rise from $1,000,000 to $1,300,000. ROE drops from 20 percent to 18.9 percent ($245,000 / $1,300,000 = 18.9%).

Now we're below the benchmark target and we've placed our incentive bonus at risk. Alternatively, the company could borrow the money at, say, 10 percent. Now the return only rises $15,000 ($45,000 from the new equipment but less $30,000 in interest expense). The denominator stays the same because the firm used debt, not equity, to finance the purchase. ROE rises from 20 percent to 21.5 percent ($215,000 / $1,000,000 = 21.5%). From the standpoint of achieving the incentive reward, this is the best choice for the source of funds. However, the firm doesn't profit as much from this alternative.

The point is, pay close attention to the type of behavior your reward benchmarks encourage.

CREATING DEPARTMENTAL BENCHMARKS

Benchmarks give each department an idea of how well the firm is doing in attaining specific goals. They specify milestones unique to each department's plan. Carefully chosen benchmarks point out potential problems that might cause deviation from the plan. No department wants responsibility for causing part of the business plan to fail.

The financial manager responsible for financing expansion of working capital requirements provides a good example. One benchmark for this department target might be increasing the firm's line of credit by $250,000. Though this is probably just one part of the company's financial structure, the line of credit increase must occur *before* accounts receivable rise as a result of the planned sales increase. Working capital benchmarks also indicate the funds needed to pay for the raw material purchased by the production department.

In this example we've identified six things the most useful benchmarks possess:

- Easily identified • Easily quantified • Specific timing
- Identification of the person responsible
- Established importance to implementation of the business plan
- Easily determined when achieved

Recognizing Useful Benchmarks

Just as with everything else in business planning, the easier a benchmark is to work with, the better. There's nothing complicated about choosing benchmarks. First, make sure everyone recognizes them easily. Think of the line of credit example used above. We identified this benchmark in terms of

- *Who:* The financial manager is clearly responsible for meeting this benchmark.
- *What:* Increase of the LOC by $250,000.
- *When:* Before the sales plan increases accounts receivable.

Next, determine how we know we hit each benchmark. In this example, the evidence was provided very simply. The company received an amendment to the borrowing agreement stipulating the increased credit line available.

Conveying the Purpose of a Benchmark

Everyone involved must clearly understand his or her benchmarks. This goes not just for those responsible, but also for those in other departments that depend on particular benchmarks being hit. Numbers seem to provide the most easily understandable benchmarks. The line of credit used above certainly was quantifiable. The amount was the increase in the line stated in dollars.

Additionally, avoid using benchmarks based on others' opinions. Such an ambiguous benchmark might call for "raising the overall quality of employees." These benchmarks are impossible to nail down. Further, they're open to dispute. Someone who appears to one manager to be a quality employee may not to another.

Finally, such qualitative objectives usually don't help us reach the targets established in a short-term business plan. Indeed, most plan goals emphasize financial targets. They allow little room for opinion and interpretation. We understand the benchmark. The timing for reaching it is easy to establish. When that time rolls around, there's no question whether we met the goal or not.

Timing the Benchmark

Business plans require a series of action steps to take place in a specific sequence. Often one part of the plan cannot begin without another being completed. This progression of benchmarks that build on one another is true of our line of credit example. Customers won't pay the day they receive the invoice. The company needs reasonable assurance that it can pay for raw materials and production expenses for the additional products. Without that assurance—in the form of an increased credit line—the firm won't commit to selling more products and building its payable balance.

Therefore, the credit line benchmark comes before final commitment to purchasing additional raw materials and hiring more production staff. That's how we work backwards from a plan target to arrive at the timing for intermediate benchmarks.

When determining the order and timing of departmental benchmarks, ask these two questions:

- Which departments depend on completion of this goal before beginning *their* work?

- How critical is the timing of one particular benchmark to other departmental goals?

The order and timing of the benchmarks provides the most basic yardstick of progress toward implementation of the business plan.

Delegating Responsibility for Benchmarks

Assign responsibility for meeting specific benchmarks to particular individuals. Make sure everyone understands exactly the expectations for each benchmark. Additionally, make clear that the department looks to one and only one individual as responsible for hitting a particular benchmark. Any more than one person's being responsible opens the door for blaming someone else if there's a problem.

This may sound like a pressure tactic. That's what's meant by *holding people's feet to the fire.* Things don't always go smoothly. Managers must overcome problems. With shared responsibility (or worse, no responsibility) the chances of overcoming those problems diminish.

Delegating Authority

It makes little sense delegating responsibility to someone without also providing the authority to get the job done. Often this includes delegating authority formerly held by more senior management. Without sufficient authority to act, most people's commitment to a target or its completion date diminishes. People perceive their responsibility as hollow. Indeed, ultimate responsibility rests with the person who has the authority to get things done.

Selecting Relevant Benchmarks

The best benchmarks tell us at a glance how we're progressing toward our goal. Engineers select such benchmarks by using critical path charts. That's not necessary here. However, the theory is useful. The critical path toward a goal identifies those parts of the plan around which all other components revolve. The plan implementation does not move forward without first meeting each critical factor.

Therefore, select as your benchmarks *those critical parts of the plan that could cause implementation to stop if not met on time.* Sometimes these are actual goals in the departmental plans. Other times they support a critical component needed to achieve a goal.

Often benchmarks focus on the infrastructure of the company. For example, a common goal for the sales department is the sales level for each product. However, part of the infrastructure that makes that possible might be a new order entry system. The firm cannot meet its sales targets without the increased throughput provided by the new O/E system. The new O/E system, therefore, is on the critical path. Its completion provides a good benchmark.

Hitting Benchmarks

Select benchmarks with their measurement in mind. That way identifying deviation from the plan isn't a problem. Ideally, the actual performance numbers for each benchmark should come from the accounting system.

For example, sales is a number every accounting system provides. There's no question whether the actual year-to-date sales figures are equal to the sales numbers used as benchmarks in the implementation plan. Such target figures placed along the timeline of the implementation plan provide a good reference guide. They tell which products are tracking against the plan and which need additional attention.

Make measuring benchmarks easy and reliable. Don't choose benchmarks that need complex computations based on assumptions. This injects an element of doubt as to how the implementation plan is tracking.

Consignment sales is a good example. Book publishers sell on what amounts to a consignment contract. As with all consignment sales, bookstores can return the books if they don't sell. Therefore, computation of sales figures requires guessing at the timing and percentage of returns for credit that the seller must bear. We really don't know for sure how many units have sold until the expiration of the return period.

Using such sales figures as benchmarks creates problems because of their uncertainty. Indeed, the U.S. government suffers from this same problem. Often government statistics such as the gross domestic product or the producer price index require correction because of inaccuracies built into their computations. Investors who base their trading strategies on these numbers often must react quickly to announcement of the corrections.

See what a problem such numbers become when they are used as benchmarks? It's better to stick with concrete numbers that are easily calculated and not subject to error.

MARKETING AND SALES BENCHMARKS

Use marketing and sales benchmarks to coordinate the engine that drives the rest of the business plan. Sales benchmarks tell us how the revenue levels compare with where we want to be. Benchmarks for sales unit volume help the rest of the firm as well. Marketing benchmarks provide the fuel that helps the sales staff do its job.

Marketing Benchmarks

The best marketing benchmarks relate to specific planned campaigns. We want to see how each tracks against the time line of the sales plan. Marketing efforts *precede* sales results. Therefore, identify specific marketing benchmarks to anticipate required sales results.

Advertising programs

Most benchmarks related to advertising programs simply follow implementation of the ad campaign. For example, we want to know that the company that prepares the artwork for an ad campaign has enough time to do the job. Most such benchmarks provide qualitative information rather than hard numbers. Nevertheless, they allow management to coordinate the implementation of ad campaigns that support the sales effort.

Advertising expenses

One good way to control advertising expenses is to make each advertising campaign a separate cost center. Assign a sub-account number in the general ledger to each advertising program. For example,

- Advertising expenses is G/L account #600
- Promotional expenses allocated to product X are coded into G/L account #610
- Promotional expenses allocated to product Y are coded into G/L account #620; and so on

The accounting system rolls the subaccounts into the lead expense account, #600. Advertising expenses still appear as one number on the income statement; however, now the marketing department can track its programs separately simply by looking at the subaccounts. Further, the marketing plan can identify advertising expense benchmarks along the way.

Sales per advertising dollar

Here's a critical index that helps us judge the effectiveness of the advertising campaigns. For example, say the sales per advertising dollar benchmark for a product is 100. This means we need $100 in sales for every advertising dollar spent. Anything less means that the advertising campaign hasn't met our expectations.

Failure to hit the established benchmark identifies a decision point in the marketing plan. Do we continue with the campaign or change it? If the problem is severe enough, it might warrant dropping the product. Either way, the benchmark served its purpose by identifying a deviation from the intended course.

Sales Benchmarks

Most small companies watch their sales benchmarks closely. Indicators of sales revenue guide other departments in executing their parts of the business plan. If Sales fails to hit its benchmarks, the rest of the business plan needs to adjust accordingly.

The good news is that much of the sales data comes right from the accounting system and isn't subject to interpretation (unless you're a book publisher or a consignment seller). Additionally, most accounting systems can provide isolated sales information throughout the operating period if need be. Further, the sales staff seldom has trouble keeping track of sales, especially when they are used to compute commissions.

Revenue is the most obvious sales benchmark. The business plan probably tracks overall performance based on sales level. However, this benchmark isn't as useful to other departments as *sales unit volume*. The production department, for example, doesn't want to estimate the number of units sold based on average gross margin for the company's product line. This isn't precise enough for gauging production requirements. Changing retail prices and special discount offers further decrease its accuracy.

Units shipped

This is a better sales benchmark for use by the rest of the company. Units shipped usually triggers an invoice. The invoice records a sale in the accounting system. Therefore, the units shipped benchmark serves two purposes:

1. It tracks sales revenue given planned pricing levels.

2. It indicates an absolute sales volume on which the rest of the company can accurately gauge its own benchmarks.

Even if there is a lag between shipment and invoice times (and there shouldn't be for cash management purposes), tracking shipments gives an early indication of the all-important sales benchmark.

Warranty costs

Often companies include special warranty offers in their sales and marketing plans. The business plan treats these as an enticement to buy. Therefore, many firms include these expenses in the sales and marketing department plans. Sometimes they associate them with particular promotional campaigns.

Regardless of where your company includes warranty costs, be sure to estimate the expense associated with making good on warranty promises. Use those estimates as benchmarks to compare actual performance with the plan. Repair costs rising beyond those originally anticipated in the benchmark indicate a problem. There's probably nothing you can do about the units already sold. However, the company certainly can alter the terms of the warranty on future products or make adjustments in the production process.

Sales commissions

Sales commissions result from sales volume. Therefore, meeting sales benchmarks should also mean meeting sales commission benchmarks. However, this doesn't always happen. Often companies provide sales incentives (in the form of increased commission payouts) for specific products.

Benchmarks that track sales commissions provide insight into how well the commission program provides the right incentive to the sales force. Compare the commission benchmark with the volume of the specific products sold.

Further, compare sales commission benchmarks with related benchmarks for collection of accounts receivable. The company doesn't want to be in the position of paying out large commissions in the face of rising delinquencies and write-offs of customers who don't pay.

Sales commission benchmarks control sales incentives. They identify situations that reward a sales effort not concentrating on targeted high-profit-margin products or on getting good-quality customers who pay their bills.

Manufacturing and Production Benchmarks

Since much of the performance measurement in the manufacturing department is quantitative, it's easy to establish manufacturing benchmarks. Further, the cost accounting system routinely reports actual results for comparison with manufacturing benchmarks.

The most useful manufacturing benchmarks involve production volume in units and costs in dollars. Plans for manufacturing and production departments usually identify goals and targets for these areas.

Manufacturing benchmarks aid both the sales and finance departments. Sales needs to be able to identify the firm's capacity to fill orders in order to quote lead times. The finance department needs an idea of the purchasing commitments Manufacturing has made on behalf of the company. This helps it plan cash disbursements.

Choosing manufacturing benchmarks depends on

- What's critical to successfully implement the plan
- The company's ability to generate actual results for comparison with the benchmarks

Cost of Goods Sold

This is usually one of the largest costs of the firm, if not the largest. Most companies carefully watch their manufacturing costs. Indeed, profit targets depend on hitting specific production cost levels. Cost of goods sold (CGS) provides one of the best benchmarks for monitoring the firm's gross margin.

However, this can be a tricky number to nail down. Many different costs go into CGS. These include

- Raw materials
- Direct production costs, such as assembly line labor
- Indirect production costs, such as allocation of health insurance premiums
- Allocation of overhead, such as rent of the plant

We don't want to have to reconcile the production cost benchmark against the cost accounting system every month. The numbers must agree from the start with little or no alteration. One way to test this benchmark's accuracy is to reconcile it at its measurement point with the beginning and ending inventory balances appearing in the financial plan for the same point in time. The equation to compute cost of goods sold is

Beginning inventory + purchases – ending inventory = cost of goods sold

We reduce the danger of using an unnecessarily confusing benchmark if everyone agrees on the computation from the start.

Production

Production benchmarks focus on unit volume. They tell the sales department how much inventory is ready to ship. The timing of production anticipates sales. As the launching of a campaign approaches, people take production benchmarks more and more seriously. This is especially true of companies that face intense competition, where prompt delivery means the difference between making a sale and giving it away to a competitor.

Companies that plan a buildup of inventory reserves also use production benchmarks. At each benchmark point on the plan time line, a specified amount of inventory above sales requirements should exist.

Overtime

Using production overtime as a benchmark helps keep the manufacturing department's cost of goods sold in line with expectations. Sometimes when production levels fall behind, there's a temptation to fill the void using whatever resources are necessary. Establishing overtime benchmarks sets a limit on the investment the firm is willing to make just to meet a production schedule.

Without this benchmark control, production costs can raise the overall cost of goods to a point that endangers the profit plan. Set overtime benchmarks throughout the plan implementation cycle at levels that are acceptable to the production department and consistent with cost targets. They should rise and fall according to the production schedule.

Machinery Downtime

The manufacturing department normally uses this benchmark. It helps track the department's own implementation plan. Most manufacturing and production plans anticipate a certain amount of machinery problems. The production cost plan includes the resulting idle labor time. Using machinery downtime as a benchmark provides a monitor for potential problems. Excessive downtime signals higher labor costs per unit and possibly disruption to production schedules.

Manufacturing Cost Variance

Production departments track their manufacturing costs against some sort of standard. Most likely the production costs contained in the business plan came in part from the cost standards. As the production department deviates from its standard costs, profit margins change. Therefore, identify the specific cost variances your production plan can tolerate and still meet its goals. Use these variances as production benchmarks. Here are a few of the more common cost variances used as benchmarks.

Direct labor contained in production

The amount of direct labor going into each unit of production drops as workers gain more experience or upon installation of more sophisticated production equipment. Often smart production planners anticipate this increased efficiency and include it in their department plans. For many, it's critical if they are to meet their cost targets.

That's why this makes a good benchmark. Use it to track the improved efficiency as the production department goes farther out on the learning curve.

Labor price variance

This can also throw off the production department's cost plan. A labor price variance occurs when the cost of labor changes from the planned standard. If your firm anticipates labor union negotiation or rising labor costs during its plan implementation, use this as a critical production benchmark.

Material contained in production

Most manufacturing departments use material standards in their products just as they do labor standards. If production requires more materials than originally planned, this quickly creates a negative cost variance.

Further, if the product was engineered correctly, it probably doesn't need the additional material. Essentially, that material is wasted. Use material contained in production as a benchmark to identify deviations from levels critical to maintaining the production plan.

Material price variance

If your plan depends on specific prices for raw material, track them using this benchmark. During periods of rising prices, a negative material price variance from standards affects the cost of goods sold. When that occurs, it places profit margins at risk. Early identification of the problem provides time to fix it. For example, hedging commodities prices guarantees a maximum cost for raw materials.

QUALITY CONTROL BENCHMARKS

Focus QC benchmarks on the number of rejects. Too many rejects increases wasted materials and effort. It also requires additional rework costs. All these add to overall production costs.

However, too few rejects also indicates a problem. Perhaps the production line is running too slowly. QC benchmarks help monitor the balance between production flow and quality.

Rework because of Raw Material or Component Defects

Many manufacturing and assembly companies need a way to determine the quality of raw materials and purchased subassemblies. Along with QC rejects, the costs of rework often serve as a benchmark for items entered into production. When rework costs exceed the benchmark, management can focus on the cause. Often it's raw material or subassembly defects.

INVENTORY

Too little inventory causes stock-out costs and possible stoppage of the production line. Too much inventory unnecessarily eats up working capital without returning the required profit. Additionally, too much inventory risks spoilage and obsolescence, and unnecessarily raises working capital requirements.

Either way, failure to track inventory is an expensive mistake. Many planners consider inventory benchmarks among the most important for companies stocking items for manufacturing, assembly, and sale.

Inventory benchmarks maintain the balance between manufacturing managers who want to build inventory and financial managers who insist on the minimum needed to keep the production line moving.

Inventory Levels

Inventory levels depend on

- Production requirements • Ordering and safety stock requirements
- Vendor lead time • Pricing of purchases

Consider these factors when establishing inventory benchmarks throughout the planning horizon.

Production requirements

Inventory benchmarks should target enough inventory to meet production demands. Establish the number of production days of inventory held in stock. Compute this as

$$\text{Prod. days of inventory} = \frac{\text{inventory on hand}}{\text{daily production requirements}}$$

The company doesn't want an undue concentration of its resources in a single asset. Further, a large inventory takes up expensive warehouse space. A better solution is to purchase inventory items throughout the production cycle. Another alternative is to execute a single master purchase order for the goods needed but accept delivery (and invoices) in several increments. Either technique tracks with the days of production inventory on hand.

Inventory turnover

Maintaining inventory at a desired level helps control inventory turnover. Compute this benchmark as

$$\text{Inventory turnover} = \frac{\text{cost of goods sold}}{\text{average inventory balance}}$$

Both this benchmark and production days of inventory are precise and easily calculated.

Gross margin per inventory turn

We want a way to track the profit associated with each inventory turn. Compute this as

$$\text{Gross margin per inventory turn} = \frac{\text{gross margin}}{\text{number of inventory turns}}$$

It's true that rapid inventory turnover is good. It reduces working capital invested in unproductive assets. However, it makes no sense to sacrifice profits for the sake of hitting an inventory turnover benchmark. The gross margin per inventory turn keeps the goal of rapidly moving inventory in proper perspective.

Here's an example of a company that actually improved its inventory turnover, but *reduced* its gross margin with each turn.

AUTUMN MANUFACTURING CORPORATION
COMPUTATION OF GROSS MARGIN PER INVENTORY TURNOVER
For the year ended December 31, 19X2

	19X1	19X2
Cost of goods sold	$10,000,00	$ 6,000,000
Average inventory of finished goods	$1,000,000	$500,000
Inventory turnover	10 times	12 times
Days of sales in inventory (360 days / turnover)	36 days	30 days
Gross margin	$3,500,000	$2,000,000
Gross margin per turnover	$350,000	$166,667

Inventory turnover accelerated from 10 to 12 between the first and second years. Further, the days of sales in inventory fell from thirty-six days to thirty days. Autumn's management hit its turnover benchmark. However, look at the gross margin per inventory turn. *It dropped by over 50 percent from one year to the next.* Autumn sacrificed profit for the sake of liquidity. By using both the turnover and gross margin per inventory turn benchmarks, management could have identified the problem before it placed the business plan at risk.

EOQ and safety stock

The EOQ and safety stock equations were introduced in Chapter 10. Many companies use EOQ and targeted safety stock levels as planning goals as well as intermediate benchmarks. They guide the management of inventory, which in turn contributes to working capital, interest expense, and additional costs if inventory spoils or goes obsolete.

By setting benchmarks at specific safety stock levels, most companies stand a better chance of moving toward a disciplined method of inventory control.

Vendor lead time

Production managers always fear problems with availability of inventory and the time it takes to get more. Timing of orders and delivery dates usually figures prominently in the inventory balances and safety stock a company maintains.

Combine vendor lead time with days of production in inventory. Compare the supply of inventory on hand with the time it takes for a new order to arrive. The two benchmarks should be almost equal. For example, a company is over-stocked if it has thirty days of an item on hand, yet the lead time to get more is only five days.

Obsolete inventory

Many firms identify obsolete inventory by its turnover or the time it sits on the shelf. This is a critical benchmark for companies in high-technology indus-tries or with inventory subject to fast spoilage. Often companies quantify obso-lete inventory as a percentage of total inventory value. Holding inventory stocks that qualify as obsolete beyond this percentage raises a red flag.

Most small businesses don't have unlimited storage space or working capital to invest. They can't have either tied up in nonproducing assets like obsolete in-ventory. Establish obsolete inventory benchmarks to guide the company toward acceptable levels.

PURCHASING BENCHMARKS

The benchmarks established for purchasing focus on price, timeliness, and terms. Like all managers, buyers use a series of guides that when hit throughout the planning period guarantee achieving their goals.

Price Variances

We often call the material prices used in the manufacturing plan the standard prices. Using standard prices as a benchmark provides a guide for buyers to use during negotiations. Tracking material price variances in the cost accounting sys-tem yields an indicator of performance against this benchmark.

When used as a benchmark, price variances identify problems while there's still time to either correct them or compensate in other ways.

Timing

Some manufacturing operations require critical materials at specific times. If items are delivered late or suddenly become scarce, this places the production schedule at risk. If you have such crucial items, use their delivery dates as bench-marks in monitoring plan performance. These benchmarks establish specific points for decisions regarding alternative sources or other actions.

Contract Terms

Some purchasing departments work toward specific goals for the terms of all their contracts. One such goal might be payment due date. Working with the fi-nancial plan, extending the payment due date from a normal thirty days to forty-five days can significantly free up some of the firm's working capital.

Using payment due date as a benchmark for the purchasing department plan keeps it in focus as a target. Further, monthly comparison of the benchmark with actual performance shows buyers how close they came.

Purchase Discounts

The weighted average purchases discount is another purchase contract term often used as a benchmark. Many companies combine this with the goals of the finance department. The buyers negotiate the discounts for early payment. The finance department takes advantage of them.

Many of the modern automated accounts payable systems allow entry of the discount percentage and automatically compute the dollars saved. The savings then gets posted to a general ledger account. This makes it easy to compare actual performance with targeted benchmarks.

Problems with discounts occur when the controller avoids paying early. Often the thinking is that the company's use of the money is worth more than the discount. Such a philosophy actually costs the company money. Here's why:

Assume a $10,000 invoice with terms of 2/10, net/30. This entitles the buyer to a 2 percent discount for paying the invoice within ten days. Otherwise the full amount is due within thirty days.

Compute the value of this cash discount:

$$\text{Annualized interest income from taking advantage of the discount} = \frac{\text{discount \%}}{\text{due date} - \text{discount date}} \times 365 \text{ days}$$

The annualized interest income from taking advantage of the discount is 37% $[0.02/(30-10)] \times 365 = 37\%$.

As long as the company can borrow for less than 37 percent (and the cash is available), take the discount. Compute the benefit in dollars and cents as follows:

Invoice amount:	$10,000
Terms:	2/10, net/30
Aggregate cost of funds rate:	10%
Discount yield (dollars):	200
Interest cost by taking the discount:	
($10,000 X 10%)/365 X (30 days – 10 days) =	<u>55</u>
Net interest profit by taking discount:	$ 145

PEOPLE BENCHMARKS

Measure people benchmarks in terms of costs (dollars) and in number of incidences. Depending on your company's business, some of these are more relevant than others. Targets in the people plan provide cost control guidelines more than anything else. Benchmarks help keep salaries and ancillary costs within boundaries set by the people plan. Let's take a look at some of the more common benchmarks.

Salary Expenses

Salary expenses provide easy-to-follow benchmarks throughout implementation of the people plan. The accounting system furnishes actual salary expenses. The salary plan provides the benchmark target. Each month it's easy to determine how close to the target salary expenses came.

Headcount

Be careful when using headcount as a benchmark. Simply counting bodies is misleading. Not all employees work a full day. Some work overtime, others work part-time. Headcount probably doesn't really tell you what you want to know. Instead, count full-time equivalents (FTEs).

Measure FTEs in your firm's normal work week. Some companies consider a forty-hour week normal. Others use a thirty-two-hour week. Say we assume that one FTE equals one person working forty hours. If someone works sixty hours, count that person as $1\frac{1}{2}$ FTEs. Count part-timers as their fraction of an FTE. Additionally, include temporary employees in the FTE count.

Headcount as a benchmark provides an indicator of the number of FTEs used to execute the plan.

Health Care

If your people plan contains targets for health care claims and work related injuries, you need a benchmark to compare actuals with the plan. Unfortunately, managers have no control over these incidents. Nevertheless their costs still affect the business plan.

Larger firms track employee liability claims—particularly stress cases. These often precede expensive litigation. Everyone is better off when the company identifies chronic problems before they become critical. It's much less expensive than fighting a class action by a group of current and former employees who want the company to punch their ticket out of a financial abyss.

Monitoring Consultants and Temporaries

Outside contractors, consultants, and temporary workers are a ready source of emergency labor. However, this is also an expensive talent pool from which to draw. A benchmark expense figure that tracks use of these outsiders helps keep their use in check. Too much use of such independents means that the company should create a full-time position and hire an employee.

Bonuses

Benchmarks figure prominently in bonuses. They provide indicators that the target was achieved and a bonus was earned. They also show everyone the progress toward targets.

Performance per Employee

Per-employee performance indices provide a quick benchmark regarding efficiency. If your business plan uses such indices, make them comparable to something. For example, the production line may establish a performance efficiency benchmark that tracks units produced per employee. By itself this index means little. However, when compared with the same index in the business plan or from last month, last year, or a competitor, it gains relevance.

FINANCIAL BENCHMARKS

These are the easiest benchmarks to understand. Most financial benchmarks employ a standard method of computation that leaves no question as to their meaning. Further, the information is easily accessible and reported each month. The most commonly used financial benchmarks include

- Sales volume • Gross margin for each product
- Operating expenses • Operating profit • Net income before tax
- Financial ratios

Departmental Financial Benchmarks

Many planners track specific financial statistics to manage specific sections of the finance department. The most common includes

- Accounts receivable • Accounts payable
- Cash-related benchmarks

Accounts receivable benchmarks

Receivables collections and growth rate greatly influence cash inflow and working capital requirements. Often the finance department identifies benchmarks throughout the planning horizon to control receivables. Most of these we identified in earlier sections. They include

- Dollars invested in accounts receivable
- Average age of a receivable before it's paid
- Percentage of total receivables in each aging bucket
- Roll rates of receivables moving from one aging bucket to the next
- Amount written off
- Amount in collections
- Accounts receivable as a percentage of total assets

Accounts payable benchmarks

Just as we track receivables, we want to be sure the firm follows planned policies regarding payables. For example, one common A/P benchmark is the average aging of payables. The cash flow plan most likely assumes a specific aging policy. This benchmark tracks that planned policy against actual performance.

Another benchmark commonly used is the amount of discounts taken. Again, the financial plan probably assumes that the firm takes any offered trade discounts. This benchmark lets everyone know just how closely the company follows its policy.

Figure 15-1 illustrates additional financial benchmarks.

Figure 15-1
Financial benchmarks

Financial ratios:	Current ratio
	Quick ratio
	Debt/equity ratio
	Times interest earned
	Ratio of debt to assets financed
	Inventory turnover
	Days of sales tied up in A/R
	A/R turnover
	A/P turnover
Financial targets:	Gross margin
	Working capital requirements
	Aggregate borrowing rate for all
	financing vehicles
	Interest expense (in $)
Cash indicators:	Number of days to make deposits
	available
	Number of checking accounts
	Average age of payables
	Average age of receivables
	Roll rates of accounts receivable
Cash capability:	Cash + cash sources coming due
	(such as collection of A/R, maturing
	investments, available credit lines)
	– cash requirements such as A/P and
	loan payments
Available cash:	Cash balance after subtracting all
	expenses and current liabilities
Loan balances and requirements:	All loan covenants and restrictions
	taken from the loan documents
	themselves. Additionally, all
	compensating balance requirements

Chapter 16

Automating the Plan

OVERVIEW

Chapter 16 demonstrates how to use a desktop computer to prepare the

- Overall business plan • Production scheduling
- Sales projections • Salary budgets
- Financial statement forecasts

Further, this section identifies shortcuts that experts use to zip through a complete business plan and create a facility that allows convenient updating. Additionally, Chapter 16 teaches how to make the best use of modern computer tools such as what-if scenarios, sensitivity analysis, and simulation. It shows the most effective ways of presenting plan information to provide precise communication of planned results and progress toward targets and goals.

SELECTING THE PROPER SYSTEM

Take care when you construct your automated financial planning system. You want it to have a high degree of both credibility and accuracy. People tend to believe information produced by a computer. However, if that information later proves false, it's difficult to regain lost confidence. So remember, check and double-check the information produced by your automated planning system. Later in this chapter we'll talk about validating a computer model to ensure its accuracy.

The software and method of automating your business plan have a lot to do with the ease of checking the results and determining if they make sense. When used properly, computers can be a huge help in preparing a business plan. The greatest contribution to the planning effort that a computer makes is in the areas of

- Organizing the data • Preparing alternative scenarios and analyses
- Crunching numbers • Presenting results in understandable formats

Selecting Planning Software

Above all, we want the software to fulfill the tasks required of the planning team. When selecting the software, first identify the people who work with it. Assess their general familiarity with computers and software. Whatever software you select must be compatible with their ability to use it.

If they have little experience in this field, you may want to consider a canned planning package that walks users through the process. If your planning team is familiar with computers and mathematical modeling, your solution may be to go with one of the popular spreadsheet systems.

Regardless of the software, here are some considerations.

Interfacing with your accounting system

If downloading information from the accounting system is important to developing accurate assumptions, you need a spreadsheet system that can convert the accounting data. Many accounting systems come with a data translation capacity. Some convert to ASCII, others convert to *data interface files* (DIF), and still others go directly to Lotus 1-2-3 and other popular spreadsheets.

Another vital use of the plan's data interface capability is the downloading of *actual performance data.* Each month you should compare the plan numbers with actuals from the accounting system. The best systems allow electronic downloading of actual data right into the planning software. This speeds creation of comparison reports.

Massaging the data

Many of the assumptions that go into business plans require some conversion from their raw state. Often this means sorting the data, alphabetizing it, and performing a variety of computational analyses. Make sure whatever planning software you use has the capacity to massage the data as needed.

Presenting results

Some of the canned planning packages have preprogrammed reporting modules. Many allow users to format their own reports. This is especially true of the spreadsheet software. It's a good idea to have at least a mock-up of your final plan reporting package when you look at the reporting capabilities of a planning system.

Another consideration is the ability to produce *ad hoc* reports and graphical analyses. Such reporting capabilities greatly increase the planner's flexibility in communicating the plan's goals and targets.

Reputation of the manufacturer

When selecting any computer software, choose products that have a long and successful operating history. Some planners use five years as a benchmark. There should be thousands of satisfied users with the same installation you're considering. Let others do the testing of new software and endure the frustration of logic bugs.

Additionally, the documentation should be first-rate. Take a look at it. If the installation instructions (for instance) aren't understandable, chances are the rest of the documentation is substandard as well.

Finally, if you anticipate needing additional help, find out if the manufacturer provides telephone access to technical experts. Ask these questions:

1. Is there a charge for this service?

2. Are the technicians really experts?

3. How long does it take to connect with a technician who can answer your question?

4. Is access immediate, or does the manufacturer put you in a queue with other frustrated users, take your phone number, and call you back next week?

Many companies want the flexibility to create a unique planning model for their company alone. If that's you, consider putting your automated business plan on one of the simple spreadsheet systems. The products most often used for this purpose are

- Lotus 1-2-3 • Excel • Multiplan • VP-Planner
- Framework • Javelin

Of course the spreadsheet and packaged software market includes many more sophisticated offerings. However, consider the reasons we use a computer to help with the business plan:

- Simplicity • Easy changes • Plan model operated by end users

Both popular spreadsheet programs and some of the complete business planning software packages allow *end users* to quickly change their assumptions and determine the effects.

Most such systems don't require extensive computer experience. Therefore, those who *actually use* the business plan are the ones who create it and update it. This method doesn't separate the planning system from the issues at hand. Those working on the plan, not a computer specialist separated from the planning effort, enter new ideas. For all of these reasons, a bigger, more sophisticated computer with complex software usually just gets in the way and doesn't generate a more accurate business plan.

Hardware

Most small businesses use desktop computers with simple spreadsheet software or one of the popular canned planning packages. Few small companies can afford the timesharing offered by mainframe service bureaus. Further, they don't need that kind of computing horsepower.

Stand-alone Systems

By a stand-alone system, we mean that we did not link the computer used for the business plan with any other database or computer. Essentially all the information and logic programs required to formulate every part of the business plan reside in *one* computer.

This is efficient in that everything related to the business plan is in one place. However, only one person can work on the plan at a time. This becomes inconvenient if several departments want to automate their part of the plan. Further, if your business plan is exceedingly large, the speed and storage capacity of a single computer may be too small. Don't forget, the computer must store plans for all the departments *and* the consolidated plan as a whole.

Still, very small businesses may have only a single computer that's used for everything from accounting to order entry and business planning. If that's the case, then much of the planning effort ends up being done in off hours when the computer is available.

Spread sheet uniformity

One thing using a single stand-alone computer for planning purposes does is promote consistency. Just one person or a very few can use the computer for planning. Therefore, the spreadsheets created to feed information from different departments into the overall business plan are more likely to use

- Similar time frames
- The same general ledger accounts for monitoring financial results
- The most up-to-date actual performance data

There's no need to keep updating disks containing the planning model when something changes.

Networked Systems

Networked systems employ several computers, all sharing a common database. Often the data and logic software reside on a single large disk called a *server*. The remote workstations on the network have access to the server. Depending on the sophistication of the software, often multiple users can work from the same software and data at the same time. If your concern is for efficiency, then this feature (called *multiplexing*) is important to have.

For planning purposes, two types of networked systems seem to work the best. Figures 16-1 and 16-2 show the hub and the wheel network configurations.

Figure 16-1
Hub Network Configuration:

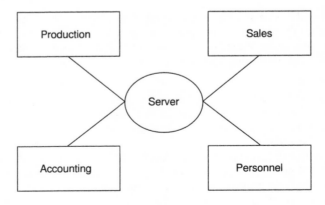

Figure 16-2
Wheel Network Configuration

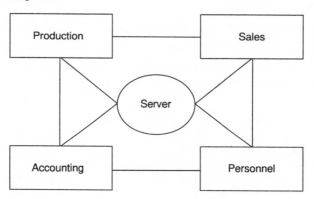

With the hub and wheel configuration, planning information comes into the server from all over the company. The planning software (either a spreadsheet or a canned planning package) accesses this information from the server. The configuration

- Eliminates the need for a dedicated planning computer.
- Promotes easy sharing of plan information and assumptions among different departments.
- Allows quick access to departmental plan information by the plan software.
- Reduces the chances of not having the most up-to-date information in the plan assumptions.
- Makes comparing the plan with actual performance information easier because both are on the same system.

With the wheel configuration, the server is still the hub. However, the different departments can share information either directly or indirectly, through the server. This allows, say the production department to plan its salary costs if it can obtain the raise schedule for its workers from Personnel.

Further, more sophisticated computer users often program the logic software to go into various databases and extract the planning assumptions every time they run the plan model. This guarantees that the most current version of each department's plan gets into the overall business plan. Further, it eliminates the manual task of entering each department's changes in its part of the overall business plan.

Securing Plan Information

Whether they use a stand-alone computer or a network, many companies worry about the security of their business plan. After all, the plan contains sensitive information regarding

- Sales strategy • New product offerings • Pricing
- Cost of production • Salaries and raises for particular individuals

These aren't things most planners want leaking out either to the general population of the company or to competitors.

Software security

Securing computers isn't difficult. Indeed, many networks come with preprogrammed security packages. Users receive *access privileges* to various parts of the computer. This allows normal operation by everyone who needs access. However, the plan section is controlled by unique passwords.

Further, the security systems often provide reports of user password access to the various parts of the system. That way, management knows which passwords accessed particular parts of the system. As long as you make everyone responsible for his or her particular password, you maintain accountability for system security by all authorized users.

Physical security measures

Some of the most effective physical security measures are also the simplest. For example, companies that are worried about unauthorized access should look first to the physical control exerted over the computer itself. Computers kept behind locked doors to which authorized users have the keys are more secure than those kept out in the open.

If you run a network, some workstations may indeed reside in common space. Putting them in a secure room wouldn't be practical. However, the security software can control the access privileges of *specific workstations*. The system refuses access to even the right passwords if they come from the wrong workstations.

Using this technique, you can still have a secure network by controlling physical entry to those workstations with valid plan access privileges.

Limiting remote on-line access

Even small companies often have access into their computer systems via a telecommunication link with remote locations. This is particularly true when firms have multiple branches or outside sales offices.

Computer hackers have compromised even the most secure government computer systems. If they want to, they can probably gain entry into yours. Reduce that possibility by

1. Maintaining connection with the outside only when needed.

2. Monitoring telecom access and verifying that all communication is with authorized users. A good way is to confirm the caller's identity by voice

before allowing him or her into the system. This does, however, restrict access to normal business hours.

3. Insisting on strict control over access passwords. Change them periodically and randomly, especially for those working on sensitive data.

4. When someone who has an access password leaves the company, canceling all computer privileges for that password.

5. Training all personnel with computer access privileges in the proper security procedures to follow. Make sure they know how serious the company considers a breach in computer security.

Choosing Hardware

Once you select the software, finding a machine to run it isn't difficult. The first and most important consideration is the existing computer equipment you may already have. We don't want several incompatible systems around the company. That's less of a problem now, since most business computers are IBM-compatible. However, be careful when deciding between IBM (or its clones) and Apple equipment. These aren't compatible without conversion procedures.

Hardware horsepower

Buy enough computing power to do your entire planning job. This is the least expensive part of the planning effort. Don't be stingy with the equipment. If you think you may need a larger random-access memory (RAM) or a bigger disk drive, get it. If you know in advance that you'll be doing extensive computations, then get a computer with a faster processing chip and higher megahertz rating.

Peripheral equipment

In addition to the actual central processing unit and disk storage device, every system uses additional machinery. The most noticeable is the screen. Get a color screen. Most of the state-of-the-art software makes good use of colors. Installations without color screens are at a disadvantage from the start.

Printers communicate all the work the planning team does. Get a reliable printer—preferably a name brand. One big caution here: *Get a printer your software supports.* You can tell what printers the software supports from its installation menu. There it asks which printer(s) you have installed. It usually gives a list of all the printers supported by the software. *Don't get one that's not on that list.* This doesn't always mean that the printer won't work, but it can mean that you're in for trouble in trying to cram what amounts to a square peg into a round hole.

If you know you'll be printing schedules with many columns (more than 13, for instance—one for each month and a total for the year), you may need a wide-carriage dot-matrix printer. Otherwise, the sophisticated laser printers feature a compressed print mode that can turn the print 90 degrees to use the width of the page (called a *landscape* configuration) that works just fine.

Many astute companies use peripheral mass storage devices for backing up (archiving) their information. Most of these are in the form of streaming tapes. Some tape drives are built into the computer. Others attach to the printer port in back of the computer. The tape copies all data and software. It keeps a permanent record and enables you to recover in the event of a catastrophe.

FLOWING THE PLAN THROUGH A COMPUTER

Think of the business plan as a tree. The trunk is the overall plan, and the branches are the different departments. The branches feed information to the main trunk. Each branch often contains a smaller business plan just for that department. The computer's job is to make sure that results from the branches flow to the trunk—to the overall business plan.

Using Submodels

Flowing information and changes from the branches using the computer saves time. Further, it greatly reduces the chance of manual error during data transfer from one branch to the next and from the branches to the overall plan. Additionally, it provides an excellent record of the derivation of the most important pieces of data.

The time taken to electronically link the departmental subplans improves the overall efficiency of the automated planning effort. Consider the fact that one of the plan's functions is to act as a tool of creativity. We want the ability to change assumptions in various branches of the plan and see the overall effects.

Structuring Information through the Plan

The business plan contains three major sections through which information flows:

- Assumptions • Departmental subplans • Actual business plan

Assumption section

Structurally, assumptions are usually the first section of the automated business plan. Planners using a spreadsheet often put the assumption section at the top. The actual "body" of the plan then reaches up into the assumption section to take the data required for its computations. Finally, print the assumption section separately from the rest of the plan.

Departmental Subplans

These generate specific data for each department. The computations are often extensive and complicated. Indeed, the subplans can be mini-business plans by themselves. Experienced spreadsheet users often prepare the subplans on their own spreadsheets, then execute a *file combine* procedure to upload the subplan's results into the main business plan model.

Some of the canned planning software does this. Often these packages accept data and assumptions from sources outside the model, such as a spreadsheet.

Alternatively, if your business plan isn't very large, you could consider assigning specific sections of the plan spreadsheet to the various departments that provide information to the overall plan. This makes for a very large spreadsheet. However, you don't have to worry about not having the latest subplan information, and there's no combining of files.

Overall Business Plan

After all assumptions and subplans comes the overall business plan. This takes information from above (if you're using a spreadsheet) and produces the schedules and forecast financial statements needed in the business plan.

AUTOMATED DEPARTMENT SCHEDULES

The parts of the business plan we want an automated link with if at all possible are

- Sales • Manufacturing and production • Finance
- Accounts receivable • Accounts payable • Salaries and wages

Most of the other data, while important, probably won't change that much during the planning process. Further, it doesn't usually affect the overall financial performance of the firm to as great an extent.

Sales

The sales subplan includes the sales forecast. The rest of the business plan and other departmental subplans require both the sales revenue and the unit sales forecasts.

Another assumption that comes out of the sales forecast is the firm's pricing strategies for its products. The advertising and market research subplans provide input for determination of the prices. The automated sales subplan generates various cases for pricing strategies. This flows directly to the financial subplan.

Finally, the sales subplans usually include the detail necessary for the sales department to manage its part of the plan. Included here are sales forecasts by

- Product • Division • Sales territory • Salesperson

Manufacturing and Production

The manufacturing subplan uses the sales unit forecast to compute its own assumptions regarding raw materials and production labor. From these come the cost of goods sold forecast used in the forecast income statement. Additionally, the purchasing plan takes its information from the raw materials requirements schedule, which comes from the production subplan.

Financial Statement Forecasts

The financial statements draw many of their assumptions from the other department subplans. Further, the financial statements use information that flows from one statement to the next. This ensures consistency. For example:

- Net income, depreciation, and amortization all flow from the income statement to the balance sheet and statement of changes.
- All changes to balance sheet accounts flow to the statement of changes in financial condition.
- The ending cash balance as computed on the statement of changes flows back up to the balance sheet.

- Subschedules of line items derived elsewhere flow into the financial plan—accounts receivable and accounts payable are two examples.

Salary Budgets

For the various departments' subplans, the most important part of the personnel plan is the salary schedule. Each department uses the schedule that identifies raises and the changes resulting from hiring and firing people.

The salary budget details all the staffing assumptions obtained from each department and converts them to dollars. Many companies then use this information in the particular departments to which the staffers belong.

USING TOOLS OF THE EXPERTS

Everybody has his or her own pet programming techniques. Good habits are easy to acquire; bad habits are difficult to break. You may find these suggestions useful.

Soft Programming

Experienced business planners always use a technique for programming their schedules called *soft programming*. This simply means that the logic of the computations (the equations) contains no quantitative variables. Instead, the variables required to perform all logical operations come from the assumption section. That way, when assumptions change, you don't have to look all over the computer model to find every place a particular assumption occurs. Further, it makes simulation and sensitivity analyses possible.

Here's an example: Assume that we have the following simple equation:

Average loan balance X interest rate = interest expense

With soft programming, the plan would use assumptions and computations involving cash requirements to compute the loan balance. The plan obtains the interest rate from the assumption section. The equation contains nothing that the assumption section cannot change or that doesn't come from somewhere else in the model. An inexperienced financial planner might have put the interest rate on the loan right into the equation.

Soft programming takes a little longer. However, users can update financial plans that use soft programming techniques faster and with less effort.

Using Macros

A macro is nothing more than a programmed set of instructions. Experienced planners use macros as a utility to make the computer do often complex but routinely repetitive tasks, such as

- Printing prescribed reports
- Transferring data in and out of the model
- Moving data around
- Performing sensitivity and simulation analyses

- Preparing graphical presentations

Most of the popular spreadsheet systems provide for the use of macros. Experienced users often have extensive menus of macros that they use for any particular planning model. If they're smart, they keep a list of the macros, how to invoke them, and what they do in a particular place in the model. For example, if you're using a Lotus 1-2-3 spreadsheet, you might use the macro command *Alt M* to pull up the macro menu.

HARNESSING THE COMPUTER'S POWER

Rather than simply using the computer as an expensive number cruncher, you can also use it to improve the accuracy of your business plan. Three techniques the computer is particularly good at are

- What-if analysis • Sensitivity analysis • Simulation

What-if Analysis

Some planning decisions lend themselves to three distinct outcomes: best case, worst case, and most likely. Many planners use as the worst-case scenario the point where they just meet plan targets. From there, they begin asking *what if* certain assumptions change. Using these techniques, planners determine the impact of specific combinations of variables.

Answers from this analysis bracket the best case, worst case, and most likely cases of the business plan. If an acceptable outcome falls anywhere in this area, the plan still succeeds. Results falling outside the worst case put the business plan at risk.

Sensitivity Analysis

Computers are great workhorses for quickly computing the sensitivity of the business plan to changes or combinations of changes in specific assumptions. Planners call those assumptions that have huge effects on the outcome of the plan *driver assumptions. Secondary assumptions* depend on driver assumptions. Sensitivity analysis provides a method of identifying the impact of changes in both driver assumptions and secondary assumptions.

Most simple spreadsheet products have a module that computes sensitivity quickly. Along with simply computing sensitivity, this technique provides a way to identify the range of tolerable error for particular variables. We answer the question, How much can this assumption change against us and still allow the company to hit its performance targets?

Results of sensitivity analyses usually appear as tables of numbers that show the variables tested and their impact on one specific number. For example, say we were testing the impact on net income of changes in selling price and interest rates. The results of the sensitivity analysis might look like Figure 16-3.

Figure 16-3
Results of Sensitivity Analysis

PEACHES ENTERPRISES
FORECAST SENSITIVITY ANALYSIS
Net Income ($ in thousands) at Selected Sales Price
and Interest Rate Levels

Interest	Sales Price					
Rates	$5.50	$5.20	$4.80	$4.50	$4.20	$3.90
15%	($ 650)	($ 350)	$ 50	$ 350	$ 650	$ 950
14%	(450)	(150)	250	550	850	1,150
13%	(250)	50	450	750	1,050	1,350
12%	150	450	850	1,150	1,450	1,750
11%	300	600	1,000	1,300	1,600	1,900
10%	500	800	1,200	1,500	1,800	2,100
9%	700	1,000	1,400	1,700	2,000	2,300

One technique used to verify the accuracy of a sensitivity table such as that shown in Figure 16-3 is to include in the variables tested, two that have a known outcome. For example, we could use the sales price of $4.80 and the interest rate of 12 percent to run the financial model that computes net income. If the model's net income is $850,000, then we know the sensitivity analysis is correct.

Using this technique, we now know the trade-off between interest rates and product prices for Peaches' net income target.

Simulation Analysis

Simulation is a little more sophisticated than sensitivity analysis. Analysts *simulate* the effects of many variables working in combination with one another at the same time. Simulation provides a more *real-world* method for assessing the assumptions used in a business plan.

Simulation analysis simply involves testing the results of changes to many variables at once, then running the automated plan model. This makes sense when you consider that many variables might shift *as a result* of a change in just one or a few variables. Simulation provides a way of analyzing the cause and effect of such changes.

Another use of simulation analysis comes after acceptance of the business plan and the beginning of implementation. Now we're forced to live with the plan's targets. Using the same simulation model, we can predict the effects of alternative courses of action needed to offset parts of the plan that may have already changed.

PRESENTING THE BUSINESS PLAN

Here's where the rubber meets the road. Once we have created the business plan, we must *communicate* it. The effectiveness of this presentation determines acceptance of the plan. We want the presentation to be:

- Clear • Concise • Simple • Informative • Verifiable

Those reading the plan should find it understandable without going through a lot of explanation. Most business plans use the computer to spin out the quantitative schedules. These often include

- Summary of plan highlights
- Forecast financial statements, including balance sheets, income statements, statement of cash flows, and statement of changes in financial condition
- Sales projections in dollars and in units by product
- Production schedules
- Salary schedules

Using Graphs

Graphs and other charts produced by the computer help to clarify the numbers on the schedules. Some of the best uses of graphs include

- Components of sales by product, shown as a pie chart
- Cash balances throughout the plan period, shown as a bar graph
- Net income, shown as a line chart
- Inventory balances, shown as a bar graph

If your plan contains graphs produced by the computer, make certain of their accuracy. Graphs saved in a picture file (.PIC) aren't automatically updated when the plan model is recomputed. Therefore, planners must rerun, resave, and reprint each graph every time they recompute the plan.

The best way to verify the accuracy of graphs is to tie every data point back to the schedules from which it came. This is a tedious task, but necessary to retain credibility.

Presenting Analytical Information

Results from the what-if analyses, sensitivity studies, and simulations often make their way into the plan document. Be sure to clearly label each analysis. Describe what it tells the reader and the reason it is so important that it had to be included in the plan document. If an analysis is not important, leave it in the work papers.

Like graphs, sensitivity tables and some simulations aren't automatically updated when the main plan model changes. Be sure to tie every number presented in these analyses back to the statements and schedules to verify their accuracy.

Using Abbreviations

Avoid slang or acronyms to describe line items in the business plan. Imagine how irritating it is to someone such as a banker to try to make sense out of your industry's technical jargon. When in doubt, spell it out.

Including a Table of Contents

People discuss business plans piece by piece. Don't make them hunt through yours to find the part they want. Provide a table of contents at the front. Make sure the page numbers listed in the table of contents correspond with the correct pages in the body of the plan. Another good idea is to use index tabs to separate the sections.

Identifying Reports

This may sound basic. However, most of us in the business have seen plans in which it was difficult to tell just what a schedule was all about. The principal error is often failure to clearly identify columns in a multicolumn schedule. This usually happens after the first page of a schedule. The person doing the programming did not understand how to get the column headings to repeat at the top of each successive page. Readers seeing this fundamental error wonder what else the programmer didn't understand how to do.

Also, be sure to include page numbers in the header at the top of each page. Remember, our objective is to make the presentation as clear as possible, not to confuse the reader.

VALIDATING THE PLANNING MODEL

Once programming of the plan model is completed, we need to make sure it works. Chances are that whoever did the programming is not a professional—nor does he or she need to be. We want to make sure the programming

- Is arithmetically correct
- Is logically consistent with the way the company operates
- Produces a verifiable result

We call the process of checking the plan model *validation*. Here are the steps professionals use.

Testing the Arithmetic

Test the arithmetic accuracy of every number. This is a simple task, but boring. Here are the most obvious points to check.

Footing and cross-footing

Foot and cross-foot each column. When ending balances in one period become beginning balances in the next, make sure they do. One obvious error that impugns the credibility of a schedule is cross-footing numbers that should not cross-foot. Percentages are a good example. For example, don't cross-foot gross margin percentage. Further, don't compute annual gross margin as the average of all the months. Rather, compute the year-end gross margin by dividing the year-end gross profit by year-end sales. The equation is the same as was used in each month. The answer may come very close to the monthly average, but the programmer should know what's correct.

Assumptions

Make sure that assumptions brought down into the plan model from the assumption section land in the right place.

Subtotals

Subtotals taken from various places in a schedule usually foot to a grand total. Make sure that the right subtotals were used and that they do indeed add to the stated grand total. The most common programming error is to leave out a subtotal.

Testing Logic

Test every equation for computational accuracy and for faulty logic. Most spreadsheet programs have the ability to copy equations across entire rows or columns. Make sure the programmer executed the copy procedure correctly.

Proving the Model

The best way to prove a computer model is to load the assumption section with data that has a known result. Try using last year's actual performance numbers. The results should come out close to the prior year's actuals. If not, find out why. It could mean there's an error or inconsistency in the planning model.

Testing Financial Statements

If you've done all of the above, there's a high probability that your automated planning system is accurate. However, there are several quick tests to find glaring errors. Doing these helps to keep you from distributing something that clearly has computational problems.

Checking the balance sheet

Does the balance sheet balance? How much credibility does a balance sheet have if total assets don't equal total liabilities and equity? This is the first checkpoint whenever you see a new balance sheet.

Tying out cash

The cash balance shown at the top of the balance sheet must equal the ending cash balance shown throughout the rest of the financial plan. Depending on the format, cash might be found in the cash flow plan or in the statement of changes in financial position.

Verifying subledgers against the general ledger

This is more important when comparing the plan's financial statements with actual performance. Make sure actuals for all subledgers tie to the general ledger. For example, the accounts receivable subledger should show a balance that exactly ties to the accounts receivable balance appearing on the general ledger.

The same holds true for these subledgers and schedules:

- Accounts payable • Inventory • Capital assets
- Accumulated depreciation and amortization

Retained earnings

Retained earnings (usually the last line of owners' equity in the balance sheet) should tie to the income statement. Here's how: Retained earnings is the prior period's balance in retained earnings plus the current period's net income after tax. If this simple computation doesn't equal the balance in the current period retained earnings, there's a problem.

Seeing that subplans agree

Make sure the schedules from each department that provide key assumptions used in the overall financial plan agree. For example, the accounts receivable plan should show a balance at the end of each operating period equal to the receivables balance on the balance sheet of the financial plan. Additionally, sales levels that produced accounts receivable should agree with the sales plan.

The same thing should be true of the balance in the accounts payable plan and the purchasing plans for equipment and inventory. These should all tie to the accounts payable figure on the prospective balance sheet.

Income statement items

Income statement items also appear in places other than the income statement itself. For example, net income before taxes also appears at the top of the statement of changes in financial condition. Depreciation and amortization don't just appear on the income statement. The statement of changes adds them back to net income before taxes to compute cash sources.

Link the sales revenue schedule appearing on the income statement to the production schedule. You should be able to see how the production schedule *leads* sales. A graph of these two schedules illustrates this timing. It also reveals potential problems.

Salaries are one of the largest expenditures. Make sure that the salary expense appearing on the prospective income statement agrees with the salary schedule prepared as part of the people plan.

The operating expenses scheduled for each department and for corporate office overhead should tie to the planned income statement. If this statement does not itemize departmental expenses, then they should tie to the assumptions used to develop the consolidated number.

Chapter 17 demonstrates how to monitor progress toward plan goals.

Chapter 17

Monitoring Progress
Toward Plan Goals

OVERVIEW

Chapter 17 demonstrates how to keep the business plan on track. We'll discuss the qualities of the mechanism that best monitors progress. The system that we set up in this chapter quickly identifies departures from plan and suggests possible solutions. Additionally, this section illustrates ways to

- Simulate the effects of possible corrections *before* implementing them.
- Identify which information should be reported.
- Determine an appropriate distribution for plan monitoring information.
- Construct a logical reporting format.

Smart and experienced planning teams begin designing the monitoring mechanism *while* formulating the business plan. Once the plan is approved, the monitoring mechanism begins capturing performance information.

STRUCTURING THE MONITORING SYSTEM

We want a monitoring mechanism that quickly and easily identifies departures from the plan. Most small businesses don't need an elaborate business plan monitoring system. Most of the people involved understand the daily operations anyway. They know when actual performance begins to deviate from the plan.

However, the monitoring system regularly communicates performance and progress to other departments affected by deviations throughout the company. We'll assume that the plan monitoring system does *not* do two things:

- It doesn't prepare reports for regulatory agencies. Companies in regulated industries report regularly to the government. That information comes from another source within the company, not the plan monitoring system.

- It doesn't prepare reports for owners and investors. Financial information intended for distribution to parties outside the firm often falls under regulatory or GAAP reporting requirements. Our monitoring system provides information *for internal use only*. It doesn't always follow generally accepted accounting principles. The system doesn't prepare reports for a CPA to attest to their fairness of presentation.

The monitoring reporting structure emphasizes simplicity. To accomplish that, we

- Keep the number of reports small.
- Conduct analytical procedures rather than exhaustive investigations of differences from the plan.
- Report *exceptions and deviations from the plan* when possible.
- Give people information in the most useful format.
- Highlight progress toward key benchmarks.
- Emphasize management of progress toward the plan goals.

Contents of the Monitoring System

Design the monitoring system to provide data on the progress the firm makes toward its goals. Focus on specific targets and goals, then compare them with actual performance. Design your monitoring system so that it becomes a tool for determining solutions to plan deviations. To accomplish the goals of performance reporting and analysis of solutions, the monitoring mechanism includes the following elements.

Comparative financial statements

Financial statements provide a quick way to identify progress toward specific financial targets. Further, if you use an automated accounting system, it's easy to load actual financial information into the automated planning schedules. From there, develop comparative reports and analyses. Make sure your monthly financial reporting system can generate these comparative financial statements and schedules:

- Summary of key financial performance benchmarks compared to those in the plan
- Balance sheet
- Accounts receivable subschedules
- Accounts payable subschedules
- Inventory control reports
- Income statement
- Sources and uses of cash
- Schedule of compliance with lending covenants and restrictions

Basis of comparison

Actual versus plan isn't the only comparison the monitoring system should make. Often it's useful to provide other convenient reference points. The most common include

- Current month actual versus current month plan
- Current month actual year-to-date versus current month plan year-to-date
- Last month actual versus last month plan
- Current month versus this month last year
- This month year-to-date versus this month last year, year-to-date

Such a complete set of comparisons allows for deviations caused by seasonality and particularly good (or bad) months.

For some key figures presented during the implementation period, it's useful to project the year-end performance. We compute that using a method called *annualization*. This tool answers the question, "If we continue for the rest of the year like this, what will be the results?" Here's an example of annualizing a number.

Say costs for the first seven months are $6,500,000. Therefore, annualized costs at this rate are $11.1 million. Compute this as follows:

$$\frac{\$6.5 \text{ million}}{7 \text{ months}} = \frac{X}{12 \text{ months}}$$

Solving for X, the annualized costs at the seventh month are $11.1 million. Therefore, if the plan requires costs of $10.0 million by year-end, the firm must save some costs in the last half of the year.

Special reports

Keep special reports to a minimum. They tend to unnecessarily expand the month-end reporting package. Often people continue to produce the reports even after management stops using them. However, sometimes special reports provide insight into specific performance issues, such as

- Progress toward benchmarks
- Progress toward targets used for performance incentive purposes

An example would be a spot gain-sharing program for sales of a specific product line. A special report used to monitor the program identifies the target and actual performance for each sales territory. It goes to the sales manager, each of the sales representatives, and the person managing the spot gain-sharing program. That way everyone can tell each month how he or she and the entire program are doing.

Punctuality

Reports from the monitoring system must be punctual. The sooner after month-end, the better. Managers use the information in the monitoring system to make the decisions necessary to keep the plan on track. They can't use late numbers or inaccurate numbers for decision-making purposes. Make sure your monitoring system sends out its performance reports within the first two weeks (preferably within the *first* week) after month-end.

Exception reporting

Some planners streamline their monitoring package by reporting only exceptions outside the planning range. Exception reports relieve management of having to determine what's right and wrong from a mass of numbers. Instead, the reports highlight unusual statistics.

Exception reporting also helps to explain why certain deviations occurred. One area deviating from the plan often causes another part to do the same. Frequently, a domino effect occurs. It's important for management to quickly focus on the issues to begin correcting them.

However, reporting only exceptions makes those receiving the report gunshy. All it brings is problems. Some companies look upon the monthly exception reports with dread.

MONITORING SYSTEM REQUIREMENTS

The structure of the business plan must recognize the monitoring requirements. Without a reliable mechanism to track actual performance and compare it with the plan, there's no way to identify deviations and correct them.

Availability of Information

The most common error of novice planners is to establish milestones for which progress numbers simply aren't available anywhere in the company. For example, say that the sales subplan has targets it must meet each month. However, few accounting systems can provide midmonth progress reports to the sales department. Consequently, after the performance reports finally appear, sales is always trying in the current month to replace shortfalls that occurred in the prior month. In this case, when they were planning the milestones, no one thought to consider the availability of the information that management needed to do its job.

Make sure the monitoring system provides the performance indicators needed to keep the plan on track.

Tracking Specifications

The monitoring system must provide information on progress toward all the goals throughout the company. Usually the sequencing of targets is important. The monitoring system tells us if one critical target has slipped that could affect other targets later in the plan implementation.

Tracking specifications include three things:

- Timing • Effects of changes in timing • Units reported

Timing the implementation

The monitoring system should report actual performance results based on the timing requirements of the departments needing the information. We saw this in the example of the sales department that needed unit sales at midmonth to manage its progress toward each month-end target.

Timing plays another important role. The monitoring system should identify performance indicators that are critical to the rest of the business plan. For example, say the plan requires an increase in the line of credit to finance accounts receivable resulting from the sales plan. Without the increased credit line, the company cannot pay the vendors who supplied the raw materials needed to make the products.

Therefore, the monitoring system must provide a status report on such critical implementation items as the line of credit.

Identifying the effects of timing changes

Part of the plan monitoring system projects the impact of changes in timing. This task is easier if you put the plan schedules on an automated spreadsheet. Convert the timing change to specific quantitative shifts in the assumptions. Then run the planning model to determine how the changes affect key benchmarks needed to implement the plan.

There's often a cascade effect when one part of the plan changes. For example, watch what happens when sales goals lag their targets by a month or two:

1. *Accounts receivable*: We don't need the staff to handle the anticipated workload from increased sales for a month or two. However, the firm hired them in anticipation of the workload. Now they're on board and idle.

2. *Collateral*: Many companies secure loans with accounts receivable. The controller negotiated a loan in anticipation of the added receivables. Now the bank won't fund the needed draw until its collateral is up to the agreed level. However, the vendors demand payment. The company is headed for a cash crisis.

3. *Manufacturing*: The company has produced the goods specified in the sales plan. Now they just sit in the warehouse, gathering dust and eating up working capital.

4. *Raw material inventory*: Accounts payable rose as a result of the materials needed by Manufacturing. Some of this material is already in the finished goods that sit in the warehouse. However, the firm had not converted some of it to work in process before production slowed. If sales don't pick up and production resume, the company may sell the excess raw materials inventory at a loss just to get rid of it and generate some badly needed cash.

Monitoring systems with "what if" capabilities are invaluable for use in assessing possible options in response to deviations in the plan.

Units reported

The monitoring system must provide information in a form that managers can use in tracking and managing performance. Some measurements, such as finished goods inventory, require units. Other benchmarks in the plan, such as accounts receivable, make more sense in dollars. Still others, like sales volume, require measurement in both units and dollars. Make sure that the tracking system reports measurements the way managers need them. You don't want managers to have to go through extensive conversion computations just to use the monitoring reports.

Presenting the Results

Pay particular attention to the design of your plan monitoring reports. Tables are the best way to present most of the comparative information. That allows readers to see what actually occurred and compare it with what should have happened. Further, tables allow the system to make comparative computations for readers and point out deviations from the plan.

Graphs also provide a quick way to illustrate a trend or make a particular point. For example, let's say that Doobie International manufactures the tape cassettes used in professional recording studios. Doobie continues to hit its sales objectives. However, the margin by which sales exceed planned benchmarks each month is steadily decreasing. Shown as a downward-sloping graph, the trend is obvious. The implication is equally obvious—shortly Doobie's sales level is going to fall below the benchmarks by greater and greater degrees. Figure 17-1 makes this point. Notice how the line plotting actual performance trends down toward the level plan line. It looks as if sales will fall below the plan between the eighth and ninth months.

Figure 17-1

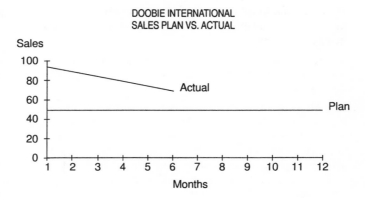

Pie charts are an effective method of showing the composition of a number. For example, say that Doobie wants to know what makes up the sales numbers in any particular month. Put the information in a pie chart. If you have the ability to cut out a slice, this provides a visual illustration of one particular component.

Most spreadsheet systems allow for pie charts. Many such systems also slice the pie at the touch of a button. Figure 17-2 shows Doobie's sales for the month of June.

Figure 17-2
Pie Chart

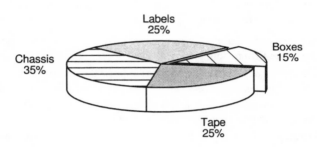

DOOBIE INTERNATIONAL
JUNE SALES COMPOSITION

Chassis is the largest single sales component. However, perhaps boxes are the highest-margin product. Discussion in the financial results package may highlight this point.

CIRCULATING RESULTS

Your monitoring system should provide useful information, not just raw data. In many cases the readers draw conclusions as a result of the presentation's slant. That's what we want to a certain extent. However, the purpose of the monitoring system is *not* to persuade readers to accept the analyst's viewpoint. We want to give managers the exact information they need to track their areas of responsibility with the business plan. This usually means providing different pieces of information to different managers.

Tailoring Reports

Report formats vary depending on the needs of the readers. Not everyone on the monitoring system distribution list gets all the reports the system produces. Don't give this information to people without a need to see it. Additionally, let those receiving it know that this information is proprietary to the company and is *confidential.*

Therefore, tailor the monitoring reports to the specific needs of the recipients. If you don't, you run the risk of diminishing the importance of vital information because it's surrounded by less useful data. Further, the less sensitive information floating around the company, the better.

The planning team usually receives all of the monitoring system reports. Package this as

- Summary of monthly performance information
- Full set of comparative financial statements
- Information showing progress toward particular milestones on the implementation schedule
- All the special reports prepared for particular individuals that track their areas of responsibility

For example, the monthly reporting package that goes to the head of marketing might include the following:

- Summary of monthly performance—provides a quick overview of how the entire firm is doing
- Comparative income statement—supports the summary
- Milestone chart showing sales by product compared with the plan for this month, year-to-date, and this time last year, year-to-date—provides the specific goals for which the marketing department is responsible
- Detailed sales analysis by sales responsibility center such as territory and salesperson
- Inflow and outflow of balances into the accounts receivable system—shows how well the target market pays its bills
- Summary of A/R aging—shows the impact on cash flow from customers to whom the marketing department is selling
- Analysis of gross margin [(sales – cost of goods sold) / sales] by product for plan versus this month and year-to-date—demonstrates how product pricing ties with manufacturing costs to hit the all-important gross margin targets

CREATING THE REPORTS

Monthly progress reports of actual performance compared to plan are one of the most valuable tools in the business planning exercise. Some may complain that the program set forth here is too structured. That's the idea. We want a regular method of assessing the company's movement toward its planned goals. Management uses these monthly reports to make decisions regarding midcourse corrections.

With such usage and credibility, the business plan and the monitoring mechanism to ensure that it stays on course become tools. As management uses the plan, it often makes changes. The monitoring mechanism then reports these changes against actual performance.

Content of the Monitoring Reports

Include in the monthly financial results package only the information needed to run the company. Leave out all extraneous information—it just wastes everyone's time if it's not used. Figure 17-3 shows one company's sample monthly report.

Figure 17-3

PEACHES ENTERPRISES, LTD
Month of May 199X
Summary of company performance

	MAY ACTUAL	MAY PLAN	ACT'L B(W) PLAN	ACTUAL YTD	PLAN YTD	YTD ACT'L B(W) PLAN	YTD ACT'L LAST YEAR	MAY YTD B(W) LAST YR YTD
Revenue	$325,000	$315,000	$10,000	$1,357,000	$1,300,000	$57,000	$1,425,000	($68,000)
Cost of goods sold	173,000	155,000	(18,000)	732,000	700,000	(32,000)	775,000	43,000
Gross margin	$152,000	$160,000	($8,000)	$625,000	$600,000	$25,000	$650,000	($25,000)
Total expenses	111,435	105,900	(5,535)	605,675	567,500	(38,175)	636,967	31,292
Net income before tax	$40,565	$54,100	($13,535)	$19,325	$32,500	($13,175)	$13,033	$6,292
Dollars in inventory	$450,000	$455,000	$5,000	N/A	N/A	N/A	$500,000	$50,000
Units in inventory	15,000	14,000	(1,000)	N/A	N/A	N/A	30,000	15,000
Days of sales in inventory	15	20	5	N/A	N/A	N/A	22	7
Accounts receivable balance	$300,000	$275,000	($25,000)	N/A	N/A	N/A	$450,000	$150,000
Accounts receivable turnover	25	22	-3	N/A	N/A	N/A	36	11
Number of employees	26	28	2					
Direct labor costs	$25,000	$29,000	$4,000	$150,000	$174,000	$24,000	$180,000	$30,000
Total salary expenses	$32,000	$35,000	$3,000	$192,000	$210,000	$18,000	$250,000	$58,000
Cash balance	$50,000	$55,000	($5,000)	N/A	N/A	N/A	$40,000	$10,000
Available line of credit	$250,000	$250,000	$0	N/A	N/A	N/A	$200,000	$50,000

PEACHES ENTERPRISES, LTD
Month of May 199X
Comparative Income Statement

	MAY ACTUAL	MAY PLAN	ACT'L B(W) PLAN	ACTUAL YTD	PLAN YTD	YTD ACT'L B(W) PLAN	YTD ACT'L LAST YEAR	MAY YTD B(W) LAST YR YTD
SALES	$325,000	$315,000	$10,000	$1,357,000	$1,300,000	$57,000	$1,425,000	($68,000)
COST OF GOODS SOLD	173,000	155,000	(18,000)	732,000	700,000	(32,000)	775,000	43,000
GROSS MARGIN ($)	$152,000	$160,000	($8,000)	$625,000	$600,000	$25,000	$650,000	($25,000)
GROSS MARGIN (%)	47%	51%	-0.04	46%	46%	-0.00	46%	0.00
ADVERTISING	7,500	4,000	(3,500)	45,000	24,000	(21,000)	36,000	(9,000)
BAD DEBT EXPENSE	14,500	9,000	(5,500)	87,000	54,000	(33,000)	80,000	(7,000)
COMMISSION EXPENSE	26,500	25,000	(1,500)	159,000	150,000	(9,000)	142,000	(17,000)
DEPRECIATION:								
CORPORATE OFFICES	3,235	3,100	(135)	16,175	15,500	(675)	22,500	6,325
MACHINERY & EQUIPMENT	4,300	4,200	(100)	21,500	21,000	(500)	27,000	5,500
FURNITURE & FIXTURES	975	900	(75)	4,875	4,500	(375)	6,657	1,782
LEASEHOLD IMPROVEMENTS	1,750	1,800	50	8,750	9,000	250	11,100	2,350
INSURANCE	3,100	4,000	900	15,500	20,000	4,500	22,300	6,800
SALARIES & WAGES	33,575	36,000	2,425	167,875	180,000	12,125	184,060	16,185
PAYROLL TAXES	7,300	8,500	1,200	36,500	42,500	6,000	43,450	6,950
UTILITIES	6,100	6,500	400	30,500	32,500	2,000	40,900	10,400
TRAVEL & ENTERTAINMENT	2,600	2,900	300	13,000	14,500	1,500	21,000	8,000
TOTAL COSTS AND EXPENSES	$111,435	$105,900	($5,535)	$605,675	$567,500	($38,175)	$636,967	$31,292
NET INCOME BEFORE TAX	$40,565	$54,100	($13,535)	$19,325	$32,500	($13,175)	$13,033	$6,292
TAX ACCRUAL	17,000	13,000	(4,000)	7,730	13,000	5,270	5,213	(2,517)
NET INCOME	23,565	41,100	($17,535)	11,595	19,500	($7,905)	7,820	$3,775

PEACHES ENTERPRISES, LTD
Month of May 199X
Milestone Sales by Product
(Units sold)

	MAY ACTUAL	MAY PLAN	ACT'L B(W) PLAN	ACTUAL YTD	PLAN YTD	YTD ACT'L B(W) PLAN	YTD ACT'L LAST YEAR	MAY YTD B(W) LAST YR YTD
Blasting caps	267	260	7	1,335	1,300	35	1,200	135
Primacord (rolls)	153	150	3	765	750	15	2,150	(1,385)
Det. wire	75	100	-25	375	500	-125	1,650	(1,275)
Lead shields	226	200	26	1,130	1,000	130	500	630
Wireless ignition systems	67	60	7	335	300	35	300	35
High drive (40% dynamite)	51	75	-24	255	375	-120	600	(345)
Amonium nitrate	120	175	-55	600	875	-275	1,400	(800)
Magnesium pellets	199	200	-1	995	1,000	-5	750	245
Total units sold	1,158	1,220	-62	5,790	6,100	-310	8,550	(2,760)

PEACHES ENTERPRISES, LTD
May 199x
Accounts Receivable Flow

BEGINNING A/R BALANCE	$267,000
INCREASE TO A/R:	
CREDIT SALES 100	23,400
CREDIT SALES $100–500	76,875
CREDIT SALES $500–1,000	61,000
CREDIT SALES $1,000–5,000	55,000
CREDIT SALES >$5,000	10,000
TOTAL INCREASE TO A/R	$226,275
COLLECTIONS ON A/R BALANCES:	
CURRENT	83,250
30 DAYS	51,750
60 DAYS	39,756
90 DAYS	31,265
120 DAYS	8,345
OVER 120 DAYS	6,152
TOTAL COLLECTIONS	$220,518
ENDING A/R BALANCE	$272,757

PEACHES ENTERPRISES, LTD
May 199x
Summary of A/R Aging

	CURRENT MONTH	LAST MONTH	CURRENT B(W) LAST
CURRENT BALANCE	$114,356	$95,354	($19,002)
30 DAYS	40,687	64,595	23,908
60 DAYS	43,753	39,432	(4,321)
90 DAYS	36,535	19,786	(16,749)
120 DAYS	14,191	17,500	3,309
OVER 120 DAYS	23,235	30,333	7,098
	$272,757	$267,000	($5,757)

PEACHES ENTERPRISES, LTD
Month of May 199X
Analysis of Gross Margin by Product

	MAY ACTUAL	MAY PLAN	ACT'L B(W) PLAN	ACTUAL YTD	PLAN YTD	YTD ACT'L B(W) PLAN	YTD ACT'L LAST YEAR	MAY YTD B(W) LAST YR YTD
Margin analysis by product:								
Blasting caps:								
Gross revenue	$51,657	$50,689	$968	$142,000	$140,000	$2,000	$155,000	($13,000)
Cost of goods sold	30,410	27,656	(2,754)	119,833	28,500	(91,333)	70,900	(48,933)
Gross margin ($)	$21,247	$23,033	($1,786)	$22,167	$111,500	($89,333)	$84,100	($61,933)
Gross margin (%)	41%	45%	-4%	16%	80%	-64%	54%	-39%
Primacord (rolls)								
Gross revenue	$22,648	$17,689	$4,959	$80,000	$66,000	$14,000	$67,500	$12,500
Cost of goods sold	11,678	9,862	(1,816)	38,000	43,000	5,000	50,350	12,350
Gross margin ($)	$10,970	$7,827	$3,143	$42,000	$23,000	$19,000	$17,150	$24,850
Gross margin (%)	48%	44%	4%	53%	35%	18%	25%	27%
Detonation wire								
Gross revenue	$75,689	$70,658	$5,031	$420,000	$475,000	($55,000)	$483,000	($63,000)
Cost of goods sold	41,432	37,659	(3,773)	203,833	272,000	68,167	240,500	36,667
Gross margin ($)	$34,257	$32,999	$1,258	$216,167	$203,000	$13,167	$242,500	($26,333)
Gross margin (%)	45%	47%	-1%	51%	43%	9%	50%	1%
Lead shields								
Gross revenue	$27,965	$25,689	$2,276	$90,000	$67,000	$23,000	$75,500	$14,500
Cost of goods sold	14,356	13,598	(758)	40,000	43,000	3,000	51,250	11,250
Gross margin ($)	$13,609	$12,091	$1,518	$50,000	$24,000	$26,000	$24,250	$25,750
Gross margin (%)	49%	47%	2%	56%	36%	20%	32%	23%
Wireless ignition systems								
Gross revenue	$56,368	$53,689	$2,679	$200,000	$186,000	$14,000	$273,500	($73,500)
Cost of goods sold	27,659	20,689	(6,970)	148,833	163,000	14,167	145,250	(3,583)
Gross margin ($)	$28,709	$33,000	($4,291)	$51,167	$23,000	$28,167	$128,250	($77,083)
Gross margin (%)	51%	61%	-11%	26%	12%	13%	47%	-21%
High drive								
Gross revenue	$43,907	$41,398	$2,509	$195,000	$210,000	($15,000)	$175,000	$20,000
Cost of goods sold	26,879	27,986	1,107	85,000	78,000	(7,000)	110,000	25,000
Gross margin ($)	$17,028	$13,412	$3,616	$110,000	$132,000	($22,000)	$65,000	$45,000
Gross margin (%)	39%	32%	6%	56%	63%	-6%	37%	19%
Amonium nitrate								
Gross revenue	$36,898	$46,099	($9,201)	$165,000	$120,000	$45,000	$135,000	$30,000
Cost of goods sold	16,898	13,872	(3,026)	75,000	57,000	(18,000)	75,250	250
Gross margin ($)	$20,000	$32,227	($12,227)	$90,000	$63,000	$27,000	$59,750	$30,250
Gross margin (%)	54%	70%	-16%	55%	53%	2%	44%	10%
Magnesium pellets								
Gross revenue	$9,868	$9,089	$779	$65,000	$36,000	$29,000	$60,500	$4,500
Cost of goods sold	3,688	3,678	(10)	21,501	15,500	(6,001)	31,500	9,999
Gross margin ($)	$6,180	$5,411	$769	$43,499	$20,500	$22,999	$29,000	$14,499
Gross margin (%)	63%	60%	3%	67%	57%	10%	48%	19%
Total revenue	$325,000	$315,000	$10,000	$1,357,000	$1,300,000	$57,000	$1,425,000	($68,000)
less total cost of goods sold	173,000	155,000	(18,000)	732,000	700,000	(32,000)	775,000	43,000
Total gross margin ($)	$152,000	$160,000	($8,000)	$625,000	$600,000	$25,000	$650,000	($25,000)
Total gross margin (%)	47%	51%	-4%	46%	46%	-0%	46%	0%

Notice how the monitoring system reports only the parts of the company of interest to management. It purposely omitted the balance sheet and cash flow reports. However, in practice, the plan would normally contain these.

Timing of the Reports

Most small to medium-sized companies run their monitoring system at least monthly. Many firms conduct formal quarterly plan reviews. In that case the monitoring reports contain quarterly totals for both actual and plan.

Many companies conduct a midyear plan review. This is the most critical review. Think of it as halftime in a football game. Management assesses where the firm stands midway through its plan implementation. There's still time to correct deviations from the plan. Further, midyear is the time to incorporate into the plan new opportunities that surfaced in the last six months.

If your firm conducts an extensive midyear plan review, the monitoring system must produce two additional comparative reports:

- Midyear plan versus midyear actual year-to-date
- Midyear actual *annualized* versus total year plan

These two comparisons illustrate how the company is doing at midyear compared to plan and how the year will end up at this rate compared to the full-year plan.

Certainly the year-end reports from the monitoring system interest management. That's especially true when companies pay incentive bonuses for year-end performance. However, from a profit management standpoint, the year-end reports are less important—there's no time left to fix any problems.

CAPTURING INFORMATION

Design the monitoring system with the type of information and reports required in mind. You don't want to be in the position of needing information that's not readily available. Sometimes the implementation team needs information never before developed by the company. When that happens, you need procedures to capture the information, review it for accuracy, and put it into a format usable by the people who work with it.

Many people view data conversion for reporting purposes as busywork. However, companies that are serious about successfully implementing their business plan present the reason for this information frankly. Most people agree about its importance.

Techniques of Data Capture

Information captured by the performance monitoring system should have these attributes:

- It must be accurate and reliable.
- Raw data must easily convert into useful information.
- It must be available within the time frame required.

- It should be captured as close to the source as possible so that it doesn't pass through too many hands, wasting time and making it subject to error or misinterpretation.
- It should be verified by another party if possible.

The data most easily fulfilling these requirements comes directly from the firm's computer. From there, the system translates it into useful information. Some larger companies keep their performance information on a large computer. To work with it more easily, they may move the raw data to a personal computer where the software is more user-friendly. There, they convert the raw data into useful information.

Emphasize efficiency in your data capture. Watch the use of the reports and information coming out of the monitoring system. If no one uses them, then discontinue them. For example, let's say the production department wants to track idle labor hours due to machinery downtime against benchmarks it put in its plan.

An astute planner would have seen that benchmark in the beginning and designed a method of capturing it *prior* to starting implementation of the plan. A good way to do that would be to put such idle labor costs into a special general ledger expense account. This makes the data capture easy.

However, what happens if there is no computer, or if for whatever reason the cost accounting system cannot capture idle labor hours due to machine downtime? Now how do we get the information? One solution would be to create a manual log of employees who are idle because of machine downtime throughout the month. A simple log would include

- Name of employee • Labor rate • Date of downtime
- Number of hours idle • Labor cost for the idle time

You might even keep the log on a spreadsheet in the production department's personal computer. If possible, transfer this information to the computer on which the business plan monitoring system resides. The performance monitoring system can then electronically incorporate the data. The time such a procedure takes should be minimal for everyone. Further, the possibility of error falls because fewer hands actually massage the information.

Using Captured Data

If we take the trouble to capture information and report it to the company, it should be relevant. One way to be sure of this is to periodically talk with the managers who receive it. Find out what they do with it. Discover how they use it to track their particular benchmarks. The answers may surprise you. Often what you thought was useful information is marked up and further massaged to convert it into something that's *really* useful. Other times, the recipients just slide it under a pile of work without even looking at it because it tells them nothing they don't already know.

If either of these things happens, the monitoring system isn't doing its job. Make the reports useful or stop generating them.

Focusing on what people need

The monitoring system should provide what people actually need and use, not what they say they need. A good example is the idle labor costs described above. As machinery gets older, downtime increases, and idle labor costs rise right along with it. Therefore, what the manager *really* needs is information on machinery downtime, not raw data on idle labor hours.

Focus on the problem source, poorly maintained or aging equipment, not the symptom, idle labor cost. Provide the information necessary to make decisions. Look at the real use of the information and the decisions it supports. Then focus on just what's needed. Anything more than that is a waste of time and just confuses already busy decision makers.

USING ANALYTICAL TECHNIQUES

Most business performance monitoring systems employ ratios and statistics to provide an index of performance. By themselves, these measurements don't tell us a great deal. Their utility is in *comparison* with other companies or different time frames. Further, if your company has two or more different businesses, don't try to compare financial ratios. What may be an acceptable index for one business may not be for another.

The most commonly used performance measurements deal with parts of the balance sheet. Many already reside in the business plan as performance benchmarks.

Asset Ratios

Often companies focus on specific parts of their balance sheet. This is usually because their banks think these items are important. Many loan agreements require maintenance of certain asset ratios as part of the lending covenant. If that's the case, then the firm must certainly watch each of these performance indicators and keep them within the limits prescribed by the bank loan.

Quick ratio

$$\text{Quick ratio} = \frac{\text{cash} + \text{marketable securities}}{\text{current liabilities}}$$

This ratio tells the firm's ability to make payments without using cash generated from sales. It presents a worst-case scenario—no sales. Note that many analysts include either the current portion or the entire balance of accounts receivable in the dividend of this equation as well.

Current ratio

$$\text{Current ratio} = \frac{\text{current assets}}{\text{current liabilities}}$$

Use this ratio to show the ability to meet payment obligations due within the operating period with assets that we can convert to cash within that same operating period.

If you find these two ratios (or any others, for that matter) in a lending covenant, you should know well ahead of time if they're going to fall outside their specified ranges. Notify the bank if there's nothing you can do to prevent it. It looks a lot better to anticipate a problem and work to fix it than to appear surprised at bad news.

Finally, if your firm breaches a lending covenant, secure from the bank a *written* waiver of its rights and remedies against your company. Without a written waiver, you run the risk of the bank changing its mind and throwing the company into default.

Financing and Debt Ratios

- *Liabilities covered by working capital* (working capital provided from operations / total liabilities). This ratio illustrates the firm's ability to repay current liabilities using internally generated working capital.
- *Financial structure.* We measure two things concerning financial structure:
  - *Term financing* (fixed assets / short-term debt). If companies finance too many fixed (long-term) assets using short-term debt, two things can occur: The debt can mature before the assets have earned enough money to repay the obligation, and if interest rates spike upward, the cost of funds is likely to rise along with it, changing the assumptions used to justify acquiring the asset in the first place.
  - *Proportionate term of debt* (short-term debt / long-term debt). Ideally, long-term debt (sometimes referred to as the core borrowings) should exceed short-term debt. If it doesn't, the company is subject to a liquidity squeeze if it attempts to roll over maturing short-term debt when cash is scarce. This happened to some real estate developers during the early 1990s when banks all but stopped lending on real estate.

By tracking these benchmarks in the financial plan, you have positioned yourself to act in advance of a crisis. Further, many loan covenants require that the borrower not fall below specified levels on certain financial ratios. If that happens, the loan may be subject to immediate call and repayment. These are benchmarks to which you definitely pay attention. It's a good idea to have your financial plan compute them each month.

Aging Accounts Receivable

Weighted average age of accounts receivable = sum of (weighted average % of each aging bucket X number of days in each aging bucket)

This number (shown in days) demonstrates the weighted average time the company takes to collect its receivables. The fewer the number of days, the less cash the company has invested in receivables. Banks like this number because it provides an indication of the receivable portfolio's stability. Watch this statistic closely if a loan is collateralized by receivables. For example, a portfolio aged forty-five days has a higher probability of being collected than one with a seventy-five-day weighted average aging.

Accounts Receivable Turnover Rate

$$\text{A/R turnover} = \frac{\text{annual sales}}{\text{average A/R balance}}$$

This measurement shows how fast the firm collects its receivables. The faster receivables turn, the less cash this component of working capital consumes. The A/R turnover rate should interest the finance department.

Accounts Payable Turnover Rate

$$\text{A/P turnover} = \frac{\text{annual expenses}}{\text{average A/P balance}}$$

As with the receivables turnover, A/P turnover tracks the speed at which the firm pays its obligations. The higher the A/P turnover rate, the more cash escapes from the firm and the greater the requirement for working capital. Conversely, the lower this ratio, the more the company retains its cash.

Compare the accounts receivable turnover with the accounts payable turnover. If receivables turn faster than payables, your vendors are financing this portion of your working capital requirements—you are collecting money from customers before vendors require payment.

Aging Accounts Payable

Weighted average age of accounts payable = sum of (weighted average % of each aging bucket X number of days in each aging bucket)

The higher the number of days payables age, the greater the leverage derived from the company's vendors. This is another measurement of how closely the A/P department follows company policy regarding vendor payment. It's not usually good policy to pay obligations before they're due. During times of cash inadequacy, many firms stretch their payables. Further, using these and other A/P measurements, the controller can control the firm's payment policies even more precisely.

Average Payment Period

$$\text{Average payment period} = \frac{\text{accounts payable balance}}{(\text{annual expenses} \div 360)}$$

This measures the number of days of average expenses vendors have invested in the firm's accounts payable. The higher the average payment period, the greater the company's use of trade credit. Consider this as a free loan—the company uses its vendor's credit policies to finance part of its working capital requirements.

Average Collection Period

$$\text{Average collection period} = \frac{\text{accounts receivable balance}}{(\text{annual sales} \div 360)}$$

This ratio also provides insight into receivables collection efficiency. The average collection period tells the number of days of average sales contained in accounts receivable. The company wants as few days of sales as possible in receivables.

Average Investment Period in Inventory

$$\text{Average investment period in inventory} = \frac{\text{present inventory balance}}{(\text{annual cost of goods sold} / 360)}$$

Many business plans focus on inventory control. The objective is to have as little money tied up in inventory as possible. The smaller the average investment period in inventory, the faster the inventory turns into disposable cash.

Inventory Turnover

$$\text{Inventory turnover rate} = \frac{\text{annual cost of goods sold}}{\text{average inventory balance}}$$

The faster a company's inventory turns, the faster its investment in inventory converts to sales and, further, the less valuable cash the company has tied up in low-demand stock.

MONITORING A FLEXIBLE PLAN

Sometimes negative variances aren't necessarily bad. At higher sales levels, the costs of commissions and other expenses are higher. Therefore, the firm may be over budget in some expense categories but still have a positive profit variance.

Be sure to watch the changes in expense levels when revenue is over budget. There should be some economies that cause expenses to climb at a *slower* rate. If that's not the case, then expenses may be out of control at the higher revenue levels.

Controlling a Flexible Plan

Flexible plans focus on the *relationships* between costs and expenses. Most planners define these relationships using percentages. For example, cost of goods sold is 55 percent of sales revenue. This defines the gross margin of 45 percent.

Flexible financial plans also allow us to maintain a valid plan despite changes in sales levels. That way the monitoring system always has a valid plan number against which to compare costs and expenses. The absolute value of the numbers may change—and that's all right—but the *relationships* remain the same. The monitoring system identifies deviations from the planned percentages and flags a problem. Make the decision to use a flexible monitoring format during the design stage of the business plan.

Chapter 18 demonstrates how to update your business plan.

Chapter 18

Updating the Plan

OVERVIEW

Business plans are living documents. Many departments continue through the planning year with little change. For them, extensive updating isn't necessary. However, in other departments, unforeseen circumstances necessitate a change to the plan. Often these changes cascade into still more adjustments to the targets and timing in other departments throughout the company.

Ignoring these changes and trying to make an outdated plan work is like navigating with an antiquated map. The milestones and landmarks have changed. The plan tells when to make midcourse corrections. However, outdated plans won't signal the need for change. The company will miss its overall targets.

Regular updates keep the plan relevant to current issues confronting the company. Obsolete business plans go stale if they don't accurately portray the business environment. Once enthusiasm has died, the business plan is almost impossible to revive.

Chapter 18 demonstrates how to update significant components of a business plan with new targets based on current results and recent developments. When managed correctly, the company achieves its main planning goals even though the *way* it gets there changes.

KNOWING WHEN TO UPDATE

How do you know when your business plan needs updating? A good indication is the differences between actual performance and the plan. If the differences accumulate to a point where the company cannot achieve the plan during the time remaining in the planning period, then the plan requires an update. Another sign is that the targets of some departments begin to shift frequently in response to missed or exceeded targets in other departments.

Scheduling Updates

Many companies schedule at least one update to their business plan sometime during the year. Often this update comes at midyear. Planned updates recognize the necessity of keeping the business plan consistent with the real world.

Companies involved in high technology or other industries where rapid change exists should schedule a plan update during the planning year.

Changing Assumptions

When basic underpinnings of the business plan change, the targets and milestones probably change as well. For example, let's say the plan bases its profit targets on sales projections. The sales plan identifies sales levels at particular points in time. However, if the plan miscalculated product demand (either up or down), the sales plan is no longer valid. There's no point in continuing to report deviations from sales targets for products for which demand has clearly shifted.

Instead, smart managers update the plan to determine what they can do *now* to reach the company's overall goals. This proactive approach helps cut losses short or allows the company to exploit new opportunities.

The fashion industry is a good example. At the start of each season, manufacturers and designers try to guess what will sell. If they guess correctly, their business plan may not require extensive updating. However, if they guess incorrectly and a line doesn't sell, the entire business plan may get revamped.

Changing Business Conditions

Business conditions change as the plan rolls out. Carefully constructed plans respond to these changes. The overall company goals remain unaffected. However, the individual targets required from each department may change. The most frequently seen environmental changes are

- Financial conditions   • Technological advances
- Changes by competition   • Union actions
- Regulatory and legislative actions

Financial conditions

Financial conditions change with the securities markets. For example, as the overall economy changes, the Federal Reserve adjusts its policies in response. The bond market moves as a direct result. As bonds move, the yield curve responds, and so do interest rates. Add to this the sentiment of lenders regarding general business conditions and the stability of specific industries.

All these forces combine to produce the market interest rate on which financing vital to achievement of the business plan depends.

Perhaps interest rates move, *but so do criteria lenders impose for the creditworthiness of borrowers*. Suddenly, the company doesn't qualify for the financing required at the rates specified in the plan. Perhaps the terms of the loan now require a larger compensating balance or more collateral to secure the lender's interest.

Another change in financial conditions that often requires an update of at least part of the plan has nothing to do with the company itself. *Customers'* ability to pay creditors varied with the economic environment. The cash flow plan assumed certain customer payment habits. If customers suddenly begin behaving differently than expected, the cash flow plan can stall. Updating for these events is a necessity.

Technological advances

Some industries enjoy rapid technological advances. The computer industry is one. Some types of manufacturing are others. The securities industry is still another. Often advances in the way a product is made or new materials produce unexpected downward shifts in manufacturing costs.

If your planners are up on the latest in their industry, most such advances won't catch them by surprise. Indeed, some of the most brilliant business plans anticipate the benefits of technological improvements. They capitalize on them, moving the savings to other parts of the company where they are needed to shore up some other part of the plan.

The impact of technological advances on business plans isn't limited to the production process. Often competitors build new innovations into their products. When this happens, it can drastically affect sales of companies whose products don't have the new wrinkle. For these companies, updating the business plan becomes a necessity. They may have to ram through a crash program to meet the competition's offering. Then the marketing department may have to figure out how to let customers know about it.

Changes by competition

Competitors don't always do what your business plan intends them to. Often they fire the first shot in what turns into a price war. Sometimes their advertising campaigns are so effective that they can significantly reduce your company's sales.

When this happens, the business plan must provide a measured response. Often this requires updating parts of the plan in order to maintain sales or counteract claims by competitors' advertising campaigns.

Union actions

Unions often disrupt even the most carefully thought out business plans. Job actions or unexpected demands in contract negotiations sometimes cause labor costs to skyrocket. Suddenly the gross margin drops to a point where it jeopardizes financial targets.

However, smart managers use the business plan to help determine just what concessions they can give to the union during negotiations. They put the financial schedules on an automated spreadsheet. Then they simulate the effects of various conditions. The simulations serve as a basis for updating the business plan after settlement of the negotiations.

Regulatory and legislative actions

These are often the most frustrating. Such changes can drastically affect small-business plans. Further, they often come as a complete surprise. Additionally, policies required for compliance with one government agency sometimes conflict with those required by another agency that also governs the company.

We see an example of this at the small community banks. The Community Reinvestment Act requires that banks lend to small businesses in the inner city. However, the Federal Reserve and the FDIC audit these same banks. The regulators criticize them for lending to small businesses in the inner city that don't meet their standards of creditworthiness. As a result, the business plans of these small banks must reflect inflated loan loss reserves (to satisfy the Fed and FDIC) for making loans to less creditworthy inner-city businesses (to comply with the Community Reinvestment Act).

Such dissonance created by competing government agencies often requires updating the business plan. This is also true of unexpected legislative changes. Sometimes companies depend on specific legislation to carry out their business plans. Real estate developers are a case in point. Zoning laws specify the types of structure allowed on certain property.

If a developer's business plan calls for an office building on land it owns and the zoning on that land suddenly changes to a less dense level, there's a major problem. Now the developer must apply for a variance or possibly change plans. Regardless, the timing of revenues and expenses slips as a result of the legislative change.

Changing Strategies

Sometimes companies must make major changes to their business strategy during the year. Such decisions cannot wait for the end of the planning year. Updating the business plan to include such decisions allows the company to track their implementation. It also allows it to better integrate the changes with the rest of the company's plans.

A change in business strategy might include the acquisition of another company or one of its products. It might include restructuring the firm's pricing strategy or the market it goes after. Any of these changes would require other adjustments in departments throughout the company. The best way to coordinate these changes is to update the business plan.

Department Changes

When separate departments change their plans and their targets, the rest of the company needs to know. For example, production departments that cannot meet targets sometimes subcontract out the difference to another manufacturer. The cost of production probably changes. To maintain profit margins, the sales department may have to adjust its pricing strategies.

Similarly, the accounts payable department may find that it cannot adhere to the planned policy of stretching all payables to forty-five days. Vendors supplying the firm with critical raw materials may establish a cash-on-delivery policy. If this happens, the cash flow plan must somehow pick up the difference in working capital required to run the firm.

A plan update—at least for the departments affected—identifies the change and helps determine the impacts. From there, the updating process makes adjustments that still allow implementation of the original business plan.

Notice that although a department's plan may change and be updated, the overall goals originally set forth in the business plan remain unaffected. We still want the company to hit its original targets. It would take major changes in critical departments to necessitate adjustment of these overall goals.

KEEPING THE PLAN RELEVANT

Updating the business plan keeps it relevant. Many plans fail because they don't reflect the current business climate. When this happens, management doesn't use the plan for its intended purpose—to help guide and control progress toward the company's goals. The monthly and quarterly reviews waste time.

Small companies that have operated for years without a business plan normally fly by the seat of their pants. They communicate changes in the operating environment as they happen. The business plan should record these changes almost as quickly. This doesn't mean redoing the plan every month. Rather, it means adjusting the targets and using the plan to coordinate efforts to ensure meeting the overall plan goals. *Then* the plan incorporates changes at its quarterly or midyear update.

Companies implementing a business plan for the first time regard relevancy as especially important. The design and implementation of a business plan was probably an uphill battle for these firms. They look at the plan with skepticism—as another way for the boss to exert control over the workers. Outdated plans supply their detractors with the excuse that they don't reflect the real world.

Updating the plan doesn't mean that management changes its original goals. After all, that's the point of making a business plan in the first place—to get the firm from point A to point B. The route taken changes, and so do the interim results, but the end point remains the same.

AVOIDING CONFUSION

People familiar with planning and the necessity of updating have doubtless heard the question, Now which version are we talking about? Confusion among the various updated plans and what each contains is a frequent problem. We don't want bewilderment over plan targets and their priorities. Everyone must sing from the same sheet of music.

The best way to avoid confusion is to keep the number of plan updates as few as possible—preferably just one update at midyear. Further, if possible, do not change the underlying goals of the business plan at that time. The various departments update their subplans to reflect changes in strategy and timing.

Everyone must identify each update as either the most current or one that was superseded. A good way to do this is to specify the revision date on the front of each updated plan. Keep a historical log of all updates. Anyone looking at the log quickly sees which is the most current. Include the update log in the front of the plan.

Another help is to summarize the changes in each updated version of the plan. Include this with the history log. Using the change summary, it's easy to see just what changed in each version and the results.

Consistency

The format of each updated version of the business plan should match that of its predecessor. This prevents having to modify the monitoring system with each plan update. Further, it ensures that the accounting system can capture all actual data against which management compares the updated plan. We don't want people to go through a laborious reconciliation of performance indicators prepared for one plan and for a new, updated version. This wastes everyone's time—especially when a performance incentive is on the line. People sometimes spend hours trying to reconcile two different plans.

Glossary

Accounting rate of return (APR): Relates asset investment to future annual income. Use this equation to compute ARR:

$$ARR = \frac{\text{annual cash flows} - \text{depreciation}}{\text{initial investment}}$$

Accounts payable (A/P): Used in an accrual accounting system to track the liabilities of the company. It is important in the business plan because paydown of A/P changes the balance of disposable cash contained in the cash flow plan.

Accounts receivable (A/R): Used in an accrual accounting system to track money owed the company. It is important in the business plan because receipt of A/R balances increases the balance of disposable cash contained in the cash flow plan.

Advance rate: A percentage of the loan value relative to the collateral asset securing the loan. Also called the *loan to value ratio.*

Audit: The examination of accounting records by an independent CPA organization for the purpose of expressing an opinion of the fairness of presentation of the company's financial statements in conformity with generally accepted accounting principals (GAAP).

Break-even point: The level of sales at which income exactly equals operating expenses. This is often used as the starting point for a small-business plan.

Capital acquisition plan: A schedule illustrating major purchases of machinery, equipment, real estate, etc. It usually contains items, purchase dates, delivery dates, and scheduled cash outflows.

Cash basis: An accounting method that recognizes revenue and expense at the time cash changes hands. This method differs from the accrual basis of accounting. However, when preparing a cash flow plan, a cash approach is used to determine *disposable* cash balances.

Cash capability: The company's ability to generate cash from all of its reserves and all available but as yet unemployed credit.

Cash conversion time: Used in business planning to determine the elapsed time required to convert a sale into disposable cash.

Cost of capital: The company's cost of borrowed funds. It is usually aggregated using the weighted average cost of all the firm's sources of debt financing.

This interest rate is often used in the business plan when projecting the cost of additional capital necessary to execute the plan.

Cost of goods sold: The cost associated with manufacturing or otherwise making the company's products available for sale. Sales revenue less cost of goods sold yields gross margin—a critical number in the planning process.

Depreciation: Allocation of the cost of a fixed asset to expense over the period benefited. It is used in accrual accounting systems to match revenues and expenses for each operating period. When preparing a cash flow plan, depreciation is added back to net income to arrive at total cash sources.

Economic order quantity: The order size that minimizes both carrying costs and ordering costs. The business plan should compute the EOQ and use it in the assumptions.

Float: The amount of funds contained in checks already written but not yet cleared by the bank.

Gain contingency: Used in business planning and presentation of financial statements. It quantifies a possible future favorable financial development for the firm, such as winning a lawsuit. GAAP does not allow the recording of gain contingencies as it does accruals for possible future losses. Instead, such possibilities require footnote disclosure; they are omitted from the financials.

Imputed interest: Computation of an effective interest rate on notes or obligations that carry no interest rate on their face or an unrealistically low rate. If the business plan is sent to third parties, its financial projections may require imputing interest on below-market loans.

Internal rate of return (IRR): The exact rate that makes future cash flows discounted back to the present equal to the investment in a capital asset. Using the correct IRR percentage, the net present value of the investment is zero.

Inventory: Goods held by the company for sale. Both beginning and ending inventory figures are used in the following computation of cost of goods sold:

Beginning inventory + raw material purchases + labor + overhead allocation – ending inventory = cost of goods sold

Learning curve: The assumption that the number of labor hours required decreases in a measurable pattern as the manufacturing process is repeated over time and people become familiar with it. Effects of the learning curve should be included in the overall manufacturing plan.

Leverage: Borrowing more than the equity owners have in the business or property. Many business plans assume a given level of debt leverage to finance growth.

Line of credit: A borrowing agreement that commits a bank to lending up to a specific amount when the borrower makes a demand for funds. Credit lines usually run for a specified period of time—one year is normal.

Mezzanine financing: An infusion of capital intended to prepare a company for a public securities offering.

Net present value: Excess of the present value of the cash inflows associated with a capital project over the initial investment.

Optimal reorder point (ORP): That point at which it's most advantageous to order more goods—raw materials, for example. Compute ORP using the equation

ORP = average requirement per unit of lead time X (lead time + safety stock)

Payback period: The length of time required to recover the purchase cost of a capital asset, used to determine the value of an asset investment. Compute payback period as

$$\frac{\text{cost of investment}}{\text{annual cash flow from investment}} \quad + \quad \text{payback}$$

Predetermined overhead rate (POR): The rate used to allocate factory overhead when planning manufacturing costs. Use the equation

$$\text{POR} = \frac{\text{annual planned factory overhead}}{\text{annual planned units produced}}$$

Regression analysis: A statistical method used to project sales, cash flow, and earnings.

Safety stock: Extra units of inventory a firm must carry to guard against stock-outs.

Tangible net worth: Book value of the company *minus* intangible assets. Use the equation

Tangible net worth = total assets – intangible assets – liabilities

Transfer pricing: The price at which goods and services are exchanged between divisions of a decentralized company.

Trend analysis: A method of forecasting sales or earnings using historical figures. It involves a regression whereby a trend line is fitted to a time series of data.

Appendix II

Organizations

International Association for Financial Planning
2 Concourse Parkway, Suite 800
Atlanta, GA 30328
(404) 395-1605

Institute of Certified Financial Planners
East Eastman Ave., Suite 301
Denver, CO 80231
(303) 751-7600

Planning Forum
P.O. Box 70
Oxford, OH 45056
(513) 523-4185

American Institute of Certified Planners
1776 Massachusetts Ave., NW
Washington, D.C. 20036
(202) 872-0611

American Institute of Management
P.O. Box 7039
Quincy, MA 02269
617) 472-0277

Association of Productivity Specialists
200 Park Avenue, Suite 303E
New York, NY 10017
(212) 286-0943

Appendix III
Bibliography

Abrams, Rhonda. *The Successful Business Plan.* New York: The Oasis Press, 1991.

Batchelor, Andrew. *Business Planning for the Entrepreneur.* New York: Tangent Publishing 1990.

Berle, Gustav. *Planning and Forming Your Company.* New York: Wiley, 1990.

——— . *Raising Start-up Capital for Your Firm.* New York: Wiley, 1990.

Bierman, Harold. *Cost Accounting: Concepts and Management Applications.* New York: Macmillan, 1990.

Blocker, E., and C. Stickney. "Duration and Risk Assessments In Capital Budgeting." *Accounting Review,* January 1979, 180–188.

Chamberlain, Neil W. *The Firm: Micro-economic Planning and Action.* New York: McGraw-Hill, 1962.

Collins, Frank, and Paul Munter. "The Budgeting Games People Play." *Accounting Review*, January 1987, 29–49.

Franz, Norman. *The Business Planning Workbook.* New York: Entole International Corp., 1991.

Greene, Charles N. *Management for Effective Performance.*, Englewood Cliffs, NJ: Prentice Hall, 1985.

Kuehl, Charles, and Peggy Lambing. *Small Business Planning and Management.* New York: Dryden Press, 1990.

Larker, D. F. "The Perceived Importance of Selected Information Characteristics for Strategic Capital Budgeting Decisions." *Accounting Review*, July 1981, 519–538.

McKeever, Mike. *How to Write a Business Plan.* Boston: Nolo Press, 1992.

McLaughlin, Harold J. *Building Your Business Plan.* New York: Wiley, 1985.

Magee, Robert. *Advanced Managerial Accounting.* New York: Harper & Row, 1986.

Malburg, Christopher R. *Business Plans to Manage Day-to-Day Operations.* New York: Wiley, 1993.

———. *The Cash Management Handbook.* Englewood Cliffs, NJ: Prentice-Hall, 1992.

Mancuso, Joseph. *How to Write a Winning Business Plan.* Englewood Cliffs, NJ: Prentice-Hall, 1985.

Rappaport, Alfred. *Information for Decision Making.* Englewood Cliffs, NJ: Prentice-Hall, 1982.

Rice, Craig. *Strategic Planning for the Small Business.* Holbrook, Mass.: Bob Adams, Inc., 1990.

Stevens, Chris. *The Entrepreneur's Guide to Developing a Basic Business Plan.* New York: S.K. Brown Publishing, 1991.

Index

About the Author

During his management consulting career, Chris Malburg has explained countless complex business issues and their solutions to both executives and peer professionals. He has known and worked with senior executives both personally and professionally for over fifteen years. This background has provided Chris with a wealth of experience in financial operations.

A CPA with an MBA in finance, Chris is also a licensed NASD Financial Operations Principal. He runs an active management consulting firm, is president of Copralite Development Corporation, a southern California real estate developer, and is the general partner of the Lapin Development Group. Chris has worked with Fortune 100 companies as well as with many small to medium-sized firms. Chris has written seven other popular books and numerous professional articles.